Studies in Eighteenth-Century Culture

Volume 46

Studies in Eighteenth-Century Culture

Volume 46

Studies in Eighteenth-Century Culture

Volume 46

Published by Johns Hopkins University Press for the
American Society for Eighteenth-Century Studies

Johns Hopkins University Press
Baltimore and London
2017

Johns Hopkins University Press
2715 North Charles Street
Baltimore, Maryland 21218-4363
www.press.jhu.edu

ISBN 978-1-4214-221-4-5
ISSN 0360-2370

Articles appearing in this annual series are abstracted and
indexed in *Historical Abstracts* and *America: History and Life*.

Contents

Editor's Introduction

SECC is moving to a new format. Eventually, it will look like this:

> --Presidential Lecture
> --Clifford Lecture
> --Panel
> --Forum
> --Individual Essays

The ASECS Executive Board has kindly agreed to restore the practice, which fell into desuetude, of publishing the Presidential Lecture in *SECC*. It decided that the Clifford Lecture should be published here as well. These changes, which will be fully in place by volume 48, will enable *SECC* to disseminate the plenary talks to members unable to attend ASECS, and considerably enrich the journal.

The introduction of Panels and Forums is designed to re-present some of the excitement of our conferences, and to enable us to explore cutting-edge topics which may be of wide interest at greater depth and breadth than is possible in a single essay. Panel presentations are revised into 5000 word essays and prefaced by the panel chair's introduction—there are two in this volume. At the suggestion of some of our readers, we will also in future invite round-tables to submit their presentations, revised into 1,500 word discourses and prefaced by the chair's introduction, and call these "Forums."

We continue to welcome individual essays, revised from conference papers into 7000-9000 word essays. *SECC* publishes essays based on conference papers given not only at ASECS and at ASECS regional meetings, but also at conferences run by all ASECS affiliates. A list of ASECS affiliates is to be found at the bottom of this page. This is a multi-disciplinary, as well as a multi-national, journal, which is interested in publishing new work and new thinking in all eighteenth-century fields.

This volume (46) contains essays in history, art history, history of science, history of philosophy, Theory and literary history, on British, French, Spanish, and Austrio-Hungarian material and verbal texts, bearing both on the Old World and the New. These essays co-operate to explore the interplay of violence and humanity, and of chaos and order, in different linguistic and formal registers and different realms of cultures.

We would be grateful for your feed-back, and for any suggestions you may have about how this journal may better serve you. Please address these, as well as your submissions, to etbannet@ou.edu. Thanks!

Eve Tavor Bannet and Roxann Wheeler

ASECS Affiliate Societies:

American Antiquarian Society
Aphra Behn Society,
Bibliographical Society of America
Burney Society
Daniel Defoe Society
Early Caribbean Society
East-Central ASECS
Eighteenth-Century Scottish Studies Society
Goethe Society of North America
Historians of Eighteenth-Century Art and Architecture
Ibero-American SECS
The International Herder Society
Johnson Society of the Central Region
Lessing Society
Midwestern ASECS
Mozart Society
North American British Music Studies Association
Northeast ASECS
North American Kant Society
Northwest SECS
Samuel Johnson Society of the West
Samuel Richardson Society
Rousseau Association
International Adam Smith Society
Society of Early Americanists
Society for Eighteenth-Century French Studies
Society for Eighteenth-Century Music
Society for the History of Authorship, Reading and Publishing
South Central SECS
Southeastern ASECS
Germaine de Staël Society for Revolutionary and Romantic Studies
Voltaire Society of America,
Western SECS
Atlantic SECS
Canadian SECS

Editorial Readers for Volume Forty-six

Panel I:

TRANSNATIONAL QUIXOTES AND QUIXOTISMS: CIRCULATION, MIGRATION, APPROPRIATION

Introduction

CATHERINE M. JAFFE

At the end of *Don Quixote* Part II, when Don Quixote and Sancho are on their way home to their village for the last time, they arrive at an inn where they contemplate some badly painted tapestries depicting Helen of Troy and Dido. Sancho remarks:

> —Yo apostaré —dijo Sancho— que antes de mucho tiempo no ha de haber bodegón, venta, ni mesón o tienda de barbero donde no ande pintada la historia de nuestras hazañas; pero querría yo que la pintasen manos de otro mejor pintor que el que ha pintado a estas. (II, 71)[1]

In the conversation that follows between the defeated knight and his squire, Don Quixote criticizes inept imitations, like Avellaneda's false continuation of *Don Quixote* (1614), that are so unlike the original that they need a caption to explain what they are. Don Quixote's comments go to the heart of what has fascinated readers of Cervantes's novel for four centuries. What is the nature of representation, and what connection does a work have to its creator and its particular historical circumstances? What is the relation between original and copy, between a text and its imitation, continuation, or translation? How do we perceive and evaluate re-presentations, imitations, appropriations, and continuations of texts and characters like Don Quixote? Don Quixote himself was unnerved by the challenge Avellaneda's (false) Don Quixote posed to his identity. Immediately after viewing the badly painted tapestries, he meets Don Álvaro Tarfe, a character straight out of the pages of Avellaneda's book. Cervantes's Don Quixote—"nuestro don Quijote" [2] as my students invariably call him by the time we reach the novel's end—has Don Álvaro swear before a magistrate that he is the true, authentic Don Quixote.

Sancho's wager, as we now know, could not have been more prescient. As we celebrate in 2015 the publication of *Don Quixote* Part II four centuries ago, we have an opportunity to reflect once again on the profound wake left by Cervantes's masterpiece, above all in the eighteenth century. Stephen Gilman has described how "within the ocean of prose fiction there is a Cervantine Gulf Stream traceable but not rigorously surveyable." [3] Indeed, Cervantes's novel and his famous character stand at the beginning not only of the novel in the eighteenth century but also wander through other literary and artistic genres, political theories, and philosophies, and they are not limited to the Atlantic world. Throughout 2015 and 2016, the worldwide celebration of the four-hundredth anniversary of Cervantes' death has reassessed the influence, afterlives, and echoes of *Don Quixote* and its famous characters in hundreds of museum and library exhibitions, film series, television documentaries, scholarly conferences, concerts, performances, new editions, and public readings.

The four articles presented in this issue, delivered at the ASECS conference in Los Angeles in 2015, bring new perspectives and innovative critical approaches to the study of eighteenth-century quixotes and quixotisms. Collectively, these articles share a focus on how writers and readers engage *Don Quixote* in debates over the rootedness of a text in a particular national culture, history, and language, and the ways a text or character can be uprooted to circulate freely and be reappropriated by other writers for personal and even perverse purposes, by other national cultures, or be claimed for world culture. The authors study the relative value of historical and cultural authenticity and the articulation of national cultures and characters, the mechanisms of transnational exchange, and the concept of world literature. They remind us that we are never finished examining, re-evaluating, and recreating Cervantes's novel, his characters, and our own relation to them, as Sancho had predicted.

NOTES

1. Miguel de Cervantes, *Don Quijote de la Mancha,* Ed. Martín de Riquer, (Madrid: Planeta, 2002): 1081. "I'll wager, said Sancho, "that before long there won't be a tavern, an inn, a hostelry, or a barbershop where the history of our deeds isn't painted. But I'd like it done by the hand of a painter better than the one who did these." Miguel de Cervantes, *Don Quixote*, trans. Edith Grossman (NY: HarperCollins, 2003): 923.

2. "our Don Quixote."

3. Steven Gilman, *The Novel According to Cervantes* (Berkeley: University of California Press, 1989), xv.

Gendering the Quixote in Eighteenth-Century England

AMELIA DALE

English interpretations, appropriations, and transpositions of the figure of Don Quixote play a pivotal role in eighteenth-century constructions of so-called English national character. A corpus of quixotic narratives worked to reinforce the centrality of Don Quixote and the practice of quixotism in the national literary landscape. They stressed the man from La Mancha's eccentricity and melancholy in ways inextricable from English self-constructions of these traits.[2] This is why Stuart Tave is able to write that eighteenth-century Britons could "recast" Don Quixote in a fashion that followed "national pride" in the "freedom" of their humors.[1] However, Don Quixote's integral place in patriotic self-constructions was troubled by gender. While national character was construed as masculine by default, quixotism's association with masculinity was complicated by the potential passive penetrability of quixotism and the proliferation of narratives about female quixotic readers. This essay will analyze these tensions. Henry Fielding's *Joseph Andrews* (1742) and Laurence Sterne's *Tristram Shandy* (1759–67) are key examples of quixotic texts that respond to the figure of the female quixote by interrogating the relationship between Englishness, masculinity, and quixotism.

National Character and Don Quixote

There was English interest in *Don Quixote* from the time of its publication in 1605, even before Thomas Shelton's translation in 1612.[3] Sarah Wood observes that "*Don Quixote* became a widely disseminated, virtually denationalized classic."[4] Similarly, Aaron Hanlon argues in this volume for an understanding of quixotism as a global heuristic, noting how difficult it is, upon each transposition of Don Quixote in eighteenth-century Britain, to ascribe the "cultural phenomenon of quixotism" to Cervantes.[5] Anglicized quixotic narratives thus *print over* Don Quixote's Spanish origins, enacting a belligerent claim on quixotic practice as inseparable from English print culture. Even though *Don Quixote*—as Elizabeth Lewis observes— became part of an Anglicized construction of Spain, English quixotic transpositions use Don Quixote to construct and reconstruct an eccentric English national character.[6]

The quixotic character, then, must be read alongside Deidre Lynch's observation about the way literary character is bound to both Enlightenment epistemology and print technology: the eighteenth-century conception of character is sutured to a Lockean, printerly formulation of experience that involves the "imprinting of surface and the acquisitions of characters."[7] Quixotes are characters who are imprinted— typically by the texts they have consumed—to such an extent that impressions from this contact indelibly shapes their subjectivity. Here, I follow Scott Paul Gordon, who characterizes quixotic practice, as the obverse to enlightenment ideals of "proper" perception. The mind of the quixote is not the Lockean ideal: objective, unprejudiced, and able to process reality because it is "a fair sheet of paper with no writing on it."[8] Instead, it is prejudiced and already inscribed by the genres he or she has consumed. Quixotes possess a subjectivity imprinted by their favorite genre, be it chivalric romance or sentimental novels. This formulation of quixotism is useful for the way it encompasses quixotic narratives' concern with (imperfect) textual replication: quixotic characters embody and attempt to reproduce their reading.

Recognizing quixotism as embedded in print technology also productively links the conceptual underpinnings of national character to quixotism. For example, David Hume's essay, "On National Characters" (1748) argues that one of the reasons national character exists is because the "human mind is of a very imitative nature."[9] The "*moral* causes" Hume outlines that prompt the development of a national character (the system of government and the position of the country in relation to its neighbor), as much as the "*physical* causes" he dismisses (the quality of the air and climate), suggest that the phenomenon of national character stems from the capacity for people to have their subjectivity overwritten by their environments. At the crux of both quixotism and national character are crises of individuation within "imagined communities," to draw on Benedict Anderson's perpetually useful term. The quixote enacts—despite differences in cultural and communal contexts— topoi imported from texts they have quixotically consumed. Resultantly, the quixote becomes comically displaced, an incomplete reproduction of a certain genre. Quixotes, with their subjectivity indelibly marked by their surroundings, are, like the quintessential national character, exquisitely receptive. Just as the quixotic character is imprinted by the text he—or she—has consumed, theories of national character conceive the moral and/ or physical specificities of countries as marking their inhabitants. Upon his arrival in England, Don Quixote can thus be subsumed into a national character; England can, as it were, penetrate Don Quixote's character and overwrite his Spanish origins.

Quixotic qualities are gendered. The longstanding trope of figuring the feminine as soft and penetrable, though obvious, is crucial to conceptualizing the gendered nature of quixotism. Quixotic characters are molded, imprinted, and formed by the texts that they consume and are therefore interconnected with the old figuration of the feminine as yielding and ductile. In the early modern period, being *imprinted* or *pressed* was also bawdy slang for being sexually penetrated or impregnated.[10] The enlightenment trope of the subject as a page being inscribed by experience could double as a description of a feminine virginal slate being stained, blotted, and altered by sexual experience. Moreover, classical theories of reproduction asserted that women provided the raw materials for an infant, and that men provided its form. Quixotes, then, embody an inscribable, malleable, penetrated, and potentially feminized subjectivity.

This tendency is apparent in a prefatory poem to a 1699 edition of an anonymous translation entitled *The much-esteemed history of the ever-famous knight Don Quixote de la Mancha.*[11] The poem describes Don Quixote as responding to the English language and transforming into an English character. As is typical of such prefatory poems, it asserts the superiority of the translated text to the original. It begins by establishing Don Quixote as a universal citizen, a character who freely and easily circulates across national borders: "I Am Don Quixote of the Spanish Race" he proclaims, "But born to travel, *Spain* too streight I found."[12] The pun on the Strait of Gilbraltar and a characterization of Spain as full of "stiff Dons" suggests that Spain is too square, too linear for Don Quixote. He then relates his journey from Spain to France, Holland, and Germany where he is well received. However, when he reaches England, he is not only welcomed but recognizes that he has come to a land with "Thousands full made as I; / Men that have Windmills in their Pates like mine." A "friend" teaches Don Quixote English, "So quite forgetting Spanish, I'm your own," and he proclaims himself to be a "Native" of England.[13] The acquisition of a new language has as much effect on Don Quixote as his reading of romances. In this poem, after crossing into English print, Don Quixote is no longer a Spaniard, or even a global heuristic. Instead, the process of being translated and printed in English abruptly molds Don Quixote into a natural English subject.

The claim that the English are mad is here—as it is throughout the century—central to the English proprietorial claim on quixotism. It occurs, for instance in Richard Steele and Joseph Addison's periodical the *Tatler,* when an upholsterer is described as being avidly and impotently fascinated with international affairs. As the fictive editor Isaac Bickerstaff states, "the News-Papers of this Island are as pernicious to weak Heads in *England* as ever Books of Chivalry to *Spain.*"[14] This reference to "weak heads" suggests that only specific English people are affected by quixotism. Yet in the same issue, Bickerstaff observes, "This Touch in the Brain of the *British* subject, is as certainly owing to the reading News-Papers, as that of the *Spanish* Worthy [...] to the reading Works of Chivalry."[15] The printerly touching that Bickerstaff describes seems to be something that all British subjects experience. The preface to Arthur Murphy's popular farce *The Upholsterer, or What News?* (1758)—based on the *Tatler's* political upholsterer—builds on the *Tatler* to claim unequivocally that quixotism is universally English: "the Quixote [...] represents ye all."[16]

Quixotism in England is centralized but simultaneously potentially marginal. Wood argues that English quixotes, unlike the original, are ensconced within the confines of the English establishment and can stand in for the nation itself.[17] Yet Wood's identification of English quixotism with political centrality sits uncomfortably alongside recognition that to be quixotic—even in England—is to deviate from epistemological and political norms. Hanlon, for instance, argues that the quixotic subject occupies a "liminal position" in society.[18] Even the etymology of "eccentricity"—out of the center or ex-centered—suggests the contradictions that come with associating a "national character" (and the centralizations that entails) with quixotism.

However, while national character is a concept that, at first glance, appears to enforce uniformity, the national character of England was constructed as involving an unlimited array of extremely singular individuals. For instance, Hume and Joseph Priestley both comment how the disparate mode of government in England results in a national character that consists of a collection of peculiar people united only through their heterogeneity.[19] At the same time as England is conceived as a community of eccentrics, the construction of this community entails exclusions and centralizations. It is unsurprising, but important to note, that in Hume's account, those who are not male are omitted from considerations of the "singularity" of the English eccentric "national character." The male English quixote thus simultaneously represents singularity and hegemony: an ex-centredness that is tolerated, even potentially celebrated, because the quixote is otherwise invested with Anglo-British masculine centrality.

Gendering the Quixotic Subject in *Joseph Andrews*

In Henry Fielding's *The History of the Adventures of Joseph Andrews and of his Friend Mr. Abraham Adams. Written in Imitation of The Manner of Cervantes, Author of Don Quixote* (1741), the two main (English, male) characters in the title are both, but differently, quixotic.[20] They speak to competing quixotic models in mid-eighteenth-century England. Abraham Adams, a quixote who models himself on Classical heroes and precepts from the bible, possesses, according to the preface "perfect simplicity" and "goodness of heart."[21] Charitable, innocent, and patriotic, Adams became, shortly following *Joseph Andrews'* publication, an accepted symbol of eccentric English kindness. Murphy praised Fielding's ability to describe those of "remarkable Oddity, or unaccountable Whim," a "Species of Men in this Kingdom" who "are of long Standing among us."[22] Murphy thus suggests that Adam's popularity as a character is inseparable from beliefs in a nationwide quixotism.[23] Identifications of Adams with the popular conviction of English eccentricity demonstrate that he was part of a collection of transpositions that rendered quixotism as a component of national character.

While Adams became a crucial entry in a growing catalogue of loveable English eccentric men, the character of Joseph Andrews responded to narratives about female quixotic readers. I have discussed the persistent figuration of quixotism as malleable and penetrable and thus suggested how the quixote is always potentially feminized. Crucially, English masculine national character conflicted with the prominent presence of a parallel corpus of female quixotic narratives, which figure quixotism as involving a feminine impressionability. Throughout the century, in response to a range of factors, including, but not limited to a growing female participation in the literary marketplace, and an association of women with particular literary genres, there was a proliferation of narratives featuring female quixotic readers.[24] Characters such as Dorinda in Jane Barker's *The Lining of the Patchwork Screen* (1726) and Delia in Delarivier Manley's the *New Atalantis* (1709) gender the enraptured, imitative novel or romance reader as feminine.

The opening chapter of *Joseph Andrews* draws on this trope, establishing a concern with English readers emulating "example[s]" from literature, in particular "female readers" being taught by Samuel Richardson's *Pamela* (1740).[25] The subsequent chapters focus not on a quixotic female reader of *Pamela* but on a man who behaves like one. *Joseph Andrews* reacts to female quixotic narratives with a parodic remasculinization of the figure of the quixotic reader. The footman Joseph quixotically responds to the letters of his sister Pamela, in other words, Richardson's novel *Pamela*. Accordingly, he cherishes his virtue and rejects the advances of his mistress Lady Booby, imitating Pamela's initial rejection of Squire B. Lady Booby's incredulous response to Joseph's rejection points to the way that his mimetic reading subverts gender roles: "[d]id ever mortal hear of a man's virtue!"[26] Joseph's quixotic cross-dressing simultaneously reworks *Pamela* and *Don Quixote*, employing omnivorous recycling to comprehend categories of gender, genre, and national literature.[27]

Joseph's quixotism compromises his masculinity on multiple levels. As well as imitating a text which, Fielding's narrator tells the reader, instructs "female readers," he is placed in the passive, feminine position of a quixotic novel reader.[28] Through his quixotism, Joseph is suggestively represented as a text, imprinted by his reading. This is reinforced by the way his identity revolves around a mark of the strawberry on the skin of his chest, a birthmark "which his mother had given him by longing for that fruit."[29] Fielding here draws on the contemporary theory of the mother's imagination's capacity to mark her fetus, a theory that figures the unborn child as a text that potentially can be inscribed by maternal imaginings. The way that Joseph is printed by his mother's imagination parallels that way that his subjectivity is marked through Pamela's letters. In short, Joseph is repeatedly figured as imprinted by female imagination. Joseph is an impressionable, feminized quixote.

Yet Joseph's quixotism becomes gradually minimized through the course of the narrative. By its conclusion, he is literally no longer kin to Pamela; the mark of the strawberry on the skin reveals, along with his parentage, that he is not Pamela's brother. Lady Booby disappears from large stretches of the narrative, and Adams gains more prominence. A quixote who emulates *Pamela*, a text that is associated from the first chapter with a female readership, is substituted for a quixote less obviously marked by gender transgressions, one who emulates scholarly and religious works rather than feminized literature. While Joseph's gender identification remains complex through the course of the novel, he appears less feminized when the Lady Booby/Pamela storyline is side-lined.[30] Jill Campbell argues that Joseph's ambiguous masculinity becomes dislocated and deflected through the figure of the foppish Beau Didapper, who, like Joseph, courts Fanny, and is, like

Joseph, associated with emulation.[31] Thus, Fielding splits the problem of male gender transgressions into "a pair of linked characters, one clearly satirically conceived and the other positive."[32] Placed alongside the effeminate Beau Didapper, Joseph appears masculine.

Beau Didapper reinforces Joseph's Englishness as well as his masculinity. The narrator sneeringly associates Beau Didapper with continental decadence: "[h]e could talk a little French, and sing two or three Italian songs."[33] Before Beau Didapper's introduction, the foppish character of the "French-English Bellarmine" in the interpolated story of the "Unfortunate Jilt" reinforces to the reader the longstanding association between dandies and Francophilia.[34] Contrastingly, when Joseph picks up and carries Fanny in his arms, his brawny strength is celebrated by Fielding's narrator as a specifically English virtue. The narrator proclaims to "my fair countrywomen," to consider "the many occasions on which the strength of a man may be useful to you; and duly weighing this, take care, that you match not yourselves with the spindle-shanked beaus and petit maîtres of the age" but instead marry a man like Joseph who is strong enough to "carry you in lusty arms."[35] This passage has elements of the mock-heroic, yet it still jovially presents Joseph as a picture of strong, healthy English manhood, an image which is achieved through contrasting Joseph with small, weak Didapper-like beaus (Didapper has "no calf," is "four foot five inches," and lacks physical strength).[36] "[P]etit-maîtres" further marks the category of "spindle-shanked" beau as French. The opposition between Joseph and Beau Didapper, then, similar to that between the "French-English Bellamarine" and the honorable Horatio earlier in the novel, is on the level of nationality as much as masculinity. An affirmation of Joseph's masculinity occurs concurrently with an affirmation of his Englishness.

Joseph Andrews, in short, picks at the threads connecting masculinity, quixotism, and Englishness. While Abraham Adams offers a model of quixotic Englishness, which could be easily integrated into constructions of a masculine national character, Joseph's narrative takes as its starting point a connection between quixotism and female readers. As a result, both Joseph's masculinity and his Englishness are only recovered after his feminized quixotism is no longer significant in the narrative. To be quixotically English, it seems, one must also be unequivocally male.

In contrast, female quixotes in eighteenth-century English texts are more likely to be identified with a subversion of Anglo-British identity (and a penetration by foreign texts) than English, masculine literary culture. For instance, in Charlotte Lennox's *The Female Quixote* (1752), Arabella quixotically emulates French romances, consumed in "very bad Translations," a description that presents Arabella's quixotic practice as an imitation of what is already a poor imitation of foreign models.[37] In this way, Lennox's quixotic narrative, as Eve Tavor Bannet discusses, questions "the continued applicability of anachronistic transnational imitations."[38] Arabella's quixotism leads to ambiguously "foreign" behavior. Her idiosyncratic dress and veil elicits speculation in the pump-room about her nationality.[39] Lennox writes:

> Some of the wiser Sort took her for a Foreigner; others, of still more Sagacity, supposed her a *Scots* Lady, covered with her Plaid; and a third Sort, infinitely wiser than either, concluded that she was a *Spanish* Nun, that had escaped from a Convent, and had not yet quitted her Veil.[40]

This description identifies Arabella's quixotic dress with a performance of a nebulously exotic identity. When coupled with femininity in English narratives, quixotism has the potential to be divested of its Anglicization, to be even renationalized as Spanish.

English Quixotism as Prosthesis

Laurence Sterne's *Tristram Shandy* (1759–67) responds self-consciously to English representations of quixotism as foreign and feminine, and like *Joseph Andrews*, questions the relationship between masculinity, Englishness, and quixotism. While Joseph is able to recover an English masculinity only after a feminized quixotism is dispensed with, *Tristram Shandy* describes English men attempting, and failing, to remasculinize and recuperate a quixotic masculinity. Like Fielding, Sterne responds to the figure of the female quixotic novel reader with English, quixotic men.

Nonetheless, here, their masculinity is besieged and supremely complex. Sterne depicts a paranoid "remasculinization" (to use Carol Kay's term) of both sentimentalism and quixotism on the part of the Shandy men.[41] Tristram, the fictive author narrator, playfully disciplines the female reader, "madam," in ways that can be read as tantamount to an attack on feminine literary culture.[42] The relegation of literary women to the narrative sidelines is embodied by the male characters' persistent marginalization of women in the book.[43] Tristram proclaims (echoing Alexander Pope) that while all the Shandy men are quixotic characters, "of an original character throughout," the Shandy women "had no character at all,—except, indeed, my great aunt DINAH."[44] Women in *Tristram Shandy* are unable to inhabit a position of sentimental eccentricity like the men, and when they occupy a position of individuation and deviance in *Tristram Shandy*, it is through their sexuality. Sterne draws on the connotations "character" has with sexual reputation. Dinah's "character" is synonymous with her sexual history: she "was married and got with child by the coachman."[45] Conversely, the Shandy men express a range of singular, eccentric behavior, a behavior identified with Englishness but also with a wounded manhood. *Tristram Shandy* thus interrogates connections between "national character", quixotism and masculinity.

Tristram connects the quixotism of Toby and the other Shandy men to England through the climate. Toby, Tristram claims, is indebted to the English air and climate for his eccentricity: he has a "humour of that particular species, which does honour to our atmosphere."[46] Tristram's speculation that the "inconstancy" of the national climate has produced "such a variety of odd and whimsical characters" is, as characteristic of the book, heavily marked with citation and authorial distance. Tristram asks:

> —Pray what was that man's name,—for I write in such a hurry, I have no time to recollect or look for it,—who first made the observation, 'That there was a great inconstancy in our air and climate?' Whoever he was, 'twas a just and good observation in him.—But the corollary drawn from it, namely, "That it is this which has furnished us with such a variety of odd and whimsical characters;"—that was not his;—it was found out by another man, at least a century and a half after him.[47]

Tristram's own idiosyncratic narration, manifest through the eccentric punctuation, and his writing "in such a hurry" that he has no time to search for a reference, marks himself out as one of England's "odd and whimsical" characters. After elaborating on observations by John Dryden and Joseph Addison, Tristram closes the paragraph with an "observation [that] is my own," placing himself in a genealogy of English male writers who remark on the climate and an odd national character.[48]

The relation between national climate and national character (something Hume, as discussed above, refuted) is referenced throughout *Tristram Shandy*.[49] The description of "odd and whimsical" characters as being as English as the bad weather results in the women in *Tristram Shandy*, who barely qualify as characters, becoming denationalized. Women here are not English, nor are they quixotes. Instead, Tristram's conventional invocation of the climate theory of national character has the effect of suturing the complicated, wounded, quixotic men described in the text with Englishness.

We see this in the description of Toby's war games. Tristram's uncle Toby, like the political upholsterer, is quixotically obsessed with imperial wars and comically incapable of affecting their outcomes. His quixotic activities are prompted by English print, by "the accounts [...] received from the daily papers."[50] Toby's futile obsession with imperial conflicts manifests itself as increasingly elaborate reenactments of the Wars of the Spanish Succession on his bowling green. Tristram writes that his father, Walter Shandy, would "often" remark:

> that if any mortal in the whole universe had done such a thing, except his brother *Toby*, it would have been looked upon by the world as one of the most refined satires upon the parade and prancing manner, in which *Lewis* XIV. from the beginning of the war, but particularly that very year, had taken the field—But 'tis not my brother *Toby*'s nature, kind soul! my father would add, to insult any one.[51]

Toby's re-enactment of British wars in the "campaigns" on his bowling green is overtly situated by Walter Shandy as being at the edge of satire and sentimentality. It potentially mocks "prancing" French masculinity, but because of Toby's quixotic, amiable "nature"—emphatically English—his war games are recovered from even a hint of Frenchness.[52] Instead, they are English, sentimental, and almost pitiful.

This overtly Anglicized quixotism is suffused by a sense of masculine loss. "[K]ind soul!" functions here as much as a lament as an exclamation, a prefiguration of the point, three chapters later in the novel, when Tristram breaks off from a narrativization of Toby's military reenactment to lament his and Trim's death.[53] Toby's construction of war simulations ultimately stems from his attempt to articulate the groin injury he gained during battle. His domestication of war, particularly his staged battles, is suffused with references to impotence; he rehearses but can never adequately explain his wound.[54] In general, quixotes are quixotes because they can never be what they aspire to be: Don Quixote is not a knight from a romance, the political upholsterer cannot successfully intervene in foreign affairs, and Joseph Andrews cannot be a male Pamela. There is a quixotic, farcical falling short of the desired model, a failure to live as a text.[55] In *Tristram Shandy*, this falling short is rendered as a mode of impotence, as masculine lack.

Indeed, in *Tristram Shandy*, through the figure of the hobby-horse, English masculinity—such as it is—is described as animated by lack. Toby, Walter, Yorick, and the autobiographical author-narrator Tristram are all each governed by their own idiosyncratic, individual obsessions, or hobby-horses.[56] The hobby-horse, the Shandean image for an obsession, is not precisely synonymous with quixotism, yet it is constituent of it. The figure of the eccentric riding his "hobby-horse" is redolent of Don Quixote on his poor-bred steed. This association is given flesh through Yorick's hobby-horse; Yorick's quixotism is his maintenance of his own, living horse, a steed which, Tristram claims, resembles Don Quixote's mount but surpasses it in its ill-health and unsuitability. Notably, the word "hobby-horse" was used in George Cheyne's treatise pathologizing the English national character, the *English Malady* (1733). Prior to the publication of *Tristram Shandy*, Cheyne describes how hobby-horses, or innocent amusements help manage the melancholy inherent in the English national character. He writes that hobby-horses can "keep the Mind easy, and prevent its wearing out the Body, as the Sword does the Scabbard."[57] English eccentricity, according to Cheyne, becomes a restorative supplement to a national complaint.

Tristram Shandy takes Cheyne's figuration of the hobby-horse as treatment for an English Malady further. The hobby-horse is not only used to ease melancholy but also it is used by the Shandy man as both a sign of, and an attempt to compensate for, phallic lack. The hobby-horse's position between the legs provides an opportunity for bawdy jokes. It also points to how the Shandy men use the hobby-horse in an attempt to supplement their wounded manhood.[58] The Shandy men all suffer castrations that can be figurative, as in the case of Tristram's unfortunate naming, or painfully literal, as in the case of Tristram's accidental circumcision from the sash-window, Walter Shandy's sciatica, and the wound in Toby's groin.

Additionally, *Tristram Shandy* emphasizes and exploits the penetrability that quixotism involves. Tristram describes the acquisition of a hobby-horsical obsession, the gaining of an English eccentricity, in other words, as a decidedly sexual penetration. Though the hobby-horse rider is described as astride his hobby-horse, their positions are fluid, and the rider becomes penetrated by his hobby-horse: "By long journies and much friction, it so happens that the body of the rider is at length as fill'd as full of HOBBY-HORSICAL matter as it can hold.[59] The hobby-horse, strongly associated with sexual pleasure for impotent or castrated men, becomes a dildo, or prosthetic phallus, paralleling how quixotism itself is a crucial, but an engrafted part of English masculinity. Quixotism has not originated from an English body (whether of literature, or of flesh) but rather is inserted into a construction of an English national character.

Tristram Shandy describes the Shandy men attempting (and failing) to remasculinize English quixotism. The novel describes penetrable, sentimental, Englishmen appropriating quixotism as a failing phallic compensation for their masculine lack. *Tristram Shandy* therefore suggestively presents the use of the quixotic in constructions of an English "national character" as a phallic prosthesis composed of English print.

Conclusions

In both Fielding's *Joseph Andrews* and Sterne's *Tristram Shandy*, an established English tradition which uses quixotism in a construction of masculine national character collides with another corpus of eighteenth-century quixotic narratives: the female quixotic reader. *Joseph Andrews* draws on these disparate canons in the characters of Parson Adams and Joseph. By diminishing Joseph's quixotism and increasing Adams' prominence through the course of the narrative, Fielding ultimately suggests that these two quixotic modes are irreconcilable. Quixotism is already ex-centered; to associate it with feminized literature is to remove it from masculine Englishness. *Tristram Shandy* responds to differently gendered quixotisms by playfully positioning the Shandy men in futile opposition to femininity. They attempt (and fail) to use quixotism to supplement their besieged English masculinity. *Tristram Shandy* presents quixotism as an inadequate phallic prosthesis for an English masculinity, which is barely masculine at all. Attempts to incorporate quixotism into a construction of English "national character" *Tristram Shandy* suggests, stem from the "national character" being tenuously, problematically masculine.

NOTES

1. Stuart Tave, *The Amiable Humorist* (Chicago: Univ. of Chicago Press, 1960), viii–ix.

2. John Skinner, *"Don Quixote* in 18th-Century England: A Study in Reader Response," *Cervantes: Bulletin of the Cervantes Society of America* 7 (1987): 53.

3. J. A. G. Ardila, "The Influence and Reception of Cervantes in Britain, 1607–2005," in ed. J. A. G. Ardila *The Cervantean Heritage: Reception and Influence of Cervantes in Britain*, (London: Legenda, 2009), 3.

4. Sarah F. Wood, *Quixotic Fictions of the USA 1792–1815* (Oxford: Oxford Univ. Press, 2005), 7.

5. Aaron R. Hanlon, "Quixotism as Global Heuristic." Published in this volume.

6. Elizabeth Franklin Lewis, "Maps, Travelers, and the "Real" Don Quixote de la Mancha." Published in this volume.

7. Deidre Lynch, *The Economy of Character* (Chicago: Univ. of Chicago Press, 1998), 34.

8. Scott Paul Gordon, *The Practice of Quixotism: Postmodern Theory and Eighteenth-Century Women's Writing* (Houndmills: Palgrave Macmillan, 2006), 20.

9. David Hume, "Of National Character," in *Three Essays, Moral and Political* (London: Printed for A. Millar [...] and A. Kincaid in Edinburgh, 1748), 9.

10. Margreta de Grazia, "Imprints: Shakespeare, Gutenberg, and Descartes," in Douglas A. Brooks, ed. *Printing and Parenting in Early Modern England* (Aldershot: Ashgate, 2005), 73–78; Wendy Wall, *The Imprint of Gender: Authorship and Publication in the English Renaissance* (Ithaca: Cornell Univ. Press, 1993), 2–3.

11. *The Much-Esteemed History of the Ever-Famous Knight Don Quixote De La Mancha Containing His Many Wonderful and Adventures and Atchievements* (London: N. Boddington, 1699), n.p.

12. *Don Quixote De La Mancha*, n.p.

13. *Don Quixote De La Mancha*, n.p.

14. Richard Steele, *Tatler*, no. 178 (May 30, 1710) in Donald F. Bond, ed. *The Tatler* (Oxford: Claredon Press, 1987), 2:471 The Political Upholsterer also appears in numbers 155, 160, 180 and 232 of the *Tatler*.

15. Steele, *Tatler*, no. 178 (May 30, 1710), 2:469.

16. John Pike Emery, ed. *The Way to Keep Him and Five Other Plays by Arthur Murphy* (Washington Square: New York Univ. Press, 1956), 75.

17. Wood, *Quixotic Fictions of the USA*, 21.

18. Aaron R. Hanlon, "Toward a Counter-Poetics of Quixotism," *Studies in the Novel* 46 (2014): 153.

19. Hume, "Of National Character," 16; Joseph Priestley, *Lectures on History, and General Policy* (Birmingham: Printed by Pearson and Rollason, London, 1788), 523; Paul Langford, *Englishness Identified: Manners and Character, 1650-1850* (Oxford: Oxford Univ. Press, 2000), 267–74.

20. J. A. G. Ardila, "Henry Fielding: From Quixotic Satire to the Cervantean Novel," in J. A. G. Ardila, ed. *The Cervantean Heritage: Reception and Influence of Cervantes in Britain*, (London: Legenda, 2009), 128.

21. Henry Fielding, *Joseph Andrews,* ed. R. F. Brissenden (London: Penguin Books, 1985), 30.

22. Arthur Murphy, *The Gray's-Inn Journal* no. 38 (7 July 1753) in *The Gray's-Inn Journal*, 2 vols. (London: Printed by W. Faden, for P. Vaillant, 1756), 1:240–3.

23. Tave, *The Amiable Humorist*, 144–5.

24. See Jacqueline Pearson, *Women's Reading in Britain 1750–1835: A Dangerous Recreation* (Cambridge: Cambridge Univ. Press, 1999).

25. Fielding, *Joseph Andrews*, 40.

26. Fielding, *Joseph Andrews*, 59.

27. Scott Black, "Anachronism and the Uses of Form in Joseph Andrews," *Novel* 38, 2–3 (2005): 149.

28. Fielding, *Joseph Andrews*, 40.

29. Fielding, *Joseph Andrews*, 40.

30. Jill Campbell, *Natural Masques: Gender and Identity in Fielding's Plays and Novels* (Stanford: Stanford Univ. Press, 1995), 63.

31. Campbell, *Natural Masques*, 65.

32. Campbell, *Natural Masques*, 75.

33. Fielding, *Joseph Andrews*, 294.

34. Fielding, *Joseph Andrews*, 117.

35. Fielding, *Joseph Andrews*, 189.

36. Fielding, *Joseph Andrews*, 293-4.

37. Charlotte Lennox, *The Female Quixote*, ed. Amanda Gilroy and Wil Verhoeven (London: Penguin Books, 2006), 19.

38. Eve Tavor Bannet, "Quixotes, Imitations, and Transatlantic Genres," *Eighteenth-Century Studies* 40, no. 4 (2007): 553.

39. Felicity Nussbaum argues Arabella's veil complicates her identity with other cultures. Felicity Nussbaum, *Torrid Zones: Maternity, Sexuality, and Empire in Eighteenth-Century English Narratives* (Baltimore: Johns Hopkins Univ. Press, 1995), 114–26. Ruth Mack notes how Lennox invites us to ask "[w]hat kind of foreigner is a romance heroine?" Ruth Mack, "Quixotic Ethnography: Charlotte Lennox and the Dilemma of Cultural Observation," *NOVEL: A Forum on Fiction* 38 (2005): 202.

40. Lennox, *The Female Quixote*, 298.

41. Kay, *Political Constructions: Defoe, Richardson, and Sterne in Relation to Hobbes, Hume and Burke* (Ithaca: Cornell Univ. Press, 1988), 233.

42. Barbara M. Benedict, "'Dear Madam': Rhetoric, Cultural Politics, and the Female Reader in Sterne's *Tristram Shandy*," *Studies in Philology* 89 (1992): 485–98.

43. Ruth Perry, "Words for Sex: The Verbal-Sexual Continuum in *Tristram Shandy*," *Studies in the Novel* 20.1 (1988): 27–42, 34.

44. Laurence Sterne, *Tristram Shandy: The Text*, ed. Melvyn New and Joan New, The Florida Edition of the Works of Laurence Sterne (Gainesville: Univ. Presses of Florida, 1978), vol 1, chapt 21, p 73. Sterne echoes Alexander Pope's "Epistle to a Lady: of the Characters of Women" (1735) which states, "Most women have no Characters at all."

45. Sterne, *Tristram Shandy*, 1:21.73.

46. Sterne, *Tristram Shandy*, 1:21.71–72.

47. Sterne, *Tristram Shandy*, 1:21.71.

48. Sterne, *Tristram Shandy*, 1:21.71.

49. Sterne, *Tristram Shandy*, 1:11.27, 3:20.230.

50. Sterne, *Tristram Shandy*, 6:22.536.

51. Sterne, *Tristram Shandy*, 6:22.538–9.

52. Toby is also compared to "*Lewis*" when he gathers materials for his war games from the top of a church, 5:19.451.

53. Sterne, *Tristram Shandy*, 6:25.544–5.

54. Ross King, "*Tristram Shandy* and the Wound of Language," *Studies in Philology* 92. 3 (1995): 308.

55. Christopher Narozny and Diana de Armas Wilson, "Heroic Failure: Novelistic Impotence in *Don Quixote* and *Tristram Shandy*," in J. A. G. Ardila ed. *The Cervantean Heritage: Reception and Influence of Cervantes in Britain* (London: Legenda, 2009), 142–50.

56. Susan Staves, "Don Quixote in Eighteenth-Century England," *Comparative Literature* 24.3 (1972): 202.

57. George Cheyne, *The English Malady, or, a Treatise of Nervous Diseases of All Kinds* (London: G. Strathan and J. Leake, 1733), 181–2.

58. Amelia Dale, "Dolly's Inch of Red Sealing Wax: Impressing the Reader

in *Tristram Shandy*" in Melvyn New, Peter DeVoogd and Judith Hawley, eds. *Sterne, Tristram, Yorick: Tercentenary Essays on Laurence Sterne* (Newark: Delaware Univ. Press, 2016), 113–52.

59. Sterne, *Tristram Shandy*, 1:24.86.

Quixotic Sade:
Echoes of Cervantes in
120 Days of Sodom

ELENA DEANDA-CAMACHO

In the foreword of *El ingenioso hidalgo don Quijote de la Mancha* (1605, 1615), the narrator recommends that his readers lower their expectations because he conceived his work in prison, a space full of noise and interruptions: "se engendró en una cárcel, donde toda incomodidad tiene su asiento y donde todo triste ruido hace su habitación."[1] Francisco Rodríguez Marín suggests that this prison is the Real Prison of Seville, where Miguel de Cervantes Saavedra (1547–1616) stayed in 1597.[2] Two centuries later, in another infamous prison in Paris, one cell was particularly 'infected' with *Don Quijote*'s deranged influence: the cell belonging to Donatien Alphonse, marquis de Sade (1740–1814).[3] Like Cervantes, Sade undertook from his dungeon the colossal task of rewriting and exhausting a literary genre: the pornographic.

120 Days of Sodom (written in 1785, published in 1904) tells the story of four libertines who sequester themselves for four months in the castle of Silling along with 42 people, 30 of whom are tortured and ultimately assassinated.[4] Four bawds recount their adventures as prostitutes, inspiring the libertines to perform a total of 600 acts of sex and torture. While Sade remained imprisoned in the Bastille (where the manuscript for *120* was found), he outlined an anonymous, but distinctly Spanish, novel that appears to anticipate *120*.[5] For this "philosophical novel," he listed Hispanic names like the duke of Corte Real, don Gaspard, or don Carlos, for its main characters. He also asked close friends for the names of the brothels, lodgings, and main streets of Madrid, Lisbon, and Toledo: "je veux … le nom de deux ou trois rues de beau monde et autant dans le quartier des courtisanes avec celui des principales promenades de … Lisbonne, Toledo, et Madrid."[6] While Sade's interest in the Spanish Black Legend and the Inquisition clearly resonate in *120*, Sade's fascination with Cervantes's work, especially with *Don Quijote* and the *Novelas ejemplares* (1613), truly unlocks a vantage point to the poetic understanding of *120*, his *opera prima*.[7] Sade considered Cervantes the root of "all evils," that is, of all of his writing; in *Id*ées sur les romans (1799), Sade pays homage to Cervantes, *Don Quijote*, and the *Novelas,* and he even confesses that he would have loved being their author.[8] *Idées* precedes twelve novels collectively entitled *Crimes de l'amour*, a Sadean take on Cervantes' *Novelas*.[9] In 1791, he also presented a play called *Oxtiern ou les malheurs du libertinage*—a rewriting of Cervantes's *La fuerza de la sangre*.[10] In his diary, Sade placed *La fuerza de la sangre* in a list of novellas that gravitated around a perversion or, as he called them, a "passion," placing it under the title "rape." Cervantes thus influenced Sade's work and, more importantly, *120*.

120 can be considered quixotic insofar as Sade aims to write the most important piece of obscene literature in mankind's history by conjuring (that is, both invoking and destroying) all previous masterpieces. In *Don Quijote*, the narrator says that he would like his novel to be "el más hermoso, el más gallardo y más discreto [texto] que pudiera imaginarse."[11] Similarly, Sade presents the reader with "le plus impur [texte] qui ait jamais été fait depuis que le monde existe."[12] Both writers want to write not only the best novel in their particular genre but also the best novel ever written. In order to achieve their goal, they had to include all previous masterpieces … if only to destroy them. By connecting with these previous works, *Don Quijote* and *120* found a niche for their own narratives. *Don Quijote* pays homage to its predecessors by naming chivalric works such as *Amadís de Gaula, Tirant Le Blanc,* or *Palmerín de Inglaterra.* Sade, however, never mentions the key works that informed *120*—*Fanny Hill* (1748), *Thérèse Philosophe* (1748), or *Dom Bougre* (1741)—but his novel does include all of the subgenres of enlightened pornography: the autobiography of the whore, the catalogue of postures, and the sexually-charged anticlerical novel. Sade may not mention any other novel (*Don Quijote* included) in order to highlight the singularity of *120*, yet his text shows both the coordinates of the enlightened pornographic genre and more importantly, the legacy of Cervantes and his work.

Cervantes' and Quijote's further connection to *120* is clear in Sade's strong belief in the performativity of the language, *120*'s quixotism, and its metafictional nature. Cervantes and Sade share a strong belief that saying and naming translates to doing or being. By naming his world, Quijote creates a reality for himself and for some people who surround him (namely Sancho).[13] Similarly, the four libertines believe in the effects of narrative on the human body.[14] Thus the bawds tell stories to incite their desires and, as the libertines listen, they perform or direct sexual scenes. Annie Le Brun argues that "Sade dramatizes both the testing of ideas by the body and the testing of the body by ideas."[15] Roland Barthes and Emmanuel Sauvage note that in *120*'s mise-en-abîme, the bawds' stories that incite the libertines to act may also incite readers to act too since they may be aroused by these sexual representations.[16]

Secondly, the Cervantine legacy in Sade's work reveals itself in both authors' clash with their own projects, in other words, in their quixotism. Although their novels are ambitious, they face tensions and pitfalls. Both writers fight with a text that resists their "plan," and, in the case of Sade, with a body that resists too.[17] The struggle between the ideal and the real makes *Don Quijote* the greatest metaphor for the boundaries of the human imagination and it helps us understand the inner workings of *120*. *120* aimed to be an "erotic encyclopedia" containing all possible desires and pleasures but this project is challenged by a resisting body (a defined number of sexual fantasies, postures, or tortures) and a resisting text that suffers from delays and chaos.[18] In the same way, *Don Quijote*'s narrator sets high expectations for both his hero and the novel, but he becomes more cautious and less confident in the second part as he faces internal and external criticisms as well as the threat of an apocryphal Quijote.

Metafiction is the most salient feature of *Don Quijote* and the touchstone by which *120* appropriated *Don Quijote*'s poetics. *120* follows *Don Quijote* closely insofar as it highlights the creation of the novel. Both texts have a metanarrative that explains the structure to the reader, that makes the reader an active participant, and that constantly verifies the success or failure of their project. This unveiling of the literary mechanism is a sign of knowledge and mastery. Cervantes and Sade know the art of narrating so well that they can play with it and show the reader the machinery behind the scenes.

As Robert Spires and Nicholas Spadaccini note, Cervantes' *Don Quijote* became a model for the metafictional novel in early modern European literature.[19] *Don Quijote*'s narrator clearly states that this novel is made of novels with a mission to attack them all: "una invectiva contra los libros de caballería."[20] Its strategy is to imitate the best in the best way: "la imitación … cuanto fuere más perfecta, tanto mejor será lo que se escribiere."[21] This polyphony of texts is mimicked by the polyphony of writers who are creating the story: there is a first author who leaves the story incomplete, a second author (Cide Hamete) who continues it, a Moorish translator who may have modified it, and a final author who may be Cervantes himself.[22] In the second part, the novel includes the first part as an actual book in circulation. Now Quijote, Sancho, and their friends are aware of being characters in a book that is being read by thousands of readers, and many of the characters who cross Quijote's path assume that they will be part of a future novel.

In *120*, although characters are not aware of being in a book, they see themselves as fictional elements in the libertines' theatre. The libertines and the bawds assume a narrative role when they turn ideas and stories into theatrical representations. Although both novels differ in location due to the fact that *Don Quijote* happens outdoors and *120* indoors, the duke's castle in *Don Quijote* resembles (and maybe inspired) *120* insofar as in both locations episodes and adventures are staged for the protagonists to see or experience. As a consequence, Henry Sullivan has described the duke's castle in *Don Quijote* as a "sadistic theatre of cruelty."[23]

The metafictional polyphony in *Don Quijote* also appears in *120* but in a different manner. We encounter two metanarratives that complement the story and guide both the reader and the narrator's "future-self."[24] The first metanarrative addresses the reader. Just as Cervantes talks to his "desocupado" or "amable lector" drawing him into writer's confidence, Sade appeals to his "cher" or "ami lecteur" with an informal "tu" that creates a sense of intimacy that is particular to *120*.[25] Because *120* is a pornographic novel, the narrator confesses that his ultimate goal is to please his reader both poetically and physically; as a consequence, his tone is both cordial and vehement. Simultaneously, a second metanarrative addresses the narrator's future self. Here a tyrannical narrator dictates specific ways to make descriptions and to unravel the plot in order to achieve a desired response: "l'accroissement d'un désir ... qui doit ... conduire à une certaine fureur lubrique."[26] This other narrator only gives orders with no room for negotiation: "Ne vous écartez en rien de ce plan: tout y est combiné ... avec la plus grande exactitude."[27]

Despite the narrator's quest for precision, Sade faced multiple obstacles in the making of *120*, notably the time and paper constraints imposed by writing in the Bastille. *120* can thus be considered incomplete: only the first part is developed, and the last three parts, made of sketches and notes, remain in skeletal form. Although the work may seem "incomplete," Mladen Kozul observes that the lists of murdered people, dates, and scarce details are crucial components of Sade's plan.[28] These lists highlight the metafictional nature of Sade's work. In other words, the auto-referential commentaries that expose the bare bones of the narrative project become a direct outlet for fiction to talk about itself.

In *120*, Sade conceived a sexual encyclopedia encompassing all desires and pleasures, a sort of erotic *ars combinatoria*.[29] When Sade uses terms such as "plan," "system," "program," or "combination," we discern *120*'s emphasis on computation.[30] Sade was obsessed with numbers. As his diaries show, he counted everything: food, money, or his days in prison. Michel Delon stresses that *120* is the only novel whose title is explicitly written in numbers.[31] This novel is mathematic and programmatic: 4 libertines go to a castle with 42 individuals: 4 wives, 4 bawds, 4 hags, 4 sodomites, 4 men, 8 girls, 8 boys, and 6 servants. 4 is the novel's pattern. Only the number 6 deviates from the pattern because the servants are not seen as victims. The libertines will stay 4 months: November, December, January, and February. Every bawd will tell 150 stories in 30 days, around 5 per day, aiming to a total of 600 passions in 120 days. The protagonists are named after consecutive letters in alphabetical order: B for Blangis, C for Curval, D for Durcet, and E for *l'evêque* (the bishop).[32] Emmanuel Sauvage notes the perfection embedded in the quadrangular structure: four temperaments, elements, seasons, and cardinal points.[33] Joan De Jean argues that this symmetry leads the reader to experience "an aesthetic response," which Lucienne Frappier-Mazur refers to as an "aesthetics of violence."[34] Symmetry, combination, and programming lead to a sense of perfection, thereby distracting the reader from the horrific and alienating violence perpetrated in the story.

120's *ars combinatoria* can be expressed as follows: "Il fait chier une fille A et une autre B; puis il force B à manger l'étron de A, et A de manger l'étron de B."[35] Éric Bordas suggests that "combination" rules the Sadean world.[36] The narrator establishes the variables: spaces (in the castle), times (months), characters (lower, upper class), and "passions" that once combined provide a "système," as Sade calls it, of human desire, pleasure, and imagination.[37] Cervantes in *Don Quijote* also changed variables, especially when narrating love stories: there is always a trio composed of two men who fight for a woman (Cardenio-Fernando-Luscinda or Lotario-Anselmo-Camila). In *Don Quijote* however, repetition does not tend to expand the imagination but in Sade, the *ars combinatoria* seeks to generate new desires and crimes or, at least, that is the narrator's promise: "se varient à l'infini," "mille et mille crimes peuvent naître de ce système."[38]

The narrative perfection sought by Sade and Cervantes cannot be achieved without rigor and control, occurring in both novels in several sorts of regimes (the "Règlements" in the case of *120*). In *Don Quijote*, the knight controls Sancho and himself in terms of food and language. Quijote barely eats, but Sancho struggles to comply with these rules.[39] In regard to language, Quijote and other characters attempt to regulate speech: from censoring "evil" books to controlling people's ways of narrating. Quijote insists on silencing Sancho, especially in the second part when he feels embarrassed by Sancho's use of proverbs ("Yo te vea mudo antes que me muera").[40] Regulating narration is paramount in *Don Quijote*, and thus the knight reprimands Sancho for being a bad narrator and applauds Pedro for being a good one: "Si desa manera cuentas tu cuento, Sancho ... no acabarás en dos días" versus "el cuento es muy bueno, y vos, Pedro, le contáis con muy buena gana."[41] Don Quijote scolds most of the story-tellers, and his influence is so strong that even Sancho, in the second part, attempts to regulate speech when he tells a businessman: "venid al punto sin rodeos ni callejuelas."[42]

In a similar, albeit more dramatic way, there are strict regimens for Silling's dwellers. These restrictions are stated in the "Règlements" that the four libertines wrote, promulgated, and were expected to follow, along with their harem. These rules control dress, speech, and bodily acts.[43] There is also a regime of language and a specific demand of detail when bawds engage in storytelling: "Duclos ... ne vous a-t-on pas prévenue qu'il faut à vos récits les détails les plus grands et les plus étendus?"[44] Yet both the narrator and the bawds exert a "rhetoric of patience," or, as I consider it, a "rhetoric of continence," in which the act of narrating consists of releasing information in small doses.[45] Joan De Jean calls this phenomenon a discipline of "both the body of narrative and the body in narrative."[46] *120*'s narrator explains that if we obey the law of saying/not saying, knowing/not knowing, we will obtain the greatest aesthetic and sexual experience. By delaying details to both the libertines (and the reader), the narrator ensures the increase of their desire and their sexual furor. Narrative mortification here mimics the sexual mortification that the libertines experience.

Sexual continence is key to the success of the libertine's sexual program and can be explained as a strategy to cope with their impotency, a condition that characterizes both the protagonists and the narrator.[47] Of the four libertines, only two (Blangis and Curval) are sexually active and the other two (Durcet and the bishop) seem to have erectile dysfunction: "deux seulement étaient en état de pouvoir procéder à cet acte, l'un des deux autres, le traitant, n'éprouvant plus absolument aucune érection."[48] Three of them have a frail body: the bishop vanishes during orgasms, Durcet fails to achieve them, and Curval has difficulties ejaculating.[49] Only Blangis delivers himself to full ejaculations.[50] Continence thus allows them to stay active in the orgy. They have to restrain their bodies and impose upon themselves a regime of food, sleep, and sexual release in order to increase their impact on victims. Curval proposes to control pleasure in a way that he masters his semen instead of being overcome by it: "Jamais le foutre ne doit ni dicter, ni diriger les principes; c'est aux principes à régler la manière de le perdre."[51] In this sense, ideas should control the real, and philosophy must rule the body. Despite this apparent sovereignty over the senses, the excessive control or continence results in a situation of total anorgasmia incompatible with the orgy.[52] The libertines experience a lack of sensuality and find it impossible either to obtain pleasure or achieve orgasm.

Quijote, on his side, although far from the orgiastic intention of the libertines, also imposes a regimen of sexual continence on himself. Paradoxically, he believes that all of the damsels he encounters fall in love with him. Yet when he has the opportunity to engage in a sexual relationship (with Altisidora, for example) he resists it, fearing his most repressed desires ("mis deseos que duermen").[53] Quijote and the four libertines control their body's impulses and take great pride in their continence. Exercising restraint can be a mark of mastery but also a frustrating experience. Especially in *120*, the tension between inciting and delaying pleasure may ultimately inhibit it. If the libertines ejaculate rarely and poorly, the narrative—which is also subjected to a rhetoric of continence—seems to discharge in a similar fashion: the last three months (and especially the climatic last one) are short and brisk telegrams or premature ejaculations.

The colossal task of writing the perfect novel is daunting. Cervantes and Quijote had high expectations for their works, and they created a number of strategies (like control and rigor) to achieve them, but they could not hide their own self-awareness of the challenges that they faced as they wrote. As the narrators show the tension between order and chaos that guides their processes of writing, we see how metafiction conducts a self-study of the novel's successes or failures. In *Don Quijote*, both the narrator and the characters verify the accuracy of the given information or the effectiveness of the narration, especially in the second part. If in the first part, self-criticism is mostly ironic and based on the formula of the *captatio benevolentiae*, or the classical rhetorical technique of winning the goodwill of listeners, in the second part, the narrator is highly critical of the first part, emphasizing its shortcomings.[54] He complains about the narrative meandering, some gaps in information (for example, the name of the thief who stole Sancho's donkey), or the unfortunate insertion of tales like "El curioso impertinente:" "una de las tachas que ponen a la tal historia."[55] The second part thus shows a more anxious and doubtful narrator who constantly keeps himself in check.[56] All in all, *Don Quijote* is not a well-oiled machine. Sancho's wife, for example, has at least four different names: Juana or Mari Gutiérrez in the first part, and Juana or Teresa Panza in the second. Additionally, the promise made in the first part that Quijote will go to Zaragoza is not accomplished in the second part—maybe due to Avellaneda's fake Quijote who actually visited the city. In terms of chronology, the narrator says that Quijote was supposed to go to Barcelona for Saint John's festival on June 24, yet previous letters are dated in July and August.[57] Just like *Don Quijote*, *120* harbors a number of inaccuracies and acknowledges its own pitfalls. Peter Cryle notes that "in spite of its thematic show of arithmetical rigor, the novel does not respond satisfactorily to a careful audit."[58] A worried narrator notes various "omissions" and mistakes and asks his future-self to correct them.[59] Moreover, although the narrator promises to say it all, on several occasions, he fails to be omniscient and finds himself apologizing for it. Although Mladen Kozul considers chaos to be part of Sade's program, the narrator is sensitive to criticism because he seeks a rigorous narration.[60]

Both *Don Quijote* and *120*'s narrators fear repetition and monotony, but, as Michel Delon argues, repetition is predictable in works like *120*.[61] The search for difference necessarily ends up in succession and repetition. The promised plethora of scenes is ultimately reduced to a definite number, and this split between the ideal and the real threatens to collapse the program. Durcet confesses how hard it is to face reality when imagination knows no border: " j'avoue que mon imagination a toujours été sur cela au-delà de mes moyens."[62] Nature limits his and all human imagination. Just like don Quijote faces the painful blow of reality every time he fights windmills instead of giants, *120*'s narrator sees both his power and the power of the novel's *ars combinatoria* constantly restricted. The more the libertines or the narrator want to control the body or the text, the more they escape from their grasping hands.

Don Quijote and *120 Days of Sodom* are works written in prison that exude an environment full of madness and genius, and they turn to death as if it were the only possible end to chaos. Death as a trope, however, differs significantly in the two works. *Don Quijote* could easily have been a one-book feat, but the publication of the *Quijote* (1614) by Avellaneda (ca. 1597–1616) prompted Cervantes to write the second part. By writing a second part, he reclaimed his book, reappropriating Quijote so that he—and only he—could kill him.[63] Cervantes sacrifices don Quijote and by killing him, he kills madness. In *120,* by contrast, Sade kills almost everyone except the four madmen and their 12 servants (4 bawds, 1 wife, 4 sodomites, and 3 cooks). If poetically these two books are linked, ethically they find themselves at opposite ends of the spectrum. Don Quijote is—in the Sadean universe—the Justine who embraces virtue and detests vice, and Sade is the murderous Juliette who prescribes her own anti-ethical approach to the world.

It becomes evident that by appropriating Cervantes and his work, Sade fictionalized a version of his favorite author, just as he did with La Mettrie according to Jean Deprun.[64] Yet there is something to be said when Sade catalogues Cervantes's works under the rubric of rape, because then he casts Cervantes's imagery in a new light. In other words, in Cervantes's novels, rape and other sexual crimes abound. By considering *"La fuerza de la sangre"* as a core piece in the making of *120*, Sade posits a veiled ethics of sexual crimes consented to and sugar-coated under the guise of chivalric misogyny. The full implications of Cervantes' ethics of sexual violence have not yet been fully acknowledged in Cervantine criticism, and they are a topic worthy of further investigation.[65]

By illuminating the extent to which Cervantes influenced Sade's *120*, we unveil new dimensions of both of their works. Thus far we know that Cervantes' books were Sade's comfort books, ones to which he returned again and again as a way to cope with imprisonment, but, more importantly, they served as a source of inspiration for his own writing. Sade himself claimed that he only read books that informed his writing: "je ne lis que ce qui a rapport à mon ouvrage;" in a novel that has been considered the most obscene novel of all times, Cervantes' *Don Quijote* certainly did just that.[66]

NOTES

1. Miguel de Cervantes Saavedra, *El ingenioso hidalgo don Quijote de la Mancha*, vols. 1 and 2, ed. Luis Andrés Murillo (Madrid: Castalia, 1991), 50. Translation: "begotten in a prison, where every discomfort has its place and every mournful sound makes its home?" Miguel de Cervantes, *Don Quixote*, trans. Edith Grossman (New York: HarperCollins, 2003): 3.
2. Francisco Rodríguez Marín, *La cárcel en que se engendró el Quijote* (Madrid: Revista de Archivos, 1916), 65.
3. Anne Gédéon de La Fitte, marquis de Pelleport (1754–1801), penned *Les Bohemiens* (1790), a rewriting of *Don Quijote,* in the Bastille. Marquis de Pelleport, *Les bohémiens,* ed. Robert Darnton (Paris: Mercure, 2010).
4. Donatien Alfonse, marquis de Sade, *Les 120 Journées de Sodome* (Paris: Le Tripode, 2014). On the manuscript, see Gilbert Lely, "Introduction aux *120 Journées de Sodome*" (Paris: 10/18, 1962), 57.
5. My sources are Sade's manuscripts in the Library of Arsenal in Paris, France: Mss. 12456, 670–760. On Sade's imprisonment, see Gilbert Lély, "La mort du marquis de Sade," *Botteghe Oscure* 18 (1956): 57.
6. "I want ... the name of two or three main streets and streets in the red district of Lisbon, Madrid, and Toledo." My translation. Sade, Mss. 12456, 724.

7. Miguel de Cervantes, *Novelas ejemplares*, 2 vols, ed. Harry Sieber (Madrid: Cátedra, 2006). On Sade's books on Spain, see Haisoo Chung, "Lectures de Sade, prisonnier à Vincennes et à la Bastille (1779–1789)," in ed. Jean Marie Goulemot, *Lecture, livres et lecteurs* (Tours: Univ. François Rabelais, 2003), 57–85.

8. He considers Cervantes without rival and *Don Quijote* the best novel ever written. Donatien Alfonse, marquis de Sade, *Idées sur les romans,* ed. Jean-Marc Levent (Paris: Éditions mille et une nuits, 2003), 15–16.

9. Donatien Alfonse, marquis de Sade, *Les crimes de l'amour* (Paris: Massé, 1799).

10. Donatien Alfonse, marquis de Sade, *Oxtiern ou les malheurs du libertinage* (Versailles: Blaisot, 1791). BNF, Arsenal, Mss. 12456, 670–760.

11. Cervantes, *Don Quijote* I, 50. "the fairest, gayest, and cleverest that could be imagined." Cervantes, *Quixote* 3.

12. Sade, *Les 120,* 84. "the most impure tale that has ever been told since our world began." Marquis de Sade, *The 120 Days of Sodom and Other Writings*, trans. Austryn Waihouse and Richard Seaver (New York: Grove Press, 1987), 253.

13. Furthermore, Sancho's becoming the fake governor of Barataria became the "reality" of the village. Cervantes, *Don Quijote* II, 433.

14. Blangis wants "what Duclos has just described," and Curval congratulates Duclos for "the effect of your discourses." Sade, *The 120,* 294, 415.

15. Annie Le Brun, "Sade or the first theatre of atheism," *Paragraph* 23.1 (2000): 45.

16. Roland Barthes, *Sade, Fourier, Loyola* (Paris: Seuil, 1971), 152. Emmanuel Sauvage, "L'évidence du tableau dans *Les Cent Vingt Journées du Sodome* et les trois *Justine* du Sade," Diss. Doctorate (Univ. de Montréal, 2002), 173.

17. Sade, *Les 120,* 35.

18. Joan de Jean, "*Les 120 Journées de Sodome*: Disciplining the Body of Narrative," *Romanic Review* 74 (1983): 35.

19. Robert Spires, *Beyond the Metafictional Mode* (Lexington: Univ. Press of Kentucky, 1984). Nicholas Spadaccini, "Cervantes and the Question of Metafiction," *Vanderbilt e-Journal of Luso-Hispanic Studies* 2 (2005).

20. Cervantes, *Don Quijote* I, 57. "an invective against books of chivalry." Cervantes, *Quixote*, 8.

21. Cervantes, *Don Quijote* I, 57. "It only has to make use of mimesis in the writing, and the more precise that is, the better the writing will be." Cervantes, *Quixote*, 8.

22. On Cervantes as the final author, see Howard Mancing, "Cervantes as Narrator of 'Don Quijote,'" *Bulletin of the Cervantes Society of America* 23.1 (2003): 117–140.

23. Henry Sullivan, "The Duke's Theater of Sadism," Diana de Armas, ed., *Don Quijote,* trans. Burton Raffel (New York: Norton, 1999): 147.

24. On the "future-self," see Will McMorran, "Behind the Mask? Sade and the *Cent Vingt Journées de Sodome*," *Modern Language Review* 108 (2013): 1127.

25. Elias Rivers, *Quixotic Scriptures* (Bloomington: Indiana Univ. Press, 1983), 108. Cervantes, *Don Quijote* I, 50; Sade, *Les 120,* 44, 84. Jean Christophe

Abramovici, "*Les Cent Vingt Journées de Sodome*: Lecture et isolisme," *Lecture, livres et lecteurs*, ed. Jean Marie Goulemot (Tours: Univ. François Rabelais, 2003), 96.

26. Sade, *Les 120,* 45, 71. "the augmentation of a desire … which must … lead to a lascivious fury … ." Sade, *The 120,* 241.

27. Sade, *Les 120,* 515. "Under no circumstances deviate from this plan, everything has been worked out … with the greatest care and thoroughness." Sade, *The 120,* 673.

28. Mladen Kozul, "L'inachèvement des *Cent Vingt Journées de Sodome* de Sade," *Cahiers d'Histoire des Littératures*, ed. Henning Krauss (Heidelberg: Univ. C. Winter Heidelberg, 1995), 60.

29. On the *ars combinatoria,* see Gottfried Leibniz, *Logic and Metaphysics*, trans. K.J. Northcott (Manchester: Manchester Univ. Press, 1964), 47–67.

30. De Jean stresses how the French "raconter" stems from "compter" or to count. De Jean, "*Les 120,*" 39.

31. Michel Delon, "Introduction and Notes," *Les Cent Vingt Journées de Sodome* (Paris: Gallimard, 1990), 1134.

32. Alain Sebbah, "Le Château dans l'imaginaire libertin chez Laclos, Sade et Vivant Denon," *Château et imaginaire*, ed. Anne-Marie Cocula (Pessac: Ausonius, 2001), 219.

33. Emmanuel Sauvage, "L'écriture du corps dans *Les cent vingt journées de Sodome* de Sade," *Tangence* 60 (1999): 128.

34. De Jean "Les *120,*" 40. Lucienne Frappier-Mazur, "Sadean Libertinage and the Esthetics of Violence," *Yale French Studies* 94 (1998): 188.

35. Sade, *Les 120,* 419. "He has girls A and B shit. Then he forces B to eat A's turd, and A to eat B's." Sade, *The 120,* 579.

36. Éric Bordas, "Sade ou l'écriture de la destruction: à propos de la structure stylistique des *Cent Vingt Journées de Sodome*," *The Romanic Review* 86 (1995): 676.

37. Sade, *Les 120,* 29.

38. Sade, *Les 120,* 45, 267. "infinitely various," "a thousand crimes may be the result of such a doctrine." Sade, *The 120,* 219, 427.

39. In the first part, Sancho's body resists, but, in the second part, he complies with the dietary restrictions prescribed by Pedro. Cervantes, *Don Quijote* II, 425.

40. Cervantes, *Don Quijote* II, 194. "I see you mute before I die," Cervantes, *Quixote,* 590.

41. Cervantes, *Don Quijote* I, 242, 165. "If you tell your story this way, Sancho … you will not finish in two days" versus "the story is very good, and you, my good Pedro, tell it with a good deal of grace." Cervantes, *Quixote* 145, 84.

42. Cervantes, *Don Quijote* II, 394. "Get to the point without going around in circles." Cervantes, *Quixote,* 764.

43. Wives have to be naked and the harem women wear costumes; if people speak about religion, it has to be heretically; and, people defecate according to a schedule. Sade, *Les 120,* 71–79.

44. Sade, *Les 120*, 104. "Duclos … we have, I believe, advised you that your narrations must be decorated with the most numerous and searching details." Sade, *The 120*, 271.

45. Abramovici, "Les *Cent*," 99. The bawds and the narrator constantly ask the libertines and the reader for their patience.

46. De Jean, "Les *120*," 34.

47. Albeit the narrator promises to say it all, but he ultimately confesses that he ignores what has happened in certain places or on some days. Sade, *120*, 309, 353.

48. Sade, *Les 120*, 19. "only two were capable of proceeding to the act, one of the remaining two, the financier, being absolutely incapable of an erection." Sade, *The 120*, 196.

49. Sade, *Les 120*, 27, 31, 35.

50. Sade, *Les 120*, 25.

51. Sade, *Les 120*, 374. "Never ought fuck be allowed to dictate or affect one's principles; 'tis for one's principles to regulate one's manner of shedding it." Sade, *The 120*, 535.

52. Since the 7th day, "no fuck shed;" the 21st day, "no sign of fuck;" on the 28th day, "no one discharged." Sade, *The 120*, 346, 474, 537. On anorgasmia, see Jean Marie Goulemot, "Sadean Novels and Pornographic Novels," *Paragraph* 23.1 (2000): 67–70.

53. Cervantes, *Don Quijote* II, 398. "my sleeping desires." Cervantes, *Quixote*, 767.

54. The narrator says that his narration is dry and lacking imagination. Cervantes, *Don Quijote* I, 52.

55. Cervantes, *Don Quijote* II, 63. "One of the objections people make to the history." Cervantes, *Quixote*, 477.

56. The narrator denounces the author and the translator as careless. Cervantes, *Don Quijote* II, 122, 169.

57. Juan Eugenio Hartzenbusch and Luis Murillo justify and dismiss this sequence as an error. See Hartzenbusch, *El Quijote de la Mancha* (Barcelona: Ramírez, 1874) and Murillo, *Don Quijote* II, 504.

58. Peter M. Cryle, "Taking Sade Serially: *Les cent vingt journées de Sodome*," *SubStance* 20.1 (1991): 98, 99, 103.

59. In December and January, he notes 151 instead of 150, and in February, 148.

60. Kozul, "L'inachèvement," 67.

61. Michel Delon, "L'obsession anale de Sade," *Annales historiques de la Révolution Française* 3 (2010): 141.

62. Sade, *Les 120*, 204–205. "I must declare that my imagination has always outdistanced my faculties." Sade, *The 120*, 364.

63. The final author claims his right to own Quijote: "For me alone was Don Quixote born, and I for him; he knew how to act, and I to write; the two of us alone are one." Cervantes, *Quixote*, 939.

64. Jean Deprun, "La Mettrie et l'immoralisme sadien," *Annales de Bretagne* 83.4 (1976): 748.

65. Bradley Nelson, "Poet or Pimp? Theatricality and Sexual Crimes in Lope de Vega and Cervantes," *eHumanista Cervantes* 4 (2015): 178–195.

66. "I only read what informs my work." My translation. Chung, "Lectures," 85.

Mapping Don Quixote's Route: Spanish Cartography, English Travelers and National Pride

ELIZABETH FRANKLIN LEWIS

During the eighteenth century, *Don Quijote de la Mancha* drew attention for its proliferation of new editions in Spanish; for its numerous translations, especially in English; as well as for the many other "spin-off" works based on the novel and its characters.[1] Eighteenth-century translators, editors, and authors identified in this classic story of the misadventures of the "ingenious gentleman" of La Mancha important messages for a modern reading public. Samuel Johnson famously remarked "how few books are there of which one can possibly arrive at the *last* page. Was there ever anything written by a mere man that was wished longer by its readers excepting Don Quixote, Robinson Crusoe, and the Pilgrim's Progress?"[2] Eighteenth-century essayists and critics considered *Don Quijote* as more than an entertaining or even inspiring work of fiction: they treated it as an object of study. A 1780 edition created for the Real Academia Española by the printer Joaquín Ibarra added to the novel some important extra-textual material including an analytical study, illustrations, and for the first time, a map that situated fictional evets of the novel in the geography of contemporary eighteenth-century Spain. This map is the first representation of what would come to be known as Don Quixote's Route—a literary tour made famous by Azorín's 1905 *La ruta de Don Quijote*.[3] About the same time as the Ibarra edition, British travelers to Spain also evoked elements of the novel—its setting, characters, and even objects—in their observations of and writings about their experiences with Spanish culture. This essay will compare two early maps of Don Quixote's route to references to the novel in British travel journals, showing the ways both Spanish and English readers found evidence of *Don Quijote* in the Spanish landscape. I argue that these editors, geographers, and authors used the novel to support claims of each nation's cultural superiority thus bolstering national pride.

Enrique Rodríguez-Cepeda identifies various types of eighteenth-century Spanish-language editions of the novel produced in Spain, each intended for a different reading public, including inexpensive pocket versions of the novel (*de bosillo*) intended for a common audience and high quality luxury editions destined for the libraries of wealthy connoisseurs and government officials as well as gifts to important diplomats and political figures.[4] The 1780 Ibarra edition by the Royal Academy presents Cervantes´ novel as an object of admiration and study. Its small run (Rodríguez-Cepeda estimates only about 1000 copies were printed, in comparison to the more than 30,000 copies of the pocket editions), large size, and high economic value indicate that is was an edition destined for collectors.[5] This edition also stands out for its preliminary study and biography of Cervantes, for its collection of fine illustrations, and for a map of Spain that highlights Don Quixote's journeys and adventures, prepared by Tomás López, the Royal Geographer to Charles III (fig. 1). In the prologue to this edition, the Academy states its main interest in undertaking this project as based in a desire to cultivate and promote the study of the Spanish language.[6] However, this edition also seeks to build upon, and even improve, an earlier 1737 Spanish-language edition published in London that included the first ever biography of Cervantes, written by Spanish enlightenment thinker Gregorio Mayans, an edition that the Royal Academy calls "magnífica" but also full of errors.[7]

Following Mayans, the Ibarra edition also includes its own biography and a preliminary study, both written by academy member Vicente de los Ríos.[8] The text itself goes back to the original first and second editions of the novel produced by printer Juan de la Cuesta in 1605 and 1615. But added to all of the previous texts was something new—a map showing the itinerary of Don Quixote starting in La Mancha, through Barcelona, and back:

> Últimamente para satisfacer más la curiosidad de los lectores, se ha puesto un mapa, que comprende una buena porción de España, y en el cual se ven demarcados con una línea encarnada los viajes de Don Quixote, trabajado con toda exactitud por Don Tomás López, geógrafo de S.M. con arreglo a las observaciones hechas por Don Joseph de Hermosilla, Capitán que fue del Real Cuerpo de Ingenieros.[9]

Figure 1. "Mapa de una porción del reyno de España que comprende los parages por sonde anduvo Don Quixote y los sitios de sus aventuras," El ingenioso hidalgo don Quixote de la Mancha compuesto por Miguel de Cervantes Saavedra. Nueva edición corregida por la Real Academia Española, 4 vols. (Madrid: Ibarra, 1780). Source: Biblioteca Nacional de España.

López and Hermosilla created the map based on Vicente de los Ríos's "Plan cronológico" that identifies the events of the novel, their duration, and location.[10] López used Ríos's plan as a basis for Hermosilla's field investigation, combining the observations that Hermosilla gathered with previous maps López had already produced for an atlas of Spain. The act of taking the novel's references to certain geographical features and place names (as interpreted by de los Ríos) and locating them "con toda exactitud" spatially on a map through scientific observations and mathematical calculations by an army engineer and the Court geographer constituted a new interpretation of the *Quijote* as not only representative of but also identifiable in contemporary Spain.

Ricardo Padrón examines the importance of the emerging science of cartography to the development of a modern, scientific, and imperialistic Spain. The increasing sophistication and availability of grid-maps in northern Europe were central to the colonization process. Eighteenth-century cartographers throughout Europe were valued by governments for identifying, representing, and even claiming political, economic, and military domains. The eighteenth century was also a time of technological transition in cartographic production involving more precise and complex topographical survey methods.[11] Spain was slow to adopt modern cartographic techniques, but, by the eighteenth century, the Spanish crown contributed significant resources in order to develop the art and science of mapping.[12]

Tomás López was the royal cartographer to Charles III and head of the newly formed "Cabinet of Geography." He had studied his craft in Paris under French cartographer Jean Baptiste D'Anville, and, during the course of his career, he produced numerous maps of Spain and the Americas as well as several publications about geography. López, following his training in France, considered himself a "geógrafo de gabinete," that is, he performed his work not in the field, but rather in his studio, by consulting numerous bibliographic resources, maps, and detailed surveys from the field that others performed and sent to him in Madrid.[13] He had produced a map of La Mancha in 1765 as part of a series of maps for his *Atlas de España*. The 1780 map, titled "Mapa de una porcion del Reyno de España que comprehende los parages por donde anduvo Don Quixote, y los sitios de sus aventuras," shares many of the same geographical features of his other regional maps but focuses on central and northeast regions of Spain from La Mancha north to Zaragoza and east to Barcelona, following the trajectory of Don Quixote identified by Vicente de los Ríos.

López's map of the travels of Don Quixote includes locations for 35 episodes of the novel. There are numerous place names and geographical features marked on the map that are not part of the novel including the regions of Castilla la Nueva (and Madrid), Castilla la Vieja, and Valencia. López, following Cervantes' ambiguous "un lugar de la Mancha" does not identify on the map the whereabouts of Don Quixote's own village.[14] Also missing is the inn where so much of the second half of part one takes place, but one can follow Don Quixote's itinerary and even see how long his journey might have taken.[15] Royal librarian Juan Antonio Pellicer was editor of a 1797–1798 edition of the *Quijote* published by the Madrid printer Gabriel de Sancha that, like the Royal Academy edition before it, also presented the novel with a preliminary study, extensive notes, and with another map, engraved by Manuel Antonio Rodríguez (fig. 2).[16] It identifies 45 places associated with the novel, and locates the ambiguous "lugar de la Mancha" in the village of Argamasilla del Alba.[17]

Both of these eighteenth-century maps tie visual representations of a concrete and identifiable contemporary Spanish geography to Cervantes' fictional seventeenth-century novel. Yet the 1780 Ibarra edition and the 1798

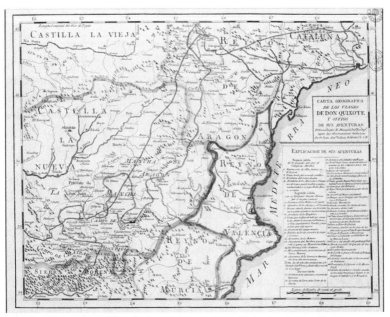

Figure 2. "Carta geográfica de los viages de Don Quixote y sitios de sus aventuras," Ingenioso hidalgo don Quixote de la Mancha, compuesto por Miguel de Cervantes Saavedra. Nueva edición corregida de nuevo, con nuevas notas, con nuevas estampas, con nuevo análisis, y con la vida del autor nuevamente aumentada, Juan Antonio Pellicer, ed. 8 vols. (Madrid: Sancha, 1787–1789). Source: Biblioteca Nacional de Madrid

Sancha edition maps stand out, not only for their detail, such that one could follow day-by-day Don Quixote's journey through the Spanish landscape, but also because as editions produced in Spain and containing maps created by important Spanish court figures—King Charles III's own mapmaker and Charles IV's librarian—they stake a political claim on Cervantes' novel as Spanish (and not British) territory. Given the immense popularity of the novel in England, the numerous editions in both English and Spanish produced in London, and the many adaptations of the novel from Fielding's *Don Quixote in England* (1734) to Lennox's *The Female Quixote* (1752), perhaps academicians in the Spanish capital saw a need to reclaim the novel for Spain, inscribing it in the very topography of the land.[18]

Travelers to Spain also represented in their narratives both real and imagined spaces, along with the real and imagined peoples they encountered in them. While Spain was not commonly part of the British grand tour during the eighteenth and early nineteenth centuries, many English travelers to Spain published their narratives upon their return to England. While typically the grand tour was meant to complete the education of aristocratic British men by acquainting them the great empires of classical tradition, Spain was, in Ana Hontanilla's words, "the still living, if failing rival Empire."[19] British travelers who came to Spain were typically merchants, military officers, or government officials, and their interests and motives for travel were more for business than for pleasure. Hontanilla finds in these narratives an expression of British moral superiority in their descriptions of Spanish cultural and social practices, which justified British economic exploitation of Spain.[20] Many travelers complained of the backwardness and uncivilized nature of the country, for example in a 1783 account by an anonymous "Polite Traveler," for whom Spain is filled with "pride, baseness, poverty, ignorance, bigotry, superstition, and ridiculous ceremonies."[21] However, many of these British travelers also came to Spain with knowledge of Spanish cultural accomplishments as well, especially in the arts and literature of the Spanish golden age, and many would have been acquainted with Cervantes' novel *Don Quijote* through the numerous editions and translations that were printed in England throughout the century.

Henry Swinburne's *Travels in Spain 1775 and 1776* (1779) was one of the most widely known of these Spanish travel narratives. His first reference to Cervantes' novel comes in chapter XI, in the description of an inn on the road to Valencia:

> The approach of night ... obliged us to stop at the Venta del Platero, a hovel that beggars all description; so superlatively wretched, that I thought an exact drawing of its outward appearance would be a real curiosity. We were lodged in part of a ground-floor, the remainder of which was occupied by the mules and pigs;... Several companies of fishermen, that hawk their fish about these scattered cottages, kept all night a perpetual knocking at the gate of our court, and brought to my mind the very lively ideas of the enchanted castles of Don Quixote.[22]

Later, in letter XIV, after leaving Valencia and approaching the village of Villena, Swinburne meets a real-life Sancho Panza, or so he imagines:

> Just as we were going into Villena, a little, round, squat figure, in a brown Montero cap, jacket, and breeches, with a little yellow waistcoat, caught my eye. It was not possible to paint a better Sancho Pança; and we were actually in a corner of the country of

that 'squire, which makes me conclude Cervantes drew the picture from real life, in some of his journeys through La Mancha.[23]

Swinburne returns to Sancho in Letter XLIV, near Segovia:

> At Villa de Santa Cruz, the only thing we remarked was a cow's tail in which the hostess stuck her combs; as this was the first instance we had met with a custom which prevailed in Sancho Pança's time, and was of such service in furnishing the barber with a false beard, we took particular notice of it. You know how fond I am of the fat fellow, and how happy I must be to find anything that explains and exemplifies the traits of his inimitable history.[24]

Swinburne finds evidence of the novel in the people and places around him, and much like the previously mentioned business travelers, his interpretations of both the book and his own travels confirm his negative views of Spain as a backwards nation mired in the past.

At about the same time, John Talbot Dillon published his *Letters from an English Traveler in Spain, in 1778, on the origin and progress of poetry in that kingdom, with occasional reflections on manners and customs and illustrations of the romance of Don Quixote.* Dillon started his journey through Spain in Barcelona, travelling south to Valencia, then west to Madrid, north through Burgos and finally to Bilbao before returning to England. All the while, in addition to comments about the places and people he encounters, Dillon provides his reader with a literary history of Spain from the medieval through the baroque period. He meets important Spanish intellectuals including, in May of 1778, Valencian thinker Gregorio Mayans, who had written the first biography of Cervantes for the Tonson Spanish language edition published in London. Of Mayans, he writes:

> I had the pleasure of becoming acquainted with the learned and courteous Don Gregorio Mayans, formerly librarian to the king; who now lives here, having a good estate in this country, and to his politeness I am much indebted for many civilities as well as great information.[25]

From Valencia, Dillon finally enters into the famed La Mancha region, where he observes real-life examples of the novel everywhere:

> I was musing on this subject and had bewildered myself in political reflections till I entered the plains of *La Mancha.* There

> I recovered my good humor, saw many a fat laughing Sancho,
> drank good wine at *Cuidad Real* (sic.), spent a night at the village
> *del Toboso,* the residence of the peerless Dulcinea; saw the
> windmills which the distracted Quixote mistook for giants, and at
> a *Venta*, or inn, of La Mancha, was pleased with the simplicity of
> a *Manchega* girl, who waited upon me at supper, and asking her
> if she had ever heard of such a person as Don Quixote, answered
> "Oh yes sir, often; they say he is lately dead."[26]

Like Swinburne before him, Dillon saw the *Quijote* in the people and places he visited, and although as he claims, his book shares interesting but mostly occasional observations of Don Quixote, these are nonetheless important to his search for the origins of Spanish literature, the focus of his travels. He seeks both academic (meeting contemporary Spanish intellectual Mayans) and fictive (meeting a fat "real-life" Sancho or a woman who seems like Dulcinea) interaction with the novel, which is still quite alive; its protagonist, as described by his compatriots, seeming only recently dead to them. Yet in Dillon's assessment of Spain's literary history, these characters, seemingly stuck in the past, are evidence of a literature whose time has passed, and Cervantes' time is the point at which "the genius of Homer and Virgil seems to have fled the bank of the Manzanares and to have fixed its residence on those of the Thames."[27]

For Dillon, great Spanish literature is a thing of the past, and England is the current heir to the genius of the classics.

In 1802, another pair of independent British travelers set out for a prolonged excursion through Spain. Lord Holland Edward Fox and his wife Elizabeth spent three years travelling in Spain where they socialized with some of the most prominent political and cultural figures of the Spanish enlightenment. Their first trip to the peninsula was ostensibly in search of a warmer climate to improve the health of their son. They returned in 1808, this time without their children, during the Peninsular War with Napoleon. Although her journal was not edited and published until a century later (1910) by the Earl of Ilchester, her accounts, especially of the first trip, reveal much about her interests in Spanish culture and the prominent Spanish figures she befriended.[28]

Baroness Holland had studied both Spanish and English texts to prepare for her journey, including Swinburne's book. Of Swinburne, she observes: "The accounts of the roads are so much more favorable than Swinburne and other travelers lead one to imagine, that in point of danger there is little to apprehend, tho´ many trifling inconveniences to encounter."[29] The Hollands were keenly interested in Spanish culture and arts, especially the seventeenth-century plays of Lope de Vega and the paintings of Esteban Murillo both of which Lady Holland reports observing in their visits to the theater in the various Spanish cities they visited for the former, and in her visits to churches, convents, and private collections for the latter. She was also acquainted with *Don Quijote*, which she mentions early in her journal:

> I always thought til now that nothing was more pedantic than to say Don Quixote could not be relished out of the original. Nothing is so true, and to the assertion must be added that it cannot be completely so unless the reader knows Spain, its manners, customs, looks of the inhabitants, their tones of voice, dress, gestures, gravity, modes of sitting upon their asses, driving; their *ventas, posadas,* utensils vessels for liquor, skins, etc. In English I thought it a flat, burlesque work; now I think it without exception much the most amusing production of human wit. It is the only book which ever excited my risible faculties, as when I read it, I cannot refrain from bursting out into a loud laugh.[30]

Holland's attitude would have pleased the Spanish Royal Academy editors, as she saw value not only in its humorous characters, but also in its (Cervantes') language. She argues that readers need to understand the subtleties of Spanish culture in order to fully appreciate the novel. Holland therefore appears to have an intellectual interest in the linguistic and artistic qualities of the novel, much as she was interested in Spanish golden age painting and theater. As further evidence of her scholarly interests, in August of 1803 Lady Holland reports meeting Juan Antonio Pellicer, royal librarian and editor of the 1798 edition of the *Quijote*, which she calls "very good," although she appears to find Pellicer a rather pedantic old man: "prolix and extremely minute in all particulars of a story."[31]

Nicolás Ortega Cantero traces the literary discovery of Spanish geography to the travel writers of Romanticism in the mid-nineteenth century, yet the eighteenth-century travel writers I have discussed also associated fiction with their travel experiences in Spain.[32] Cervantes' novel of journeys influenced Swinburne, Dillon, and Holland as they planned their travels, even if they did not directly follow Don Quixote's route through Spain. They, like Cervantes's protagonist, traversed wide expanses of geography, meeting and interacting with the spaces and people along the way, whom they viewed through the lens of Cervantes's own narrative.[33]

As the eighteenth-century aristocratic grand tour gave way to upper middle class travelers in search of cultural refinement and exotic adventure, journeys through Spain became even more desirable, and the travel narrative gave way to the guidebook, providing visitors detailed instructions on what to see and how to appreciate national treasures. Barbara Schaff, who studies Victorian guidebooks to Italy and their literary references, observes that "Victorian middle-class tourists were now able to travel extensively, but they still willingly relied on literary sources as guidance to the right perception of place."[34] This happened in Spain as well, where travel narratives of the nineteenth century continued to strengthen the connection among Cervantes' novel, Spanish reality, and the travel experience. Richard Ford's *Handbook for Travellers in Spain,* first published in 1845, is one such travel guide for British travelers to exotic Spain. In it, Ford makes multiple references to the novel's descriptions of the people and places the traveler could expect to experience, from the Spanish inns to the bullfights. Ford recommends various tours that include stops at important sites from the novel on the maps from both the Ibarra and Pellicer editions, and he even suggests the novel to help the traveler learn Spanish:

> The best method of acquiring the Spanish language is to establish oneself in a good *casa de pupilos*, to avoid English society and conversation, to read *Don Quijote* through and aloud before a master of a morning, and to be schooled by female tongues of an evening.[35]

In his section on La Mancha, Ford encourages the traveler to acquire a copy of the novel:

> Never let Don Quixote be out of our readers' *alforjas*, let it be one of the *little books* which Dr Johnson said no man ought ever "not to have in his pocket." It is the best HAND-BOOK for La Mancha, moral and geographical: there is nothing in it imaginary except the hero's monomania. It is the best comment on Spaniards, who themselves form the most explanatory notes on the work, which reflects the form and pressure of them and their country.[36]

For Ford, Cervantes' novel is more guidebook than literature, a pocket reference to the land (the "geographical") and its people (the "moral"), and not only does it illustrate what the traveler will observe in his travels, but what he observes will also serve as living footnotes to explain the novel. Ford extends the context of Johnson's remark made almost a century earlier from regarding *Don Quijote* as a commentary on life, to be a specific commentary on life in Spain.

In 1840, at about the same time as Ford was composing his handbook for British travelers, Fermín Caballero published his *Pericia geográfica de Miguel de Cervantes demonstrada con la historia de Don Quijote de la*

Mancha, in which the president of the Geographical Society of Madrid rates Cervantes among the greatest geographers of history:

> Su inmortal libro, *El ingenioso hidalgo*, encomiado por todos los sabios del orbe culto, y vulgarizado en todas las lenguas vivas de Europa, ofrece testimonios sobreabundantes de que nuestro alcalaíno era versado en la geografía universal, en la corografía de diferentes estados, y aun en la topografía de países propios y estraños. Esta obra gigantea ... merece bien un nuevo examen en gloria de su autor, que es gloria de nuestra España.[37]

Caballero cites the aforementioned eighteenth-century studies by Ríos and Pellicer, among others, as informing his interpretation of Cervantes' geographic expertise, evidence not only of the glory of the author, but also of Spain itself.[38] Both Ford and Caballero demonstrate the evolution of eighteenth-century interests in the novel, mediating their representations of Spain through these eighteenth-century texts that "mapped" *Don Quijote* in the people and places of contemporary Spain.

It is no coincidence that a proliferation of editions of the novel that included interpretive maps of Don Quixote's travels coincided with an increased awareness by English travelers to Spain of the presence of the novel in its people and geography. While the Don Quixotes and Sancho Panzas that British travelers found during their journeys through Spain confirmed their own notions of a quaint but decidedly backwards Spain still mired in the seventeenth century, the eighteenth-century luxury editions and their maps produced in Spain laid claim to the novel as a pinnacle of a great Spanish culture, despite its popularity in England and elsewhere. Yet both the Spanish maps and the English narratives were informed by fiction even as they created their own fictive discourses that interacted with the reality of contemporary Spain, confirming each group's sense of national pride.

NOTES

1. See Ronald Paulson, ed. *Don Quixote in England: The Aesthetics of Laughter* (Baltimore: The John Hopkins Univ. Press, 1998) and Susan Staves, "Don Quixote in Eighteenth-Century England," *Comparative Literatures* 24.3 (1972): 193–215. I use the modern Spanish, *Don Quijote,* when referring to the novel in general, but English *Don Quixote* referring to the character or to specific editions that used that spelling.

2. Quoted in James Boswell, *The Life of Samuel Johnson LL.D. Including a Journal of His Tour to the Hebrides,* 10 vols. (London: John Murray, 1844), IX: 102.

3. Azorín (José Martínez Ruiz), *La Ruta de Don Quijote,* José María Martínez Cachero, ed. (Madrid: Cátedra, 1998).

4. Enrique Rodríguez-Cepeda, "Los *Quijotes* del siglo XVIII: 1) La imprenta de Manuel Marín," *Revista Cervantes* VIII.1 (1998): 61–107.

5. Rodrígez-Cepeda, "Los *Quijotes,*" 63.

6. Vicente de los Ríos, "Prólogo," *El ingenioso hidalgo don Quixote de la Mancha compuesto por Miguel de Cervantes Saavedra. Nueva edición corregida por la Real Academia Española,* 4 vols. (Madrid: Ibarra, 1780), I: i.

7. Gregorio Mayans y Siscar, "Vida de Miguel de Cervantes Saavedra," in *Vida y hechos del ingenioso hidalgo Don Quixote de la Mancha,* Miguel de Cervantes Saavedra, 4 vols. (London: J and R Tonson, 1737). See Antonio Mestre Sanchis, "Valores literarios y política en la *Vida de Cervantes* de Gregorio Mayans," in Enrique Giménez, ed. *El Quijote en el Siglo de las Luces,* (Alicante: Univ. of Alicante, 2006), 221–244; and Álvarez Barrientos, Joaquín, "El Quijote de Avellaneda en el siglo XVIII," (ibid., 13–41); de los Ríos, "Prólogo," *El ingenioso hidalgo,* I:ii.

8. Antonio García Berrio, "Nueva estética de la novela moderna: el comentario de Vicente de los Ríos sobre la poética del *Quijote,*" in Giménez, *El Quijote en el Siglo de las Luces,* 109–180.

9. "Lastly, to satisfy the curiosity of the readers, there has been included a map that covers a good portion of Spain, and in which the travels of Don Quixote are marked with a red line, created with great precision by Don Tomás López, geographer of his majesty, conforming to the observations made by Don Joseph de Hermosilla, Captain of the Royal Corps of Engineers." Vicente de los Ríos, "Análisis del Quijote," *El Ingenioso hidalgo* (1780), I:viii.

10. de los Ríos, "Plan cronológico," *El Ingenioso hidalgo* (1780), I:cliii–clxiv.

11. Ricardo Padrón, "Mapping Plus Ultra: Cartography, Space and Hispanic Modernity," *Representations* 79 (2002): 28–60.

12. Matthew Edney, "The Irony of Imperial Mapping," in *The Imperial Map: Cartography, and the Mastery of Empire,* James R. Ackerman, ed. (Chicago: Univ. of Chicago Press, 2009), 41.

13. Antonio López Gómez and Carmen Manso Porto, *Cartografía del siglo XVIII: Tomás López en la Real Academia de la Historia,* (Madrid: Real Academia de la Historia, 2006), 22.

14. Francisco Parra Luna, "Sobre el 'lugar de la Mancha' en el *Quijote:* Una hipótesis científica," in Féliz Pillet Capdepón and Julio Plaza Tabazco, eds. *El espacio geográfico del Quijote en Castilla-La Mancha,* (Cuenca: Ediciones de la Univ de Castilla-La Mancha, 2006), 141–183.

15. de los Ríos, "Plan cronológico" in *El Ingenioso hidalgo* (1780), I:clxiv.

16. *Ingenioso hidalgo don Quixote de la Mancha, compuesto por Miguel de Cervantes Saavedra. Nueva edición corregida de nuevo, con nuevas notas, con nuevas estampas, con nuevo análisis, y con la vida del autor nuevamente aumentada,* Juan Antonio Pellicer, ed., 5 vols. (Madrid: Sancha, 1797–1798).

17. "Descripción geográfico-histórica de los viages del Don Quixote de la Mancha," in *Ingenioso hidalgo don Quixote de la Mancha* (1798). For this and the

Ibarra edition map, see "Los mapas del Quijote," in the digital exhibition *Los mapas del Quijote*. Biblioteca Nacional de España, 2005. http://www.bne.es/es/Actividades/Exposiciones/Exposiciones/Exposiciones2005/mapasquijote/index.html (Accessed June 5, 2015).

18. See essays by Deanda, Dale, and Hanlon in this volume of *Studies in Eighteenth-Century Culture.*

19. Ana Hontanilla, "Images of Barbaric Spain in Eighteenth-Century British Travel Writing," *Studies in Eighteenth-Century Culture* 37 (2008): 119–143, 122.

20. Hontanilla, "Images of Barbaric Spain," 122, 137. See also Margaret Hunt, "Racism, Imperialism, and the Traveler's Gaze in Eighteenth-Century England, spec. issue, *Making the British Middle Class*, ca 1700–1850, *Journal of British Studies* 32.4 (1993): 333–357.

21. Quoted in Hontanilla, "Images of Barbaric Spain," 123.

22. Henry Swinburne, *Travels through Spain and Portugal in the Years 1775 and 1776, in which Several Monuments of Roman and Moorish Architecture Are Illustrated by Accurate Drawings Taken on the Spot* (London: P. Elmsly, 1779), 80.

23. Swinburne, *Travels through Spain*, 109.

24. Swinburne, *Travels through Spain*, 410. For more on Sancho Panza in English texts, see J.A.G. Ardila, "Sancho Panza en Inglaterra: *Sancho at Court* de James Ayres y *Barataria* de Frederick Pilon," *Bulletin of Hispanic Studies* 82 (2005): 551–567.

25. John Talbot Dillon, *Letters from an English Traveler in Spain, in 1778, on the origin and progress of poetry in that kingdom, with occasional reflections on manners and customs and illustrations of the romance of Don Quixote* (London: R. Baldwin, 1781), 34–35.

26. Dillon, *Letters from an English Traveler*, 77–79.

27. Dillon, *Letters from an English Traveler*, 106–107.

28. Earl of Ilchester, ed. *The Spanish Journal of Elizabeth Lady Holland* (London: Longmans Green and Company, 1910).

29. Ilchester, *The Spanish Journal*, 29.

30. Ilchester, *The Spanish Journal*, 31.

31. Ilchester, *The Spanish Journal*, 81–82.

32. Nicolás Ortega Cantero, "Geografía y literatura. El descubrimiento literario del paisaje geográfico de España," *El espacio geográfico*, 15–33; and Félix Pillet Capdepón, "La imagen literaria de la Mancha desde la publicación del *Quijote*," *El espacio geográfico*, 35–62.

33. Karl-Ludwig Selig, "Don Quixote and the Exploration of (Literary) Geography," *Revista Canadiense de Estudios Hispánicos* 6.2 (Primavera 1982): 341–357.

34. Barbara Schaff, "John Murray's *Handbooks to Italy: Making Tourism Literary*" in *Literary Tourism and Nineteenth-Century Culture*, ed. Nicola J. Watson (New York: Palgrave McMillan, 2009), 106–118.

35. Richard Ford, *Handbook for Travellers in Spain*. 2 parts, 3rd edition (London: John Murray, 1855), 1: 241; Ford, *Handbook,* 1: 67.

36. Ford, *Handbook,* 1: 240.

37. "His immortal book, *The Ingenious Gentleman*, praised by all the intellects of the cultured world, and popularized in all the spoken languages of Europe, gives abundant testimony that our man from Alcalá was versed in world geography, and the chorography of various states, and even of the topography of familiar and unfamiliar countries. This gigantic work ... merits a new examination for the glory of its author, which is the glory of our Spain." Fermín Caballero, *Pericia geográfica de Miguel de Cervantes demostrada con la historia de don Quijote de la Mancha* (Madrid: Yenes, 1840), 8.

38. Caballero, *Pericia geográfica*, 9.

Quixotism as Global Heuristic: Atlantic and Pacific Diasporas

AARON R. HANLON

The fact that quixotism behaves like a meme in eighteenth-century literatures in English has significant bearing on how we understand "global" or "world" literatures today. Each time a version of Don Quixote appears in a British or early American text, from Parson Adams in Henry Fielding's *Joseph Andrews* (1742) to Dorcasina in Tabitha Gilman Tenney's Female Quixotism (1801), it becomes increasingly difficult to say that the cultural phenomenon of quixotism belongs to Cervantes. In other words, when Quixote becomes "globalized," he also becomes deracinated, complicated by what Eve Tavor Bannet identifies as his role in negotiating "the relation between local cultures and transnational models."[1]

Quixote does this work of cultural translation between the local and the global more prominently than most characters in eighteenth-century fiction because the Quixote character was so widely reproduced, an archetype so influential that it creates its own set of heuristic problems. Along with *The Pilgrim's Progress* (1678) and *Robinson Crusoe* (1719), *Don Quixote* (1605–15) was one of the few books that Samuel Johnson famously wished was even longer, a sentiment that reflects the extent to which eighteenth-century readers and writers demanded both translations and reproductions of Quixote.[2] Such extensive rewriting of Quixote lends the character what David Brewer calls the quality of "inexhaustibility." As Brewer writes of another inexhaustible character, Shakespeare's Falstaff, "the proof of ... detachability and inexhaustibility lies in his capacity to migrate into new texts."[3] Crucial here is the relationship between inexhaustibility and detachability, the capacity of Quixote to become something bigger and more culturally variegated than Cervantes' hidalgo as he migrates into new texts written for differing regional and national audiences with conflicting political purposes.

Not only, then, can we think about world literature in terms of character migration, how characters take on new meaning when written for different national or international audiences. We can also look to quixotism specifically as a model for addressing the heuristic problem of world literature: the problem of literature's "belonging" once it leaves home and is changed by the journey. Quixote is a model of heuristic problems arising from deracination, imitation, and distortion, a figure belonging simultaneously to the Spanish golden age and the wider literary world. As a globally claimed and consumed character, he is also an archetype of archetypes, a figure for whom imitation of a preexisting and prominent character model—the chivalric knight—is a defining and regenerative feature.

In this sense, we might say that the heuristic problem of quixotism in the seventeenth and eighteenth centuries—the period over which the quixote became a character archetype beyond Spanish borders and across the Atlantic—is also the heuristic problem of world literature, which necessarily reflects tensions between the local ownership and the global impact of narratives that migrate. Accordingly, this essay argues for the importance of eighteenth-century quixotism for contemporary discussions of world literature. By linking eighteenth-century quixotism in the English-language tradition with the role of Quixote in mediating nineteenth-century Spanish colonialism in the Philippines, I will demonstrate the transhistorical and transhemispheric reach of eighteenth-century quixotism as a case study in world literature. Given that Quixote's influence in the Atlantic world is well documented, linking Atlantic quixotism with Pacific quixotism—in this case through an examination of Filipino author Jose Rizal—also demonstrates how the study of quixotism can challenge Eurocentric models of world literature even as quixotism was used for Spanish colonialist objectives in the Philippines.

World Literature

As Franco Moretti declared at the turn of the millennium, "world literature is not an object, it's a problem."[4] World literature is specifically a heuristic problem because circulation, translation, shifting contexts and national borders, and shifting demographics and geopolitical relations all create complications for texts that migrate. If world literature is, as David Damrosch describes it, "not an infinite, ungraspable canon of works but rather a mode of circulation and reading," a mode that becomes relevant when a text is launched, like *Don Quixote*, "out into a broader world beyond its linguistic and cultural point of origin," then the very making or becoming of world literature has the potential to agitate just about every heuristic category that scholars have constructed for the study of literature.[5] Indeed, this is a significant reason why the idea of world literature has been, in more than a few circles, controversial.

Thinking of world literature as primarily a heuristic problem that affects how we read and contextualize literature is fruitful but also limited. What if, instead, we conceive of the heuristic problem of world literature as a symptom of the human problem of globalization? That is, what would it mean to acknowledge that readers of literature throughout the world are mostly unconcerned with issues of literary heuristics, but certainly constrained in our daily lives by the limitations of language capability, educational opportunity, opportunity of mobility, crosscultural awareness and experience, historical conflicts and misunderstandings, and other like issues that affect what is ultimately the un- or imperfect translatability of experience? The problem of translation—of language and of experience—is a quotidian problem for the person before it becomes a heuristic problem for literary studies.

A solution to a heuristic problem like world literature requires, as Moretti notes, "a leap, a wager, a hypothesis to get started."[6] The wager I offer in this essay is that the study of character is a heuristic enterprise, but also a deeply human enterprise that makes character study a useful way of understanding world literature. As Brewer demonstrates in *The Afterlife of Character*, readers participate in the "off-page" lives of characters at times as if the characters themselves were real. To read this way—with investment in the imagined lives of characters—is not to suffer from ontological confusion akin to what Don Quixote suffers: we understand that literary characters are not flesh and blood, even as we become intimately engaged in their "lives."[7] Rather, to invest in the imagined lives of characters who transcend the page is a heuristic choice to "humanize" what we might otherwise understand as technical matters of structure, genre, or allusion.

The heuristic choice to "humanize" character by studying what happens when characters take on relevance beyond the page is a form of strategic essentialism, a compromise that connects the minute particulars of a character in a local context with the sprawling, unwieldy, and important effects that global characters achieve off the page in the lives of real people (including, as I will discuss, the life of Rizal).

The considerable investment of eighteenth-century readers in the "lives" of fictional characters—especially, as John Skinner shows, the lives of quixotic characters—renders eighteenth-century quixotism a particularly germane case study for contemporary debates about world literature.[8] The ranging character migration of Quixote from Spain to Britain to early America, all before 1815, predates what is now a commonplace critical focus on matters of genre, structure, and the national or regional identity of literary texts. Before character became another of these heuristic categories in literary studies, it was, in the case of quixotism, a social phenomenon more akin to how fan-fiction writers or readers in a non-specialist capacity reimagine and respond to character today. In this way, a critical focus on character and character migration helps mitigate the seeming disconnect between scholarly discussions of world literature and readers' quotidian experiences with the "lives" of characters whose origins lie abroad.

Portability

Vladimir Nabokov, one such reader abroad who appears to have disliked *Don Quixote* for the cruelty it inflicted upon its protagonist, called that protagonist "a stroke of genius on the part of Cervantes, looming so wonderfully above the skyline of literature, a gaunt giant on a lean nag."[9] J.L. Borges noted that Don Quixote—the character—"is more real to us than Cervantes himself."[10] These impressions, supported by immense literary and cultural interest in *Don Quixote*, reflect not only that Cervantes has been an influential author, but also more specifically that it is foremost the character of Quixote who appeals so widely and transhistorically. For this reason, as I have argued elsewhere, what we think of as "quixotism" is not matter of any number of Cervantean narrative tactics or structural aspects of *Don Quixote*, but of those character attributes of Quixote himself that give rise to so many other characters who behave as Quixote behaves.[11]

By *quixotism*, then, I mean not the general influence of Cervantes, but the specific characteristics of Quixote. Quixote is not a picaro, a lowlife struggling upward, making his way socioeconomically by his wiles, but an idealist. We know that Alonso Quijano (or Quijada or Quesada) becomes

Don Quixote after enthusiastically reading chivalric romances; but we should also recall that Quixote's impetus for setting forth on horseback was to right the injustices that the law and civil society failed to address. As Cervantes writes:

> he could no longer resist the desire of executing his design; reflecting with impatience, on the injury his delay occasioned in the world, where there was an abundance of grievances to be redressed, wrongs to be rectified, errors amended, abuses to be reformed, and doubts to be removed. [...][12]

Further, what enabled this justice-oriented idealism was not general madness, but a distinctly literary sensibility, an ability to read imaginatively and a tendency to understand reality as simply a lesser iteration of a fictive world. This literary sensibility, combined with an at times ruthless sense of justice, are so strong in Quixote that he comes to believe that he is a moral and in some cases legal exception in a world of unjust and unscrupulous people, laws, and customary practices. For this reason, Tobias Smollett wrote in the introduction to his 1755 translation of *Don Quixote* that he set out to avoid "debasing him to the melancholy circumstances of an ordinary madman."[13]

Fittingly, then, Smollett's *Launcelot Greaves* (1760) provides a lucid example of this difference between the quixote, who believes himself an exception to the laws and customs of ordinary people, and the mad imitator. The comic hero Launcelot, accused of imitating Don Quixote, denies the charge, despite behaving frequently like a madman, but he also retains enough awareness and sense of purpose to identify his mad imitator and aspiring knight-errant,Captain Crowe, as a misguided impostor.[14] Even when quixotes like Launcelot are mocked and punished for their exceptionalist deviation from the norm, such figures do not internalize these experiences as marginalization but take them as further evidence of the villainy and inadequacy of the surrounding society (in some cases, these quixotes are both reasonable and correct in their madness). Edmund Gayton, author of *Festivous Notes upon Don Quixot* (1654), affirmed this notion when he suggested that Quixote "imagined he obliged every place that received him, and thought his landlords indebted to him for his acceptance of their courtesies."[15] Indeed, where Don Quixote is able to avoid paying his bill at the inn by invoking the antiquated laws of chivalry, the picaresque Sancho Panza, whose station does not afford him Quixote's chivalric privileges, gets captured and tossed in a blanket for trying to skip out on his own bill.[16]

In this scenario, Sancho participates mimetically in quixotic madness but feels the effects of marginalization as a result. Quixote, on the other hand, moves on from the inn without paying, and, more importantly, moves forward with his understanding—that he is an exception to the rules that govern common men like Sancho—not only intact but also reinforced by others who play along in jest. Here we see the crucial points that quixotism is a form of idealism to be differentiated from the picaresque and that a quixote inspires imitation in others. Because the surrounding cast of characters is mimicking and impersonating according to the quixote's idealistic expectations—thereby affirming the quixote's expectations in real life—quixotic figures are perhaps not as mad as we think they are.

We witness this mode of quixotism most powerfully in the eighteenth century not only in Smollett's *Launcelot Greaves* but also in characters such as Charlotte Lennox's *Arabella*, who vows in *The Female Quixote* (1752) "to live single, not being desirous of entering into any Engagement which may hinder my Solicitude and Cares."[17] Eventually, Arabella's suitors assent to her quixotism to the extent that they begin to imitate her antiquated language and behavior to gain her favor.

The phenomenon that was eighteenth-century quixotism in the British tradition made its way to early America in characters such as Tabitha Gilman Tenney's Dorcasina (from *Female Quixotism*), Royall Tyler's Updike Underhill (from *The Algerine Captive* (1797)), and Hugh Henry Brackenridge's Captain Farrago (from *Modern Chivalry* (1792–1815). As Sarah Wood observes, "the Don Quixote [early Americans] came to know was mediated through the eyes and minds of the English translators who works were sold in American bookshops, the English novelists whose narratives rolled off the American presses, and the English critics whose articles were reprinted in American journals and magazines." As Wood also notes, in the eighteenth century, more editions of Don Quixote were printed in English than in Spanish.[18]

Thus, eighteenth-century quixotism would distort certain contextual elements of Cervantes' *Don Quixote* as it appeared in new and differing cultural spaces, but quixotes themselves would maintain the fundamentals of the character archetype: the imaginative idealism, literary sensibility, and exceptionalist deviation from the mainstream that render Cervantes' *Don Quixote* different from what Smollett understood as the "ordinary madman." The portability of this particular kind of eighteenth-century quixote, tested as the character was translated into English in the seventeenth century, then circulated throughout Britain and the wider Atlantic world in the eighteenth, has become a key feature of Quixote's legacy. This feature enabled versions of Quixote to comment on and mediate the effects of Spanish, British, and

American colonialisms of the seventeenth and eighteenth centuries, as well as, in the following example, Spanish colonialism in the Philippines in the nineteenth century.

"Quijote Oriental"

To demonstrate just how well traveled quixotism is, we can link the features of eighteenth-century quixotism to another notable idealist very much in the quixotic mode: the Filipino novelist, intellectual, and polymath Jose Rizal. Rizal's quixotism—or at least the perception of his quixotism in both his life and writings—illustrates how a heuristic emphasis on character provides a model for understanding writing in the disparate literary traditions of Spain, Britain, America, and the Philippines as part of a global character canon. The study of Rizal's quixotism therefore achieves two important objectives for the study of world literature. First, it challenges a Eurocentric view of world literature—and of one-way literary influence from Europe to the broader world—by accounting for the role of one of Southeast Asia's most prominent writers in shaping the global image of quixotism. Second, it shows, in the opposite direction of influence, how Eurocentric views of quixotism were part of the Spanish colonial project in the Philippines, and thus how the heuristic choice to study character can draw attention to the impact of characterization off the page. By "characterization off the page," I refer to the material consequences of Rizal being characterized with a global fiction "owned" and claimed by multiple parties with conflicting political objectives.

Rizal's execution by Spanish colonialists in 1896 became the rallying cry first for the Philippine revolution for independence from Spain, then for the Indonesian independence movement. Rizal was himself an admirer of Quixote, though the Spanish colonial apparatus used the association of Rizal with Quixote as way of policing Rizal's politics and writing. Spanish intellectual Miguel de Unamuno called Rizal a "quixote of thought" who "looked with repugnance upon the impurities of reality," despite that Rizal opposed an armed revolution largely on the pragmatic grounds that the Philippine opposition was not yet prepared for the fight. W.E. Retana, a Spanish colonial administrator, called Rizal "Quijote oriental," a quixote of the Philippines who represented the Spanish image of the European colonies of Southeast Asia.[19]

Rizal's first novel—also widely cited as the first Filipino novel—*Noli Me Tangere* (1887) ("the Noli") was aimed at exposing the injustices of Spain's occupation of the Philippines.[20] Its protagonist, Ibarra, avenges the political and religious persecution and death of his father by building a school dedicated to enlightenment values, a gesture that associates Ibarra with the kind of high-minded and literary idealism that characterized enlightenment quixotism. Whereas Cervantes' Quixote frequently takes vengeance through belligerent acts, quixotes like Fielding's Parson Adams or Hugh Henry Brackenridge's Captain Farrago prefer to appeal to truth and reason (tendencies that place them comically and at times tragically at odds with those around them). Ibarra, however, is an earnest hero whose ambitions, while not synonymous with those of Rizal, still resemble the complexities of Rizal's thinking about Philippine identity and revolution. Ibarra is, as such, not the comic butt of a Cervantean joke rather a moral guidepost of the sort that quixotes become in the eighteenth century as means of critiquing what their authors perceive as societal strife and decay. As Ronald Paulson notes, the eighteenth century witnesses a shift from readings of quixotes as dunces in satirical narratives in which the joke is on them to quixotes as heroes who serve as engines of critique.

Ibarra's life mirrors in many ways the life of Rizal, who, like Ibarra, had a distinctly literary sensibility and understood his literary projects as explicit participation in the politics of anticolonial resistance, of making a more just world. Retana, Rizal's first biographer, praised the Noli for its rendering of Ibarra as conflicted about Spanish occupation, an attempt to cast the recently executed Rizal as less an anticolonialist than as a critic of the dysfunction of the Philippine state itself; then, Retana exposed the so-called radical Rizal through a far less sympathetic analysis of Rizal's second novel El Filibusterismo (1891).[21] The contested narratives of both the life of Rizal and the lives of his protagonists—the conflicting readings of Spanish colonialists like Retana and subsequent scholars who have helped remake Rizal into a national hero of the Philippines—reflect the immense political importance of Rizal not only as an historical figure but also as a character in a broader nationalist narrative of colonial resistance.

Of particular interest here is the Spanish colonialist tactic of framing Rizal as quixote as part of a more comprehensive effort in the late nineteenth century to take control over the narrative of Rizal's life and writing (that is, to characterize him). Notable for eighteenth-century quixotes—as well as eighteenth-century readings of Cervantes' original—is the contested nature of the quixote, upon which turns the political critique of the quixotic narrative. If readers of The Female Quixote come to view Arabella as a thoroughly ridiculous figure without redeeming causes or qualities, then French romances become the butt of Lennox's critique. If, on the other hand, readers understand Arabella's quixotism as a gesture of empowerment, of claiming agency throughout processes of courtship and inheritance that otherwise diminished women as unworthy of controlling their own romantic and financial destinies, the critique is very different. Attempts at characterizing the quixotism of Rizal and his characters similarly reflect the political stakes of quixotism both on and off the page.

On one hand, as I have mentioned, Rizal was to Retana a "quixote oriental," and to Unamuno, a "quixote of thought," a romantic idealist without practical aptitude, who, like his characters, was too frequently misguided or self-contradictory. As Unamuno writes in Rizal: *The Tagalog Hamlet* (a title that reflects Unamuno's awareness of the potency of character archetypes for framing life writing):

> Retana insists that Rizal is the Ibarra but not the Elias [Ibarra's practical-minded ally] of *Noli Me Tangere*. I think that he is both Ibarra and Elias, and this is especially true when they contradict each other. Because Rizal himself is the spirit of contradiction, a soul that dreads the revolution, although deep within himself he consummately desires it; he is a man who at the same time both trusts and distrusts his own countrymen and racial borders; who believes them to be the most capable and yet the least capable—the most capable when he looks at himself as one of their blood; the most incapable when he looks at others. Rizal is a man who constantly pivots between fear and hope, between faith and despair. All these contradictions are merged together in that love, his dreamlike and poetic love for his adored country, the beloved region of the sun, pearl of the Orient, his lost Eden.[22]

On the other hand, to his contemporary supporter and Filipino revolutionary, Antonio Regidor, Rizal's ability to channel quixotism was a profound strength, the sound foundation of Philippine anticolonial resistance, and proof of the intellectual and creative capacities of Filipinos:

> If *Don Quixote* immortalizes its author because it exposes to the world the ailments of Spain, your *Noli Me Tangere* will bring you an equal glory. With your modesty and your voracious and able appraisal, you have dealt a moral blow to that old tree full of blemishes and decay. Every Filipino patriot will read your book with avidity and upon discovering in every line a veracious idea and in every word a fitting advice, he will be inspired and he will regard your book as the masterpiece of a Filipino and proof that those who thought us incapable of producing intellects are mistaken or lying.[23]

From these two efforts in framing Rizal's quixotism we can see that Rizal is given the same double edge that quixotes possess, the potential to be used as tragicomic figures at their own expense, or as heroes whose visionary qualities transcend the limitations of conventionally or pragmatically minded contemporaries. In the imaginations of Rizal's colonizers (who also happen to be some of his first biographers) as well as his allies, Quixote is a common touchstone with conflicting meanings. Rizal's nineteenth-century Spanish biographers, such as Retana and Unamuno, adopted seventeenth-century readings of quixotism to cast Rizal as well-meaning but flawed, while the more sympathetic account of quixotism we get from Regidor aligns Rizal and his best-known protagonist, Ibarra, with the heroic quixotism that exposes the flaws of the Spanish empire, in both its Atlantic and Pacific iterations.

As John Nery demonstrates methodically in *Revolutionary Spirit*: Jose Rizal in Southeast Asia, such double-edged characterizations of Rizal gave rise to an extensive sub-genre of Philippine historiography concerned with framing Rizal's life and character appropriately. This sub-genre includes, tellingly, a thorough analysis of "The Character of Rizal" in the *Philippine Review* by Trinidad Pardo de Tavera, a scholar who also knew Rizal. Pardo rejects Unamuno's view that Rizal was a "Quixote of thought," responding:

> What reality repelled him? Neither Rizal nor myself understand what the 'impurities of reality' are so long as they are not realities become impure after they had an ideal life. Unamuno's opinions are a complete misrepresentation of the character of Rizal and are unsupported by any known fact.[24]

Here again, the attribution of quixotism is primarily a matter of character, a moment in which the Quixote archetype becomes at once a figure of contested readings and interpretations and a figure of immediate social importance.

Character as World System

If the mode of quixotism that proliferated throughout the eighteenth century helps explain the application of quixotism transhistorically and beyond Europe and the Americas, the question remains how this wide resonance of quixotism might contribute productively to contemporary discussions of world literature. As I have shown, quixotism is fundamentally a matter of character above structural matters of or allusions to Cervantes'

Don Quixote because the character of Quixote is the element of Cervantes' text that migrates most prominently and becomes, in Borges' terms, "more real" than Cervantes. The heuristic challenge of reconciling Rizal as quixote with Arabella as quixote with the Don himself, then, is a challenge akin to that of approaching world literature via character canons instead of other generic or heuristic categories.

The idea of fitting a heuristic category with a "global" approach to literature is, of course, not new. When Wai Chee Dimock asked what literary history would look like "if the field were divided not into discrete periods, and not into discrete bodies of national literatures," organizing literary history in terms of transnational or world literatures was already a widespread practice. Recognizing the unavoidable "national" root of the transnational as an organizational framework, however, Dimock proposed genre as a preferred organizing principle, a "theory of interconnection," which enlists Moretti's concept of comparative morphology—a comparison of forms—to map the interconnectedness of literary forms across nations and world-historical periods.[25]

While a transnational approach to literary history enables us, by definition, to examine developments in literary form across nations, Dimock's call for "genre as world-system" accomplishes two important objectives that transnationalism traditionally has not. Firstly, "genre as world-system" is more explicitly transhistorical, lending a deep history to the study of genres, like the novel, that have been largely examined by way of flatter period studies. Secondly, it helps us interrogate what has been an organic tendency in transnational studies to emphasize Western literatures, such that transnational means more often transatlantic. To illustrate this point, Dimock cites the geographical narrowness of the "rise of the novel" approach in eighteenth-century studies that has been so prominent in the study of the novel, an approach reflected not only in Ian Watt's landmark study that gives such an approach its name but also in period studies of the novel's "rise."[26]

I am, like Dimock, intrigued by what it would mean to move even further away from geography as an organizing principle for literary history. By calling attention to the "coevolution and cross-fertilization of literary forms," Dimock's "genre as world-system" approach demonstrates convincingly how genres like the epic and the novel are far from products of a discrete historical period or geographical space, nor are they necessarily discrete genres themselves.[27] But genre has one weakness in particular as an organizational principle for world literature: generic commonalities reveal themselves in elegant analyses like Dimock's, but they lack the social capacity of characters and character types. In other words, both genres and characters have defining characteristics, and both kinds of characteristics are subject to heuristic ambiguities and exceptions; however, only characters have what we can plausibly call "lives." This distinction is not a populist gesture meant to suggest that literary studies can only be useful if intuitive to readers in non-specialist capacities, but rather a way of addressing the sensitivities of world literature in particular. Such sensitivities concern less what it means for a specialist in the novel to write about the epic than what it means for a literary text of great cultural importance to a given place and people to suddenly become the domain of outsiders. Even when understandings of what characters represent are contested, the lens of character has the ability to represent even complex "literary" readings such that they can be consumed and contested by readers in more immediate and personal ways. For example, the sort of quixote that Rizal embodies matters precisely because Filipinos care about Rizal's lives, the life led by the historical Rizal as well as the life he takes on as a character of Filipino anticolonial resistance and a symbol of national pride and genius.

The study of eighteenth-century quixotism has long been a fraught endeavor, as scholars from György Lukács and Vladimir Nabokov to Walter Reed, Ronald Paulson, and Sarah Wood have attempted to organize and to codify the fruits of *Don Quixote*'s vast influence.[28] Trying to make sense of quixotism as a transnational phenomenon with close attention to its mimetic popularity in the English-speaking world for the next two hundred years after 1612 (the year of *Don Quixote*'s first translation into English, by Thomas Shelton) has been and continues to be an exercise in theorizing world literature, even if not explicitly. A focus on character in the process of theorizing world literature provides some common ground for readers across nations and languages in those instances in which characters become globally reproduced. If we take Damrosch's definition of world literature as a mode of circulation and reading—and if we add Brewer's insight about eighteenth-century readers becoming ever more invested as characters' lives are circulated and reproduced off the page—then we can hypothesize two things about the relationship between eighteenth-century quixotism and world literature: one, the more a text makes it out into the world, inspiring circulation and imitation as quixotes do as characters, the more likely are its characters to take on enough transnational and human significance that they can be studied as part of a transnational character canon; two, quixotism is prime testing ground for this type of inquiry. The latter is the case not only because of quixotism's global reach as an archetypal character mode but also because of the mimetic self-perpetuation that rendered Quixote an archetype in the first place.

NOTES

1. Eve Tavor Bannet, "Quixotes, Imitations, and Transatlantic Genres," *Eighteenth-Century Studies* 40.4 (2007): 553.

2. James Boswell, *The Life of Samuel Johnson*, Vol. 9 (London, 1844), 102.

3. David Brewer, *The Afterlife of Character, 1726–1825* (Philadelphia: Univ. of Pennsylvania Press, 2005), 86.

4. Franco Moretti, "Conjectures on World Literature," *New Left Review* 1 (2000): 55

5. David Damrosch, *What is World Literature?* (Princeton: Princeton UP, 2003), 5–6.

6. Moretti, "Conjectures," 55.

7. Brewer, *Afterlife*, 1.

8. John Skinner, "*Don Quixote* in Eighteenth-Century England: A Study in Reader Response," *Cervantes: Bulletin of the Cervantes Society of America* 7.1 (1987): 45.

9. Vladimir Nabokov, *Lectures on Don Quixote*, ed. Fredson Bowers (New York: Harcourt, Brace, Jovanovich, 1983), 27–28.

10. J.L. Borges, *Professor Borges: A Course on English Literature*, eds. Martin Hadis and Martin Arias (New York: New Directions, 2013), 95.

11. Aaron R. Hanlon, "Toward a Counter-Poetics of Quixotism," *Studies in the Novel* 46.2 (2014): 141–58.

12. Miguel de Cervantes, *Don Quixote*, trans. Edith Grossman (New York: Harper Perennial, 2005), 9. All references are to this translation.

13. Tobias Smollett, ed. "Introduction" in *Don Quixote* (London, 1755), xxi.

14. Tobias Smollett, *Launcelot Greaves*, eds. Robert Folkenflik and Barbara Lanning-Fitzpatrick (Athens: Univ. of Georgia Press, 2002), 62.

15. Edmund Gayton, *Festivous Notes upon Don Quixot* (London, 1771), xi.

16. Cervantes, *Don Quixote*, 121–122.

17. Charlotte Lennox, *The Female Quixote*, ed. Margaret Dalziel (New York: Oxford Univ. Press, 1989), 41.

18. Sarah F. Wood, *Quixotic Fictions of the U.S.A., 1792–1815* (Oxford: Oxford Univ. Press, 2006), 6–8.

19. Quoted in John Nery, *Revolutionary Spirit: Jose Rizal in Southeast Asia* (Singapore: Institute of Southeast Asian Studies, 2011), 21.

20. Here it is worth noting that the Noli, like *Don Quixote*, has a complicated translation history, and it has been read widely in English translation as opposed to in Rizal's original Spanish. Anna-Melinda Testa-de Ocampo's "The Afterlives of the *Noli Me Tangere*," *Philippine Studies* 59.4 (2011): 496–527 provides a thorough discussion of this translation history, including the heavily altered American version of the Noli that was retitled *An Eagle Flight* (1900). The Noli's textual migration mirrors in many ways the history of rewriting quixotes for new national audiences and political scenarios.

21. Maria Theresa Valenzuela, "Constructing National Heroes: Postcolonial Philippine and Cuban Biographies of Jose Rizal and Jose Marti," *Biography* 37.3 (2014): 750.

22. Quoted in Petronila Daroy and Dolores Feria, *Rizal: Contrary Essays* (Quezon City: Guru Books, 1968), 8–9.

23. Quoted in Libert Amorganda Acibo and Estela Galicano-Adanza, *Jose Rizal: His Life, Works, and Role in the Philippine Revolution* (Manilla: Rex Book Store, 1995), 33.

24. Quoted in Nery, *Revolutionary Spirit*, 22–23.

25. Wai Chee Dimock, "Genre as World System: Epic and Novel on Four Continents," *Narrative* 14.1 (2006): 85–86.

26. Dimock, "Genre as World System," 91.

27. Dimock, "Genre as World System," 91.

28. Among these studies, I include György Lukács' *The Theory of the Novel* (Cambridge: MIT Press, 1971), Vladimir Nabokov's *Lectures on Don Quixote*, ed. Fredson Bowers (New York: Mariner Books, 1983), Walter Reed's *An Exemplary History of the Novel: The Quixotic versus the Picaresque* (Chicago: Univ. of Chicago Press, 1981), Ronald Paulson's *Don Quixote in England: The Aesthetics of Laughter* (Baltimore: Johns Hopkins Univ. Press, 1997), and Sarah Wood's *Quixotic Fictions of the U.S.A, 1792–1815* (Oxford: Oxford Univ. Press, 2006) as a representative sample of studies that address morphological and heuristic elements of quixotism.

Panel II

THE HABSBURGS
AND THE
ENLIGHTENMENT

Introduction

REBECCA MESSBARGER

"They Reigned from the Middle Ages to Modern Time. Nineteen emperors from one family who changed the course of world history...forever."[1]

With these epic claims gradually solidifying in majestic gold letters across a black screen to the rhythm of a thunderously heroic musical score, the trailer begins for a three-part, TV miniseries "The Habsburg Empire." While the program would prove forgettable in contrast to other made-for-TV dynastic dramas such as *The Tudors*, *The Borgias*, and *Medici: Godfathers of the Renaissance*, the Habsburg reign, especially at the height of the enlightenment, merits adroit and vivid depiction, including on screen. The historical import and intrigues of the House of Habsburg-Lorraine during the eighteenth century are made plain by the four essays in this collection, which elucidate the dynasty's influence in political, social, religious, and cultural arenas. Intersecting dynastic and political dramas are shown to play out across the European landscape, dotted as it was by Habsburg rulers from Vienna to Milan, Paris to Parma, Florence to Naples, and to shape and reshape geopolitics as well as major cultural and political trends and reforms.

A strong undercurrent running through the essays is the theme of generational rift, which frequently erupted into full-blown clashes, between the old guard and a younger reformist vanguard in the metamorphic second half of the eighteenth century. Rita Krueger's essay "Maria Theresa's Enlightenment" demonstrates the influence on European geopolitics and dynastic rule of the turmoil between an autocratic royal parent and her defiant children. Krueger analyses Maria Theresa's complicated motivations for the imperious control of her progeny, which she strategically ensconced through marriage in key territories of the realm in order to maintain Habsburg control where it had been lost in war. Struggles between old and young also arose over questions of taste in the world of court culture as Julia Doe documents in "Marie Antoinette et la Musique: Habsburg Patronage and French Operatic Culture." Here we learn about the controversial influence of Marie Antoinette's preference for popular Opéra-Comique over traditional Tragédies Lyriques on courtly taste in French operatic culture at the end of the eighteenth century. A "battle between generations" ("Lotta di generazioni") is also how historian Franco Venturi defines the contest between young Italian illuministi seeking to reform Habsburg territories, and their patrician fathers, who jealously defended upper-class privilege, a lex talionis (eye for an eye retribution) system of justice, and traditional local ways of life. In his article, "The Debate on Judicial Torture in Austrian Lombardy," Shane Agin scrupulously reconstructs the political history and generational strife that produced not only Beccaria's famed *Essay on Crimes and Punishment* but also a series of crucial writings against judicial torture that preceded it. Agin counters arguments by legal historians who have downplayed the originality and international sway of the anti-torture movement that issued from Habsburg Lombardy in the mid-eighteenth century. Lastly, Heather Morrison provides a reconstruction of the botanical voyage to the Pacific Northwest sponsored by Joseph II and its influence on international scientific exploration, trade and politics. In "Open Competition in Botany and Diplomacy: the Habsburg Expedition of 1783," Morrison argues that this plant-collecting expedition was a form of colonialism by other means, and that it influenced shifts in old diplomatic alliances and spurred rival states to pursue "economic botany," that is, useful and profitable plant collection, as well as new directions in global exploration and trade.

Individually and together, these four essays demonstrate the truth for the Habsburg Monarchy of Dino Carpanetto's and Giuseppe Ricuperati's assertion that the enlightenment "was rocking the very foundations of ancient certainties and introducing radically different ways of thinking and... played an important part in the changing of ideas and traditions."[2]

NOTES

1. *The Habsburg Empire*, "Episode 1," June 17, 2011, https://vimeo.com/35717152.

2. Dino Carpanetto and Giuseppe Ricuperati, *Italy in the Age of Reason, 1685–1789* (New York: Longman, 1987), 163.

Maria Theresa's Enlightenment: The Habsburgs, Generational Challenge, and Religious Indifference

RITA KRUEGER

A recurring debate in enlightenment studies is the relationship between ideas and socio-political change. In his 1972 essay on the European enlightenment, Franco Venturi argues for research methods that ground the enlightenment, as a movement, in particular historical contexts with the goal of illuminating what it all "meant."[1] Scholars like Venturi investigate enlightenment coalescence, namely the ideas and the historical realities that cohered the increasingly self-aware cadre of writers, philosophers, statesmen, and others around particular notions of tolerance, reason, progress, and individual or national edification. By contrast, the *cri de coeur* of anti-enlightenment—of those who perceived their world to be under attack —emphasized the manifold dangers and terrible consequences of these new ideas. The struggle over whether to perceive intellectual ferment as hopeful evidence of progress and renewal or a threat to the stability of all that was good in the world played out not only among writers but also within influential households. In eighteenth-century royal families, intergenerational struggles could be and sometimes were grafted to the new language of the enlightenment, thereby setting up new locations for enlightenment ideas and for the passionate pushback against them.[2]

The eighteenth-century Habsburgs had their fair share of drama between couples, as well as among parents and children. The conflicts in Habsburg relationships reveal the ways in which familial struggles shaped and were in turn shaped by political and intellectual change. Empress Maria Theresa, who embraced an ideology of both beneficent government and fecundity, has a mixed reputation. While her sons Joseph and Leopold are invariably styled as enlightened monarchs, or at least as enlightened absolutists, historians have at times placed Maria Theresa on both sides—sometimes portraying her as a conservative and, at other times, as an (accidental) enlightenment reformer. Both views have ample evidence to support them. Maria Theresa rejected ideas that she thought posed a threat to power, patrimony, and salvation. She pursued reform for the good of the state, but she viewed some of the intellectual challenges of the eighteenth century—religious toleration and new social principles among them—as fundamentally corrosive of individual and social morality. At times, she loathed and feared the "acrid ferment of enlightenment" and defended her intolerance of religious plurality, but she did so out of the deepest of religious and political convictions that evinced her love of her people and dynasty.[3]

Maria Theresa's impact on the Austrian state was profound, but, with a few exceptions, she resisted using the grand canvass of the Habsburg realm as a political laboratory of the enlightenment. In the last decade of her life, her desire to address the miseries of the Habsburg peasantry, and her repugnance for and dread of warfare were tied to her disquiet over her own (and others') salvation. In the first years of her reign, however, war had been the only way to protect her patrimony and have a chance to regain the territory of which she had been robbed. But, by the late 1760s, after the enormous cost of the Seven Years' War and herself a widow, she began to see in war only the potential for loss (both territorial and human). She perceived her legacy partly as the dynasty itself, in both personal and political terms. It was within the family that she sought to shape political identities and control ideas, and it was within the context of imperial mothering that she expressed a religiously-informed political worldview that was, at the same time, a throwback to baroque culture and vibrantly new. She understood that a renewed Habsburg realm, which included the Austrian Netherlands, Central Europe, and the Italian peninsula, could influence events and people to create a more just world, but it should not be a secular world. In her mind, the empire would not thrive if it was unmoored from its critical anchors in dynastic power and Catholic hegemony, and she lamented the new statecraft of rulers like Frederick II who drew energy from secular enlightenment principles.

It is worth reflecting on the intersection between the personal and the political in the relationships of an imperial mother and her marriageable children. We can find in Maria Theresa's marriage strategies, marriage essays, and correspondence with her family a hint of her broader political and religious understanding within the intellectual variability of the eighteenth century. While there has been a significant amount of scholarship on Joseph, Leopold, and particularly Marie Antoinette, less attention has been paid to Maria Theresa's other children. An examination of Maria Theresa's relationship with her daughters in the Italian states provides a fuller picture of the Empress's concepts of state, gender, religion, and enlightenment.

Maria Theresa's marriage strategy unfolded primarily in the 1750s in the context of the diplomatic revolution that saw the French, Spanish, and Austrian Catholic monarchs of Europe united in dissatisfaction about the political and religious status quo. Whatever their many confrontations and differences, by the middle of the century, the Bourbons and Habsburgs were united in what they saw as the problematic power of the British and the Prussians, the similarly unwelcome secular reach of the papacy and the Jesuits, and the potential of the Italian states to right the territorial balance sheet among the dynasties. For Maria Theresa, the loss of Silesia was not the only unacceptable outcome in the War of the Austrian Succession. Although her writings suggest that she did not have a particular affinity for southern living during her brief sojourn in Tuscany, she had, according to M.S. Anderson, a sentimental attachment to her Italian possessions. The territorial losses that Maria Theresa sustained in Italy in 1743 were not more palatable by the end of the war, but war weariness and economic problems in the late 1740s forced Maria Theresa to make the concessions over her Italian territories that she had long resisted.[4] This did not, however, mean that she dismissed the possibility of exercising more influence or once again increasing the Habsburg presence on the peninsula, nor that she was reconciled to any of her losses. She deeply resented what she perceived as British treachery in the peace negotiations that had lost her Parma, and, although her erstwhile British allies believed she turned to Italy only as a last resort, Maria Theresa continued to focus on all that was stolen from her.[5]

If war was unsuccessful, marriage held out the hope that these territorial prospects might still yield gains. Maria Theresa saw the advantageous marriage of her children as a way to reclaim Naples, which had been lost in the midst of her father's frantic efforts to secure her position in the 1730s, and which she had failed to take by force of arms or persuasion in the 1740s.[6] Maria Theresa's attitude toward the Italian states was shaped by the political expediencies of the diplomatic revolution and by the desire to fold parts of the Italian peninsula into the Habsburg imperial project, thereby extending the reach of the dynasty beyond Lombardy. She continued to have a strong sense of entitlement regarding the importance of the Habsburg presence on the peninsula: it was central to her understanding of her patrimony. Her concerns about Lombardy and the hope of increased Habsburg influence in Italy served to drive a wedge between Maria Theresa and the papacy. Reform, rethinking alliances, and marriage strategy became various ways to address her profound dissatisfaction with the current state of peace and to prepare for new conflict.

Maria Theresa was joined in bitter disappointment at mid-century by the Spanish, the Sardinians, and, ironically, even the French. In 1751, the Neapolitan ambassador in Vienna presented the possibility of a double marriage contract that would link her son Joseph with Charles VII's eldest daughter, and Charles's son with one of Maria Theresa's daughters. By the middle of the 1750s, Maria Theresa also considered a potential third marital contract between Naples and the imperial dynasty.[7] The connection with the Bourbons via Naples was Maria Theresa's attempt to achieve "complete security, at least on one side" and to put together the military and financial building blocks of an alliance necessary to engage the Prussians once more.[8] By the late 1750s and 1760s, Maria Theresa's marriage strategy was therefore shaped by the desire to use the power of formal connections hammered out between states, but even more so, the informal ties of sentiment at various courts to propel continued support for alliance and war to increase the Habsburg presence on the Italian peninsula. She was motivated by dreams of territorial redress in Italy and continued bitterness over the Prussian control in Silesia, and she was willing to use whatever means she had at her disposal to keep soldiers in the field. Her military required French assistance, and Maria Theresa hoped that French support and the broader connection to the Bourbon family compact could be maintained through royal marriage. The stakes involved not only the possibility of regaining Silesia but also the potential rethinking of the borders of the empire and the possibility of territorial expansion without war. Marriage contracts encouraged these hopes, and her increased, explicit distaste for war as a tool of politics in the 1760s and 1770s made marriage even more important. In her plans, she replicated what Habsburgs and other ruling families had long pursued, namely political connections and control through family ties.

But the Italian peninsula was not a blank canvas, neither, of course, from the perspective of the Italians nor from the perspective of the Habsburg children placed there through marriage or appointment, and who subsequently failed at various moments to see family interests in the same way as their mother in Vienna. If Maria Theresa's marriage strategy was intended to solidify the Austrian-Bourbon alliance and shape events in the peninsula, its success was dependent on more than money and military maneuvers, and it required the personal commitment of her children. The dangers of relying on them in this way became painfully clear. Maria Theresa's efforts were often frustrated when the personalities, political choices, and, in some cases, outright rebellion of her children undermined her vision of Habsburg power. Maria Theresa sought at times to stem the tide of undesired change; however, a new generation of rulers (including, at times, her own children) had been raised to see power, religion, and statecraft in different terms and was unwilling to heed her warnings.

This is not to suggest that she did not care about her children or that she saw them simply as pawns in a political game. During her last decades, she was often distraught at the political and social burdens that the dynastic demands had placed on her progeny. The burden of power, the responsibility of children to parents (and children to the state), the moral imperative of religious practices, the weight of personal experience, and profound affection complicated the relationships Maria Theresa had with her children. Undoubtedly, she had more affection for some and was saddened (or enraged) by the behavior of others, but she was as quick to declare her love as she was to criticize them when they failed to meet her expectations. Certainly few of them escaped the cloud of her recurring disappointment. As Maria Theresa embarked on her fourth decade in power, she was deeply anxious about what she believed to be her children's encroaching secularism. Their lack of commitment to religious ritual, reported to the Empress through her many servants and agents abroad, highlighted for her the dangers of a new world that embraced inquiry rather than certainty.

Maria Theresa's criticism of the potential effects of enlightened rule was most explicit in her relationship with her two oldest sons.[9] For example, Peter Leopold was originally betrothed to Maria Beatrice d'Este, a union that held the potential for a large, relatively unified territory extending from Lombardy and under Habsburg-Lorraine control. However, the diplomatic fracas during the negotiations for his elder brother Joseph's Parma marriage, combined with the death of Leopold's other brother Charles in 1761, disrupted Habsburg expectations. Maria Theresa consequently agreed to marry Leopold to Maria Luisa of Spain and invest him in Tuscany as a *secondogeniture*, which she acknowledged would never be held directly by any Austrian sovereign. Tuscany became, from Maria Theresa's perspective, quasi sovereign, and her hopes of tying its interests to her own depended on cultivating the relationship she had with Leopold. Maria Theresa often held up Leopold as a model for his younger brothers and sisters, but his relationship with Vienna was not always easy, and his position meant his enlightened policies in Tuscany were relatively shielded from maternal interference.

Naples and Parma required different tactics from the Empress' perspective. Both had long been targets of Habsburg interest and had endured significant political upheavals through shifting ruling houses and contested local politics.

Naples, a "juridically independent kingdom," had been ruled by the Austrians during Maria Theresa's youth but conquered by Charles of Bourbon in the 1730s.[10] Marriage would, in theory, give Maria Theresa what war in the 1740s had denied her, namely the return of Naples to Austria, if in an indirect form. In the context of marriage negotiations, Spain established its second son in Naples and contracted to never absorb the territory under direct Spanish control, just as the Austrians had done in Tuscany. Maria Theresa held steadfast to the Naples connection even when the players changed after the tragic deaths of her daughters. Thea Leitner notes that the first two girls, Johanna and Josepha, escaped their fate in death, but the third, Maria Carolina, had to bear it to the bitter end.[11] The death of Josepha right before her wedding to King Ferdinand of Naples left her younger sister very little time to prepare to take her sister's place. Carolina, often in trouble with Maria Theresa for her behavior, was wretched at the prospect of a marriage connection that seemed cursed. She hoped her mother would reconsider the match, but Maria Theresa vehemently denied Carolina's desire to postpone (or reject) the Neapolitan nuptials.

Parma too had both personal and dynastic significance. Austrian control in Parma had come in the flurry of international disagreements during the Polish war of succession and had been lost in the subsequent conflict over Maria Theresa's succession. Maria Theresa continued to claim the title of Duchess of Parma, Piacenza, and Guastalla, despite the loss of the duchies in the 1740s. Parma was so important to her because its geographical position would help ensure the success of her plan to secure the Austrian position on the Italian peninsula. Again, marriage was the primary tool by which Maria Theresa hoped to acquire it. The initial connection was forged by Joseph's first, tragically short, marriage to Isabella of Parma. However, by the 1760s, the Parma connection was complicated by religious politics, and the duchy became a focal point for the Bourbons' increasingly explicit articulation of state sovereign authority over the church. The Jesuits were expelled from the Duchy in February 1768 to which the Vatican responded by excommunicating Duke Ferdinand. The struggle between the Bourbons and the Jesuits was connected to enlightenment politicking in Italy and Spain, but Maria Theresa long resisted moving in any way against either the papacy or the Jesuit order. The connection with the Bourbons encouraged Maria Theresa to see the interdiction in Parma as the beginning of the papal counter-attack against sovereign political authority, but she did not base her response on new or enlightenment principles, and she was troubled by the political machinations of the Italian states.[12]

If resistance to Jesuit or papal power or the perceived threat to secular political authority were problematic, Maria Theresa primarily sought to sidestep these issues in Parma. She requested and received a dispensation from the newly installed pope, Clement XIV, to allow her daughter Maria Amalia to marry the excommunicated Duke.[13] Maria Theresa hoped that the marriage would be the means to make more tangible, if indirect, claims to the title that she continued to make.[14] Moreover, from Maria Theresa's perspective, her daughter Amalia's marriage, like Carolina's, was an opportunity to counterbalance the Bourbon presence in Italy, while remaining true to the alliances Vienna had formed with the Spanish and French courts.[15] If, that is, Amalia herself remained in the Habsburg orbit.

In fact, married unwillingly in July 1769 to a man five years her junior, Amalia subsequently became the poster child for maternal influence gone awry. Both Amalia and Carolina (as well as Marie Antoinette) are interesting tests of the power or limits of royal marriage connections in an age of political reform and revolution. The formal connections on paper in the marriage negotiations worked, but the political connections forged through marriage could only be truly of use to Maria Theresa if the children remained loyal to Austrian interests and influence. Riding roughshod over the feelings of children in matters of matrimony sometimes complicated what were already challenging familial relationships. Maria Theresa's hopes that these marriages might form a new core of Habsburg authority foundered additionally on political and social realities that were partly, though not entirely, of her daughters' making. Maria Theresa recognized the dangers herself, seeing the imbalance in the abilities of Carolina and Amalia vis-à-vis their husbands: these men were massively outmatched by the political abilities of their wives.

The empress desired to shape her children's spiritual, intellectual, and political identities and practices for their own good as well as to serve the interests of the Austrian state. Though her ability to do so from a significant distance was stymied, her instructions remain a clear expression of her conclusions about the shifts in politics and religious practices that she found deeply disturbing. In her marriage instructions to her daughters, Maria Theresa repeatedly described the happiness of marriage and the well-being of the state as mutually constitutive. She advised them to succumb to the men they married, regardless of the husbands' objective qualities or lack thereof, and to find a way to bind themselves in sympathy to their spouses. The empress warned that it was critical that they not show their husbands that they knew themselves to be superior. She also urged them to leave their husbands alone as little as possible so they had a greater chance of becoming indispensable confidants. She persisted in seeing the potential for social and political instability in the gap of indifference that could open up between king and queen or duke and duchess—a gap that was created by absence.[16]

Maria Theresa's instructions did not encompass the possibility of mutual loathing and/or repulsion, and she assumed that practicing self-restraint and mimicking affection were adequate stand-ins for real sentiment and would yield the same political and emotional benefits. When Carolina wrote home after her marriage, "I freely admit that I would rather die than to have to experience again what I have lived through," Maria Theresa replied that every beginning was difficult and that if things were not to Carolina's liking, either it was up to her to embrace or to shift her husband's inclinations and habits.[17] The epistolary treatises that Maria Theresa offered to her daughters were, in fact, exemplary statements of a method of exerting female power behind the throne, but the success of her advice largely depended on their commitment to self-abnegation. The best hope of influencing king, duke, and court lay in her daughters becoming socially and psychologically irreplaceable to their husbands. She argued that the disgust, awkwardness, or boredom that they experienced by being omnipresent in the beginning would be a small price to pay for the tranquility they would enjoy the rest of their lives as powerful confidantes who, she implied, exercised influence over their husbands.[18] Maria Theresa's marriage advice explicitly rejected any notion of a new place for women in marriage. Her arguments consistently made clear that her daughters should not seek a usurpation of the power and position of their spouses. The self-restraint, control, and manipulation that she recommended were supposed to be the tools at their disposal, and they were to intervene in politics only when they were asked or if they could be useful. Even the clause in Carolina's marriage contract that gave her the right to enter the council was a wedge that she could use only conditionally after her essential connection to the kingdom had been forged by providing a male heir.

While both daughters were embittered by the marriage choices Maria Theresa made for them, the empress insisted that happiness in marriage, in power, and in one's soul were all bound together. She worried constantly that a secular, tolerant world would bring ruin on multiple levels. As she described to Carolina, "[w]ithout religion, there is no morality, and without morality there is neither happiness nor tranquility in any state, least of all in marriage ...."[19] The emphasis on religious practices that Maria Theresa hammered home in her correspondence was the other part of her marriage strategy; namely, her hope that her children's modeling of good Catholicism in their married lives would stand against the broader trends of secularization that she saw everywhere. She believed that the pious behavior of royals engendered similar behavior in others and that it ensured sovereign authority as well as marital happiness and salvation. Maria Theresa was anxious that her married children's religious sensibilities had been infected by the skepticism and indifference that she saw prevalent in so many of her contemporaries' lives. In her correspondence, Maria Theresa emphasized that they needed to pray sincerely, submit to God's will, engage fervently in church services, and to be thoughtful during sermons; in essence, they should commit to her vision of what a Catholic prince had to do in order to survive and thrive. Her frustration inevitably increased when she confronted her inability to bend the children to this vision once they had left her immediate control.

Maria Theresa's religious strictures were matched by her dismissal of the value of new thinking. Writing to her son Ferdinand, newly married and acting as her representative in Lombardy, she celebrated his being a good Christian, father, husband, and son. She emphasized that only these achievements were essential for happiness and that "all of the titles that are fashionable at this time—heroes, the savant, the philosophe—are invented only for pride, to cover weakness, because ... they want to seem like something."[20] The loss of religion, which Maria Theresa feared in her own family and condemned in society at large, was, she thought, the result of a century gone awry, and she worried about the malicious consequences that would follow this erosion of religious commitment and moral purity. In her correspondence with family and friends, she made it clear that she believed the loss of deep religious sentiment struck at the heart of what held Austrian, indeed European, society together. From the most intimate social connections to the relations among states, she was embittered in her last years by how irreligious and dishonorable the world appeared. Military aggression, the loss of royal prestige, graft, theft, and scandal were all the result of "misery and too little religion."[21]

Maria Theresa had reason to worry about her children's positions. The rumors and official reports that came north to Vienna, particularly regarding the reputations and political activities of Carolina, Amalia, and Ferdinand, frequently angered their mother; she had cautioned them repeatedly about the social and political dangers of poor judgment and what she perceived to be reprehensible behavior. Both Carolina and Amalia, unimpressed by their spouses, carved out spectacular spheres of political power independent of their mother and husbands. Amalia's complete rejection of her mother's advice, deep resentment at the marriage, and subsequent political career (or tragedy, as her mother termed it) led to a complete break between the two. In May 1772, as Maria Theresa described to her son Ferdinand her distress at what she termed Amalia's "excesses," she told him that all correspondence between the family and Amalia was prohibited. She bemoaned her own suffering at watching her daughter run, as she thought, headlong into disaster, with no chance to help her.[22] What constituted disaster for Maria Theresa included not only the loss of Amalia's soul but also the connections that alliance and marriage had built. With Amalia, Maria Theresa's personal and political interests collided. Despite the many ways the two were alike, mother and daughter clashed over far more than just marriage. As much as Maria Theresa wanted to see Habsburg influence flourish in the Italian states, Amalia (and Carolina's) positions gave them not the right to rule, but only the duty to serve the men God had placed in power. For her daughters to engage aggressively and openly in a political sphere for which they were not intended was for Maria Theresa an unnatural subversion of God's will. This was, in essence, one of her most profound grievances with Amalia in particular. Her daughters ought not, in fact, to model their behavior on their mother because Maria Theresa's claim to power was quite different. She held a scepter in her own hand by God's grace, a position quite different than the consort status her marriage policies had created for her daughters.[23]

Unhappy royal (or commoner) marriages and poor personality matches were not new historical phenomena, but the eighteenth-century celebration of the power of family and marital sentiment reveals the way that concepts of marriage were in flux. Maria Theresa famously grieved when she contemplated her daughter Josepha's expectations of happiness in Naples. She recognized all the advantages the connection would bring but admitted that her "mother's heart is utterly disturbed. I see poor Josepha as a sacrifice of politics."[24] That she wrote in these terms is startling, but she continued to insist that it was possible to shape happiness through an act of individual will. Here, too, religious and political experience was critical. Maria Theresa continued to see intellectual, social, and cultural departures as perilous rather than liberating, condemning in the process an "enlightened century" that failed by "pushing everything to excess."[25] Informality, irreverence, disrespect, and sarcastic wit were threats to civilization and constituted further evidence that the century's alarming innovations corroded the values that she held most dear.

Maria Theresa's fears for the future did not end with her children. The pervasive sense of having lost control of what she believed to be the true Christian center of the Habsburg world, in terms of both her children's beliefs and habits, and the creeping secularism that characterized public and intellectual life in the latter decades of the century, informed her impassioned recommendations for her grandchildren as well. She recognized the dangers of a new political and intellectual culture from the Catholic perspective, but part of her still hoped the trend could be reversed if the next generation would reinvigorate and internalize Catholic practices of prayer and piety.[26] One cannot help but wonder whether she would have been inclined to offer a wretched "I told you so" if she had lived to see her other daughter's experience in Paris.

NOTES

1. Franco Venturi, *Italy and the Enlightenment: Studies in a Cosmopolitan Century* (New York Univ. Press, 1972), 1–3.

2. Based on Venturi, the theme of a generational Enlightenment was raised by Rebecca Messbarger at the 2015 ASECS conference.

3. Venturi, *Italy and the Enlightenment*, 7.

4. M.S. Anderson, *The War of the Austrian Succession, 1740–1748* (New York: Longman, 1995), 98.

5. Thea Leitner, *Habsburgs Verkaufte Töchter* (Munich: Piper, 2009),189.

6. Anderson, *Austrian Succession*, 196.

7. Johann Joseph Khevenhüller-Metsch, *Aus der Zeit Maria Theresias. Tagebuch des Fürsten Johann Joseph Khevenhüller-Metsch*, 7 vols. (Vienna: Holzhausen, 1911), 4: fn 36, 201.

8. Franz Herre, *Maria Theresia: Die große Habsburgerin* (Munich: Piper, 2004), 273.

9. There is insufficient space here to describe the complicated relationship between Joseph and his mother. For a detailed account, see Derek Beales, *Joseph II. In the Shadow of Maria Theresa, 1741–1780* (Cambridge: Cambridge Univ. Press, 1987).

10. John Robertson, "The Enlightenment Above National Context: Political Economy in Eighteenth-Century Scotland and Naples," *The Historical Journal*, 40 (1997): 674.

11. Leitner, *Habsburgs Verkaufte Töchter*, 189.

12. H.M. Scott, "Religion and Realpolitik: The Duc de Choiseul, the Bourbon Family Compact, and the Attack on the Society of Jesus, 1758–1775," *The International History Review* 25 (2003): 56.

13. F.A.J. Szabo, *Kaunitz and Enlightened Absolutism*, 1753–1780 (Cambridge: Cambridge Univ. Press, 1994), 233.

14. Herre, *Maria Theresia*, 326.

15. Arsenio Frugoni, ed. *Maria Teresa d'Austria: Consigli Matrimoniali all Figlie Sovrane* (Florence: Felice le Monnier, 1947), 118.

16. See Arsenio Frugoni, ed. *Maria Teresa d'Austria: Consigli Matrimoniali all Figlie Sovrane* (Florence: Felice le Monnier, 1947) and the volumes of letters *Briefe der Kaiserin Maria Theresia an Ihre Kinder und Freunde*, ed. Alfred von Arneth, 4 vols. (Vienna: Braumüller, 1881).

17. Herre, *Maria Theresia*, 324.

18. See, for example, vol. 3 of Alfred von Arneth, ed. *Briefe der Kaiserin Maria Theresia an Ihre Kinder und Freunde*, 4 vols. (Vienna: Braumüller, 1881).

19. Maria Theresa to Caroline, from *Briefe der Kaiserin Maria Theresia an ihre Kinder ind Freunde,* vol. 3, ed. Alfred von Arneth (Vienna: Braumüller, 1881), 36. The letter to Caroline is undated, but the volume editor places it as early 1768.

20. To Ferdinand, Alfred von Arneth, ed. *Briefe der Kaiserin Maria Theresia an Ihre Kinder und Freunde*, 4 vols. (Vienna: Braumüller, 1881), 1:102.

21. To Ferdinand, Arneth, *Briefe*, 1:159.
22. To Ferdinand, Arneth, *Briefe*, 1: 122.
23. Herre, *Maria Theresia*, 324–325.
24. Leitner, *Habsburgs Verkaufte Töchter*, 190.
25. To Maria Beatrice, Arneth, *Briefe*, 3: 280.
26. To Maria Beatrice, Arneth, *Briefe,* 3: 360.

Marie Antoinette et la Musique: Habsburg Patronage and French Operatic Culture

JULIA DOE

Few repertories in the history of western music have been more persistently identified with absolutist politics than the tragic operas (*tragédies lyriques*) of Jean-Baptiste Lully. Composed for Louis XIV and unabashedly devoted to the celebration of his *gloire*, these works have been described by one prominent historian as veritable "symbol[s] of musical Bourbonism"[1]— by another, more colloquially, as the "courtiest court operas that ever were."[2] This standard assessment of Lully's oeuvre is unassailable on a number of fronts. No other body of French lyric theater can match its particular combination of blatant propaganda value, extravagant scale, and longevity in the performing repertory. But there is one metric in which Lully's operas might be challenged in their "courtiest" title. In terms of frequency of court performance under the ancien régime, these *tragédies lyriques* do not reign supreme.[3] That honor goes instead to the lighter dialogue operas (*opéras-comiques*) of André Grétry—a composer less well known than Lully but associated with the comparably influential royal patron Marie Antoinette.

This essay examines Marie Antoinette's impact on French operatic culture at the end of the eighteenth century. Musicologists have long been familiar with the general outlines of the queen's artistic training and influence. As William Weber shows, her support of a modernized corpus of *tragédies lyriques*—and of the compositions of Christoph Willibald Gluck, in

81

particular—helped to "revolutionize" the nation's most prestigious musical institution (the Paris Opéra), overturning the traditional hegemony of Lully's works within its repertory.[4] However, new research in the archives of the royal household confirms that Marie Antoinette's progressive preferences were even more acutely reflected at the Bourbon court theaters than they were on the public stages of the French capital.[5] Indeed, the tastes of the Austrian-born queen seem to have cemented an ongoing reorientation of courtly fashion, not only away from the Lullian *musique ancienne* but away from serious opera altogether—and towards the upstart genre of *opéra-comique*. Marie Antoinette's patronage of the comic idiom situated her at the vanguard of contemporary musical developments, bringing the aesthetic of Versailles and Fontainebleau more closely in line with the cosmopolitan and popularly-infused musical styles then widely favored in other western-European cultural centers.[6]

Although the background of this change has been well-documented, its broader significance remains unexamined. In this essay, I will address two related questions: What did it mean for the conservative Bourbon court to be reconfigured as a bastion of musical modernity on the eve of the revolution? And what did it mean for *opéra-comique*—a genre with humble origins at the seasonal fairs of Paris—to be appropriated as an emblematic courtly art? On the one hand, I argue, this development represented a considerable (and potentially subversive) challenge to the hierarchies of French theaters and theatrical forms. For opponents of the Bourbon regime, Marie Antoinette's newfangled operatic tastes and disregard for generic conventions marked an affront to dramatic, and by extension, to social propriety; this was one of many examples of what critics considered improper conduct from a frivolous and suspiciously foreign queen. On the other hand, and somewhat paradoxically, this porousness of generic boundaries was a direct consequence of the manner in which *opéra-comique* was incorporated into existing structures of royal representation and display. Put another way, if the new emphasis on lyric comedy constituted a disruption to the theatrical status quo, this was only because the genre was so successfully adorned with the trappings of traditional courtly spectacle.

Marie Antoinette and the Court Repertory

If Louis XIV had been an avid connoisseur of lyric theater, succeeding generations of French monarchs did not necessarily share his expansive vision. While Louis XV was personally fond of music, he was far less active as a patron than either his first wife Marie Leszczynska or his *maîtresse en titre* Madame de Pompadour (the principal organizers, respectively, of an important series of court concerts and a well known society troupe). Louis XVI was rather more apathetic towards the art form—so much so, apparently, that it made the news in 1783 when he remained engaged all the way through a performance of *Didon*, a new *tragédie lyrique* by Niccolò Piccinni.[7]

When Marie Antoinette arrived in Versailles in 1770, government officials feared that she, too, might share her new husband's "decisive aversion" to music.[8] Treated to a flurry of spectacles for her wedding festivities, including an opulent revival of Lully's *Persée* (1682), she reacted with utter indifference.[9] As it turned out, however, Marie Antoinette was an enthusiastic performer and benefactor of opera; it was merely the representative monarchical repertory, *la musique ancienne*, that left her cold. Her presence was soon felt on the Parisian musical scene, where she frequented the public theaters and became a force in debates over the reform of serious opera, the well-documented *querelles* of the Gluckistes and Piccinnistes. But from the archival record emerges a more vivid picture of her private and courtly musical endeavors—and of the remarkable extent to which lyric comedy (rather than reform tragedy) became embedded in her daily life at Versailles.[10]

The expense accounts of the royal household show, for example, that Marie Antoinette received regular instruction in singing and in harp, and that she sponsored informal concerts for her associates several times each week.[11] The works copied for her personal library and accumulated for these events reflect a decisively modern musical taste, being skewed towards arias and arrangements from the latest Italian operas and French *opéras-comiques*. The queen's appreciation for this lighter idiom was such that, after the births of each of her children, she requested that a stage be built in her private apartments, so that she might be entertained with a series of comedies as she convalesced.[12] The extent of this musical activity is perhaps best demonstrated in the rehearsal and scheduling of performances by the famed *troupe des seigneurs*—the amateur company formed by the queen to mount comic works (both spoken and sung) in her theater at the Trianon.[13] Figure 1 provides an overview of these events from the summer of 1780, reconstructed from the payment records of the royal instrument porters.[14] The society troupe prepared its performances extensively—with up to five days of rehearsal before the presentation of each. The comte de Mercy-Argenteau (Marie Antoinette's "minder," charged with reporting back on her activities to Vienna) seems not to have been exaggerating in the least when he complained that *opéra-comique* had become the "single and unique" obsession of the queen.[15]

27, 28, 29, 31 July	Daily rehearsals for *Le roi et le fermier*
1 Aug.	Performance of *Le roi et le fermier*
3 Aug.	Courier sent to Paris to purchase scores
5, 8, 9 Aug.	Rehearsals for *On ne s'avise jamais de tout* and *Les fausses infidélités*
21, 24, 27, 30 Aug., 4 Sept.	Rehearsals for *Rose et Colas* and *L'anglais à Bordeaux* (up to twice daily)
6 Sept.	Performance of *Rose et Colas* and *L'anglais à Bordeaux*
12, 14, 16, 18 Sept.	Rehearsals for *Le devin du village* (up to twice daily)
19 Sept.	Performance of *Le devin du village* and *Rose et Colas*
20, 25, 27 Sept.	Rehearsals for *Le sorcier* and *L'amant jaloux* (Grétry summoned to the Trianon to assist)

Figure 1. Activities of the *troupe des seigneurs*, 1780 (F-Pan, O¹ 3058.188)

Marie Antoinette's musical preferences were reflected not only in her private life but also in the shaping of the public theatrical calendar at court—in the seasonal entertainments offered by France's royally sponsored troupes (the Opéra, Comédie-Française, and Comédie-Italienne) at Versailles and Fontainebleau. After the death of Louis XV, especially, she often submitted suggestions for programming—or requested that the music on offer be adjusted to suit her current inclinations.[16] Analysis of the operas staged during this period reveals a striking turn in the courtly repertory towards contemporary compositions.[17] As shown in Figure 2, the works selected for court performance by the Opéra anticipated the modernizing trends that would subsequently affect this institution's output in Paris. The tragedies of Lully disappeared from court stages after 1770—nearly a decade before their final ancien-régime appearances in the capital.[18] These time-honored examples of *la musique ancienne* were replaced with updated works by the new generation of cosmopolitan composers favored by the queen—Gluck, Piccinni, and Sacchini foremost among them.

Even more dramatic than this evolution in the repertory of the Opéra, however, was a larger-scale—and still largely under-acknowledged—shift in the overall balance of theatrical genres in favor at the royal residences. Between 1770 and 1789, the vast majority of lyric works produced at court were not *tragédies lyriques* but *opéras-comiques*, featuring the actors of the newest and least prestigious of the crown theaters, the Comédie-Italienne (fig. 3). Indeed, for all the legitimate scholarly attention surrounding the relationship of Marie Antoinette and Gluck, he does not even make the

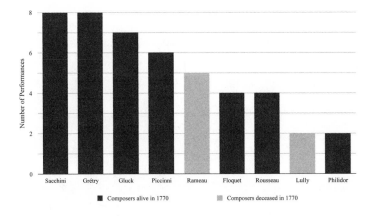

Figure 2. Most popular court composers, 1770–89 (repertory of the Opéra)

list of the top-ten most frequently staged court composers during her time in France—with seven performances of his reform tragedies paling in comparison to nearly 200 performances of Grétry's *opéras-comiques*.

Opéra-comique had enjoyed a rapid increase in status in the years since mid-century, so its inclusion within these operatic seasons is neither unprecedented nor entirely unexpected.[19] But it should be emphasized that critics considered the genre to be subsidiary to *tragédie lyrique* (and thus somewhat foreign to the court context) for two key reasons. First, although *opéra-comique* was now performed by the royally-sponsored Comédie-Italienne, it still bore the traces of its fairground roots. French comic operas frequently featured lower-class or bourgeois characters and an accessible musical language that contrasted sharply with the mythological settings and elevated idiom of the traditional *tragédie lyrique*. Moreover, these stylistic distinctions were strongly reinforced by a rigorous array of bureaucratic regulations. The Opéra held a legal monopoly on music drama of all kinds, which enabled its director to dictate the structure of lyric works created elsewhere.[20] A contract signed between the Opéra and the Comédie-Italienne in 1779, for example, consisted of a full eleven pages of rules defining how an *opéra-comique* should be composed—ranging from the famous prohibition of continuous music, to more esoteric mandates against expansive choral numbers and certain kinds of borrowed material.[21] The purpose of this legislation was to protect the integrity of the Opéra's *privilège*—that is, to

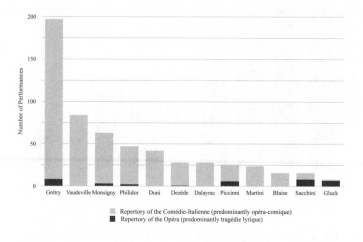

Figure 3. Most popular court composers, 1770–89 (total repertory)

prevent the authors of *opéra-comique* from producing any piece of theater that drew too closely upon the elaborate conventions of *tragédie lyrique*. Given the distinct musico-dramatic characteristics and legal limitations of the comic genre, then, its predominance within the court repertory (and the extreme rapidity at which it attained this predominance) is remarkable and should be read as a significant disruption to the theatrical status quo.

Boundaries of Genre

The final decades of the ancien régime thus witnessed the culmination of a large-scale transformation in the types of lyric theater given a place of prominence at the Bourbon court, a musical revolution that matched, or even surpassed, the scope of the so-called Gluckian revolution at the Opéra. This period was also marked by changes in the ways these genres were regulated—and by a degeneration of the boundaries that had once existed between them. One might expect that legal and generic distinctions would be carefully upheld at Versailles, the seat of government from which they technically emanated. (The theatrical contracts, after all, bore the direct imprint of the monarch, taking the form of *arrêts du conseil d'état du roi*.) But this was not the case. When the demands of court performance contradicted the existing statutes, it was the former that took precedence. In fact, the directors of the Comédie-Italienne were repeatedly allowed to test their customary restraints in the works that they presented for the royal household.

The most common form of transgression pertained to personnel. The Opéra had long maintained its aura of exclusivity through a strict "guarding" of the artists it employed, and the Comédie-Italienne was forbidden from casting any actor, singer, or dancer associated with the more venerable lyric stage.[22] While this mandate was generally obeyed in the capital, it was frequently disregarded for performances at court. The payment records indicate, for instance, that a number of *opéras-comiques* were augmented in this context, supplied with extra ensemble players or paired with divertissements featuring dancers from the Opéra.[23] Some of these changes in personnel may well have been arranged for pragmatic reasons: the Comédie-Italienne did not always cancel its Parisian engagements when it was in residence elsewhere, and its own chorus and orchestra could not be in two places at once. But it also seems that the extravagant spectacle assumed of court opera necessitated special dispensations for the comic theater, especially when it was included among the festivities marking an important royal event. Ironically, in order to assume an appropriate rhetoric of monarchical celebration, the creators of *opéra-comique* were obliged to break a set of rules established by the monarchy itself.

A crucial repercussion of this sort of privilege-infringement—or, better, of the broader attitudes it represented—is that the hierarchical relationships between lyric forms were increasingly called into question. In the 1770s and 1780s, court entertainments were marked by an extreme porousness of generic boundaries, as the gap between the *tragédie lyrique* and competing varieties of musical comedy began to collapse. Nowhere was this development more apparent than in the revival of operatic parody, a subset of French comic opera most closely associated with the Parisian fair entertainments of the early eighteenth century. In general terms, a parody offered a satirical or burlesque take on a *tragédie lyrique*, transplanting the source plot to a less rarified locale and recasting its music into vaudevilles, or re-texted popular songs.[24]

Of course, there had always been significant overlap between fair theater and the official stage, between vaudeville parodies and the tragic works that they mocked. The fairs of the French capital attracted spectators from a range of social classes, and many who frequented these entertainments undoubtedly also attended the crown theaters on a regular basis.[25] It is clear, however, that parody was considered something of a counter-cultural art and that, in consequence, it was viewed with a measure of skepticism by many of those accustomed to the "real thing." An aristocratic visitor to the fairground

Opéra-Comique in 1745, for example, was appalled to see Lully's *Thésée* mutilated there and lambasted the satirical genre for ruining French taste:

> Vous sçavez, Madame, que ce Poëme est un des plus beaux du gracieux Quinault, si vous l'aviez vû défiguré, travesti, qu'il vous auroit paru hydeux! Ah, Madame, la mauvaise chose qu'une Parodie!... Devroit-on souffrir ce pitoyable genre d'écrire dans la République des Lettres?[26]

If well-heeled consumers often descended upon the fair spectacle (and even appropriated associated parodic works for their private theaters), this repertory was nonetheless positioned at a remove, aesthetically, from the more prestigious offerings of the Opéra or Comédie-Française.

Given the "lowbrow" reputation of operatic parody, it is hardly surprising that the genre was not a traditional fixture of ceremonial entertainment at court. The fair troupes that developed this lyric form were not typically invited to appear at the royal residences. Even the Comédie-Italienne, which later adopted parodies within its repertory, presented these only sporadically at Versailles and Fontainebleau during the reign of Louis XV.[27] Between 1770 and 1789, however, the situation changed markedly, with a crescendo of interest in the genre—more than thirty performances of at least fifteen different works.[28] Consequently, the distinctions between source and satire—and the presumed patrons, audiences, and authors of each—grew ever more hazy, a development driven once again by the theater-loving queen.[29] If Marie Antoinette was a leading supporter of a new generation *tragédie-lyrique* composers, she was also the most prominent patron of the send-ups of these very same artists. During this period, there were more court performances of parodies of the tragedies of Gluck and Piccinni than there were performances of the tragedies themselves.[30] The archival record also confirms that the queen might be consulted prior to the initial performance of a parodic work,[31] and that the authors of the satirical genre were regularly granted special financial remunerations—a mark of court standing and esteem.[32]

The parodies that flourished at court during the waning ancien régime were far removed from their predecessors, both in spirit and in substance. As Pauline Beaucé notes, the new venue of performance seems to have required a taming of the genre's subversive edges, or a certain diminution of critical intent.[33] What is more, such works were often lavishly expansive, more closely aligned with the scenographic conventions and grand scope of *tragédie lyrique* than with the more streamlined character of the earlier fair repertory. For example, the satirical *Syncope, Reine de MicMac* (1786; based on Piccinni's *Pénélope*) made explicit visual parallels to the staging of its target at the Opéra by dressing its actors in costumes borrowed from that august institution.[34] The cast of *Christophe et Pierre Luc* (1780; based on Rameau's *Castor et Pollux*) was so large that it required a full six pages of the libretto to cover all of the featured players, many of whom had also performed in the final court revival of Rameau's opera.[35]

The case of the librettist Pierre-Louis Moline exemplifies this newly cozy relationship between customarily disparate genres. Moline is best known for helping Gluck adapt the Viennese *Orfeo ed Euridice* into the Parisian *Orphée et Eurydice*, which premiered at the Opéra in the summer of 1774. Just a few months later, Moline wrote his own vicious parody of the opera for the Comédie-Italienne, which subsequently performed it at court. Moline even went so far as to act within this satire, appearing onstage in a cameo.[36] A critic for the *Correspondance littéraire* was puzzled by the relationship between the author's two librettos, noting that "les deux ouvrages sont absolument calqués sur le même plan, et il n'est même pas aisé de voir si la parodie a été imaginée pour l'opéra ou l'opéra pour la parodie."[37] Never before, in other words, had the aims and expectations of the two genres been so closely intertwined.

Conclusions

During the final years of the ancien régime, court entertainments were rapidly modernized. Their organization was also turned on its head—with the system of theatrical privileges increasingly called into question and the hierarchy of lyric forms increasingly confused. This decline in the hold of the old tragic repertory, and the subversion of generic norms it engendered, can be interpreted in a number of ways. We might, for example, draw useful parallels with Weber's study of the Gluckian revolution at the Opéra, which sees emerging traces of social discord refracted in artistic rupture, finding evidence of a "society in the process of liberation" in the toppling of the quintessentially absolutist *musique ancienne*.[38] Or we might go one step further to read the new courtly emphasis on *opéra-comique* as symptomatic of broader erosion in the symbolic authority of the Bourbon regime—one of many signs of a monarchy losing control over traditional systems of royal etiquette and representation.[39]

It is certainly suggestive that the slanderous *libelles* of the late eighteenth century make reference to Marie Antoinette's theatrical endeavors and even, on occasion, go so far as to take on operatic form.[40] Both *L'autrichienne en goguettes* (1789) and *Le branle des Capucins* (1791), which illustrate a pornographic relationship between the queen and her frequent acting partner, the comte d'Artois, are structured as old-fashioned *opéras-comiques*, with alternating dialogue and re-texted airs.[41] (And in the latter of these, the sensationalized queen is made to sing adapted music that the real-life queen actually did sing with her *troupe des seigneurs*.)[42] In *Les Fantoccini français* (1789), Marie Antoinette's insidious foreign identity is underscored not in direct relation to her Habsburg roots, but through allusion to her association with the Comédie-Italienne. In the context of this *intermède*, the character "Maria-Antonia" comes across as distinctly Italian, reimagined as the leading lady of a *commedia dell'arte* troupe. In each of these cases, the queen's taste for cosmopolitan, comic theater serves as a symbol of her supposed deficiencies in character—her inappropriate friendships and frivolous leisure activities, her Austrian birth, and, especially, her refusal to conform to standards of courtly decorum. This royal patronage of *opéra-comique* might consequently be read as a breakdown in the rhetoric of kingly (or rather, queenly) display, a disruption in the manner that the monarchy constructed itself through public art.

It is important to keep in mind, however, that both the nature of *opéra-comique*'s rise and the upheaval it engendered were fraught with paradoxes, which were strongly linked to the longstanding conventions of court opera. In other words, it might be more useful to investigate how *opéra-comique* was molded to conform to the standards of ceremonial pageantry as opposed to how its presence threatened these standards. As we have seen, many affronts to theatrical regulation were inspired by the spectacular traditions of Bourbon theater. Indeed, the more genre-bending *opéras-comiques* of the late eighteenth century, in terms of music and structure, are often among the most retrogressive in political orientation. For many contemporary music critics, the most pressing issue was not how *opéra-comique* at Versailles reflected poorly on the reputation of the monarchy, but how monarchical intervention was altering the fundamental identity of *opéra-comique*. Their concern was not how the Bourbon image was being improperly debased, but how the conventions of lyric comedy were being improperly ennobled.

Here we might cite an *opéra-comique* like Jean-Paul-Égide Martini's *Henri IV*, written for the accession of Louis XVI in 1774. This work was roundly criticized at the time of its premiere, in part because its expansive pantomimes, brash military music, and historical plot transgressed the traditional boundaries of the comic domain. The *Journal des théâtres*, in a review of the general subject, decried such "heroic" traits within *opéra-comique* as an affront to theatrical propriety that had rendered the genre virtually unrecognizable.[43] But, of course, the authors only adopted these stylistic markers because their opera had a ceremonial function tied to a specific political event; in a manner reminiscent of the Lullian *tragédie lyrique*, they meant to use historical allegory to celebrate their optimism for the reign of a new king. It is clear, then, that at the end of the ancien régime, the once unbreakable association between lyric tragedy and monarchical propaganda began to loosen. But we should not necessarily take this to mean that the Bourbon court ceased to further its political agenda through operatic spectacle. Rather, *opéra-comique* might now also fulfill this role, and it would behoove us to explicate the aesthetic and political tensions inherent in this process.

NOTES

1. William Weber, "La musique ancienne in the Waning of the Ancien Régime," *The Journal of Modern History* 56 (1984): 78.
2. Richard Taruskin, "Courts Resplendent, Overthrown, Restored," in *Music in the Seventeenth and Eighteenth Centuries* (New York: Oxford Univ. Press, n.d.), accessed 30 July 2015, http://www.oxfordwesternmusic.com/view/Volume2/actrade-9780195384826-chapter-03.xml.
3. Philippe Beaussant, *Les plaisirs de Versailles: Théâtre et musique* (Paris: Fayard, 1996), 237.
4. Weber, "La musique ancienne," 84–85.
5. The records of court programming are conserved in the Archives Nationales in Paris (F-Pan), within the general accounts of the *maison du roi* (series O^1).
6. For an introduction to the various national forms of comic opera, see Daniel Heartz, *Music in European Capitals: The Galant Style, 1720–1780* (New York: W.W. Norton, 2003). For a discussion of the French genre, in particular, see David Charlton, *Grétry and the Growth of Opéra-Comique* (Cambridge: Cambridge Univ. Press, 1986).
7. Friedrich-Melchior von Grimm and Denis Diderot, *Correspondance littéraire, philosophique et critique de Grimm et de Diderot depuis 1753 jusqu'en 1790,* ed. Maurice Tourneux, 16 vols. (Paris: Garnier Frères, 1877–82), 13: 417.
8. This description was leveled against Louis XVI by the comte de Mercy-Argenteau. See Florimond Claude, comte de Mercy-Argenteau, to Maria Theresa, letter of 20 October 1770, reprinted in Alfred d'Arneth and M.A. Geffroy, eds. *Marie Antoinette. Correspondance secrète entre Marie Thérèse et le Comte de Mercy-Argenteau*, 3 vols. (Paris: Librairie de Firmin Didot Frères, Fils et Cle, 1874), 1: 66.
9. For a description of the royal wedding, see Beaussant, *Plaisirs de Versailles*, 198–209; and Benoît Dratwicki, "Le *Persée* des fêtes de 1770: un collectif d'artistes à la gloire du *goût français,*" *Cahiers Philidor* 36 (Versailles: Éditions du Centre de Musique Baroque de Versailles, 2009).

10. These activities have been previously sketched in M. Elizabeth C. Bartlet, "Grétry, Marie-Antoinette, and *La rosière de Salency*," *Proceedings of the Royal Musicological Association* 111 (1984–85): 92–98; and Corinne Pré, "L'opéra-comique à la cour de Louis XVI," *Dix-huitième siècle* 17 (1985): 221–28. The present essay represents a deepening of these earlier findings, made possible by a new appraisal of the archival records of the court theaters.

11. In 1788, for example, she hosted more than 150 *petits concerts*, either in her own apartments or in those of the comtesse d'Artois. See F-Pan, O^1 3082.359–3082.362.

12. Denis-Pierre-Jean Papillon de la Ferté, *Journal de Papillon de la Ferté, intendant et contrôleur de l'argenterie, menus-plaisirs, et affaires de la chambre du roi (1756–1780)*, ed. Ernest Boysse (Paris: P. Ollendorff, 1887), 424.

13. This troupe has been described in Adolphe Jullien, *La comédie à la cour de Louis XVI: le théâtre de la reine à Trianon* (Paris: J. Baur, 1875).

14. "Mémoire de Duvergé et Bellocq, pour les voyages de Paris et autres pendant le quartier de Juillet 1780," F-Pan, O^1 3058.188.

15. Comte de Mercy-Argenteau to Maria Theresa, letter of 16 September 1780, reprinted in *Marie Antoinette*, 3: 464.

16. There are receipts in the archives of the *menus plaisirs* (i.e., F-Pan, O^1 3060.126) for couriers sent to alert the Comédie-Italienne to alter its schedules to accommodate the queen's requests. See also Beaussant, *Plaisirs de Versailles*, 233–35.

17. Throughout, statistics are compiled from Annegret Gierich, "Theater am Hof von Versailles zur Zeit der Marie Antoinette, 1770–1789," (PhD diss., Universität Wien, 1968); Paul F. Rice, *The Performing Arts at Fontainebleau from Louis XIV to Louis XVI* (Ann Arbor: UMI Research Press, 1989); and F-Pan, O^1 3026–3086.

18. The wedding revival of *Persée* seems to have made a strong impression on Marie Antoinette, though precisely the opposite impression that officials had intended: it was both the first and the last of Lully's *tragédies lyriques* that Marie Antoinette witnessed at Versailles.

19. The genre had previously made headway at court—in the early 1750s and again in the early 1760s—but was thwarted by the Seven Years' War and a series of deaths in the royal household, respectively, both of which necessitated a return to sobriety of theatrical entertainment.

20. For a history of this system, see Robert M. Isherwood, *Farce and Fantasy: Popular Entertainment in Eighteenth-Century Paris* (New York and Oxford: Oxford Univ. Press, 1986), 81–97.

21. "Arrêt du conseil d'état du Roi, approbatif du bail ou concession du privilège de l'Opéra-Comique, faite par la Ville aux Comédiens, dits, Italiens, pour trente années, à commencer le 1er Janvier 1780," F-Pan, AJ^{13} 3.

22. "Arrêt du conseil d'état du Roi," F-Pan, AJ^{13} 3.

23. See, for example, the receipts contained in F-Pan, O^1 3031.96; O^1 3066.467; and O^1 3075.707. While such casting overlap at court was not an invention of the 1770s, it did not represent a threat to legal privilege before the Comédie-Italienne took over the contract of the fairground Opéra-Comique in 1762.

24. On the development of operatic parody, see Pauline Beaucé, *Parodies d'opéra au siècle des Lumières: Évolution d'un genre comique* (Rennes: Presses universitaires de Rennes, 2013); and Susan Louise Harvey, "Opera Parody in Eighteenth-Century France: Genesis, Genre, and Critical Function" (PhD diss., Stanford Univ., 2003).

25. On the mixed public of the fair theaters, see Isherwood, *Farce and Fantasy*; and Nathalie Rizzoni, "Inconnaissance de la Foire," in eds. Agnès Terrier and Alexandre Dratwicki, *L'invention des genres lyriques français et leur redécouverte au XIXe siècle* (Lyon: Symétrie, 2010), 119–51.

26. "You know, Madame, that this poem is one of the most beautiful of the gracious Quinault. If you had seen it disfigured, distorted, how hideous it would have appeared to you! Ah, Madame, the terrible thing that a parody is!... Must we really put up with this miserable genre of writing in the Republic of Letters?" Anne-Marie du Boccage, *Lettre de Madame *** à une de ses amies sur les spectacles, et principalement sur l'Opera Comique* (Paris, 1745), 18–19. All translations are my own unless otherwise indicated.

27. There was, however, a burst of activity in the 1750s, likely in reaction to the *querelle des bouffons* (a pamphlet war concerning the relative merits of French and Italian music). For a listing of these performances, see Rice, *Performing Arts*, 182–92.

28. These statistics represent a bare minimum of performances and are based on Beaucé, *Parodies d'opéra*, 370–71; Gierich, "Theater am Hof," Annex 119–33; and Rice, *Performing Arts*, 182–240.

29. It is worth noting that the incentive here may have been less the personal taste of the queen than her desire to please her husband. On Louis XVI's preference for parody, see Louis Petit de Bachaumont, *Mémoires secrets pour servir à l'histoire de la république des lettres en France*, 36 vols. (London: John Adamson, 1781–89), 10: 270–71.

30. Marie Antoinette saw *La bonne femme*, the spoof of Gluck's *Alceste*, at least five times.

31. An invoice paid to Jean-Étienne Despréaux in 1780 indicates that preparations for his parody *Christophe et Pierre-Luc* included a trip to Versailles to preview the play before the queen (F-Pan, O¹ 3058.194).

32. In 1786, artists granted special financial compensation from the court included Antonio Sacchini and Antonio Salieri (composers of *tragédie lyrique*) and Jean-Étienne Despréaux (dancer and author of operatic parodies). See "Bordereau de la dépense contenüe en état des comédies, concerts, spectacles et bals à la Cour, pour l'année mil sept cent quatre vingt six," F-Pan, O¹ 3074.

33. Beaucé, *Parodies d'opéra*, 226–28.

34. Ibid., 380. These costuming choices are also indicated in the libretto of the parody. See Despréaux, *Syncope, Reine de Mic-Mac, parodie de Pénélope* (Paris: Ballard, 1786).

35. Despréaux, *Christophe et Pierre Luc, parodie de Castor et Pollux en cinq actes, en prose et en vaudevilles* (Paris: Ballard, 1780).

36. Joseph de la Porte, *Dictionnaire dramatique, contenant l'histoire des théâtres,*

les règles du genre dramatique, les observations des maîtres les plus célèbres et des réflexions nouvelles sur les spectacles, 3 vols. (Paris: Lacombe, 1776), 3: 499.

37. "The two works are essentially modeled on the same plan, and it is not easy to determine if the parody was constructed after the opera or the opera after the parody." Grimm and Diderot, *Correspondance littéraire,* 11: 81.

38. Weber, "La musique ancienne," 60.

39. Beaussant, for instance, describes Marie Antoinette's interest in music as based nearly entirely in the pursuit of pleasure, with little regard for the symbolic potential of the art form. Beaussant, *Plaisirs de Versailles,* 211–12.

40. See Chantal Thomas, *La reine scélérate: Marie-Antoinette dans les pamphlets* (Paris: Éditions du Seuil, 1989).

41. *L'autrichienne en goguettes* is described as an "opéra proverbe," while *Le branle des Capucins* is termed a "petit opéra aristocratico-comico-risible."

42. The character sings a tune based on the vaudeville finale of Philidor's *Le sorcier,* which Marie Antoinette's society troupe had performed in September of 1780.

43. *Journal des théâtres, ou le Nouveau spectateur,* 1 April 1777: 37–43.

The Debate on Judicial Torture in Austrian Lombardy

R. S. AGIN

As legal and intellectual historians have demonstrated, the use of judicial torture began declining significantly in western Europe in the centuries before its widespread abolition at the end of the eighteenth century. Scholars have debated the reasons for this decline. It has been generally assumed that the increasingly limited application of torture in judicial proceedings was the direct result of the abolitionist efforts of philosophers such as Cesare Beccaria and Voltaire. Nevertheless, in *Torture and the Law of Proof* (1977), lawyer and legal historian John Langbein dismissed this belief as a "fairy tale."[1] Instead, he argued, the end of judicial torture was the result of changes in legal procedure dating to the seventeenth century that made it easier for judges to apply less severe punishments, *poenae extraordinariae,* for capital crimes where absolute proof (which generally came in the form of confession) had previously been necessary. The history of the debate on torture in Austrian Lombardy, however, challenges Langbein's strictly legalistic account of torture's abolition. At least in the Duchy of Milan, the debate on torture and its ultimate elimination were, in fact, part of a more complicated intellectual and legal history that grew from the interactions between rulers and philosophers, political centers and peripheries, and even parents and children.

Sometime around 1777, the eighteenth-century Milanese philosopher, political economist, and public administrator Pietro Verri finished writing *Observations on Torture*, a detailed examination of the 1630 arrest, interrogation, and execution of Gian Giacomo Mora and Guglielmo Piazza, the two men accused of having spread the plague in the city. Studying Giuseppe Ripamonti's eyewitness account of Milan during the plague, as well as the actual transcripts of Mora's and Piazza's trials, Verri wrote what stands today as the enlightenment's most thorough denunciation of torture's efficacy in judicial proceedings. However, for reasons that owed to his problematic relationship with his family and to the local power structure of his native Milan, Verri chose not to publish the *Observations* during his lifetime. Instead, it was the *Essay on Crimes and Punishments*, published in 1764 by his onetime friend and collaborator Cesare Beccaria, that would continue to be most associated with the enlightenment critique of judicial torture—an association that, as Langbein's argument shows, still persists today.

As we know, Beccaria's *Essay* became a sensation throughout Europe, primarily because of its immediate translation into French by the abbé Morellet and the stamp of approval it received from the philosophes. Slightly less known than its reception is its origin. Conceived and written in Pietro Verri's study, *Essay on Crimes and Punishments* was the most celebrated work to come out of the facetiously called *Accademia dei pugni*. Begun by Pietro and his brother Alessandro, the *Accademia* was an informal group of young Milanese men who were deeply influenced by the work emanating from Parisian philosophical circles and who shared a commitment to social betterment. However, unlike their French counterparts, they were almost all born into noble families occupying important political positions. This was particularly true for the Verri brothers whose father Gabriele was a long-standing member of the Milanese Senate, the most powerful political and judicial institution of the city. Consequently, for the Milanese philosophers, questioning traditional beliefs and practices often meant rebelling not only against the social and political order but also against one's own family. It is this particularity that led historian Franco Venturi to characterize the Milanese enlightenment as a "struggle between generations" in which Pietro Verri and Beccaria "affirmed their vocation as reformers and Enlightenment thinkers in opposition to the environment in which they were born and raised."[2]

Beccaria's *Essay on Crimes and Punishments* was created in this particular setting. In a letter dated April 16, 1803 to his friend Isidoro Bianchi, Alessandro Verri looked back on the origins and early development of the book. Alessandro was working at the time, like his brother before him, as a "protector of the incarcerated."[3] The brothers' work with the city's imprisoned had led to a general discussion of crime and the methods used in judicial procedures. According to Alessandro, "[i]t seemed to Count Pietro a topic worthy of the pen of his friend Beccaria, and he proposed that he treat it."[4] Beccaria accepted and, sitting alongside Alessandro in Pietro's study, started to write his text. Verri recounted that it was "there on Count Pietro's small table that I saw the Marquis Cesare Beccaria write and compose the work *On Crimes and Punishments*."[5] Alessandro also recalled his brother helping Beccaria edit the work as well as offering general encouragement: "But because the Marquis was so reluctant to part with his first draft, which was always full of corrections and crossed-out words, I recall that my brother had the honor of correcting the work with his own hand. He always inspired Beccaria to continue working on it and predicted that it would earn the applause of Europe."[6] Pietro's own version of the story largely repeated Alessandro's, although he noted both Beccaria's general ignorance of the city's criminal system and the collective nature of the work that resulted in the *Essay*:

> The book is by the Marquis Beccaria. I gave him the topic, and the majority of the ideas were the result of conversations that took place daily between Beccaria, Alessandro, Lambertenghi and me. In our little group, we spent the evenings together in the same room, each working. Alessandro was busy with his *History of Italy*, I with my works on political economy, others read. Beccaria was bored and bothering the others. Out of desperation, he asked me for a subject to work on, and I suggested that one, knowing that it was particularly suited to a man with eloquence and a vivid imagination. However, he didn't know anything about our criminal system. Alessandro, who was a protector of the incarcerated, promised to assist him. Beccaria started writing down ideas on individual pieces of paper, we supported him with enthusiasm and incited him so much that he wrote down scores of ideas. After lunch, we would go for a stroll, talk about the horrors of criminal jurisprudence, argue, question, and in the evenings, he would write. But writing was so difficult for him and cost him such efforts that after an hour he couldn't withstand the strain. I would gather up what material he had, would write it down and put some order in it, and a book was formed.[7]

While we may wonder if the Verri brothers' depiction of the large role that Pietro played in the redaction of the *Essay on Crimes and Punishments* was not, in part, fueled by jealousy of Beccaria's success, it is indisputable that the *Accademia*'s general interest in judicial torture—the subject of chapter

16 of the *Essay*—owed directly to the elder Verri brother, who had already published several texts on the topic.

These texts relied heavily on ridicule. In January of 1764, Verri's satirical almanac *The Pain of the Spleen* contained a short riddle whose answer was "Regina tormentorum," the "Queen of tortures," otherwise known as torture by rope.[8] And in his *Panegyrical Oration on Milanese Jurisprudence* (1763), a pompous and ignorant magistrate defended the city's judicial system against two groups: the French philosophes with their "libercoli oltramontani," and countries like England and Prussia, where torture was not used in judicial interrogations.[9] On the latter, the magistrate remarked: "And to convince ourselves fully of the state of blindness to which the English and Prussians have been reduced, observe, gentlemen, how these two crestfallen nations have even arrived at abolishing any little crucible for which criminals purge their infamy. There is no one who can deny that the *corda*, the *veglia*, the *canape* [all forms of rope torture], and similar ingenious inventions, are types of purgatives, and I'm not talking about the senna and rhubarb kind, but about purgatives in general."[10] In Milan, on the contrary, "a poor criminal does not want for any of the assistances necessary for being truthful; here, in our land, we have the humanity to purge him when he is tainted with infamy; but in the states of those most unfortunate nations, a villain [infame] remains always a villain. Our eyes fill with tears at the sight of such barbarous and implacable legislation!"[11] According to the magistrate's logic, in places where judicial torture was not practiced, criminals were not allowed the same possibility of purifying themselves and were therefore condemned to wallow in a state of corruption forever: "un infame resta sempre un infame."[12] The following year, Beccaria referred specifically to this idea of the "purgative" effect of torture, when he wrote in chapter 16 of the *Essay on Crimes and Punishments* that "there is another ridiculous motive for torture that holds that it purges a man of his infamy, that is, a man whom the law has judged to be a villain [*infame*] must confirm his deposition by the dislocation of his bones."[13]

The biting irony of Verri's *Panegyrical Oration*, with its repetition of the word "infame," would have been lost on few people living in a city where a column called the *Colonna infame* (*Column of Infamy*) still stood. It is therefore no wonder that the *Panegyrical Oration*, like his later *Observations on Torture*, remained unpublished during Pietro's lifetime. The *Column*, which Milanese city officials had erected on the former site of Gian Giacomo Mora's house, was accompanied by a plaque that detailed in cold, administrative language exactly how Mora and his accomplice Piazza were punished before being executed. It was intended to serve both as a warning to the city's would-be miscreants and as a symbolic reaffirmation of the Milanese Senate's authority and control over the city. But by the second part of the eighteenth century, its symbolic resonance had become quite different. For Verri and others who knew how Mora and Piazza had been tortured in order to extract confessions to an impossible crime, the *Column* stood, in Verri's own words, as "a monument to the superstitious cruelty and ignorance of the past."[14]

Judicial torture thus came to serve as an issue around which Verri and the members of the *Accademia dei pugni* could articulate their own larger vision of enlightened social and judicial reform. But, at the same time, it also quickly became a rallying point around which the city's conservative elders tried to preserve their cultural and political autonomy against what they viewed as the abstract, philosophical, as well as foreign-born arguments that were exerting a pernicious effect on actual policy. As a result, the debate on torture in Habsburg Milan was built upon a series of political, historical, philosophical, institutional, and even generational oppositions that made it unique to eighteenth-century Europe.

Here, it is important to recall that the Milanese Senate had been instituted in 1499 by the French monarch Louis XII and was modeled after the French parlement system to act as a court of last instance. Resulting from what we might today call the politics of pragmatic colonial administration, it quickly demonstrated its usefulness in the day-to-day operations of the city, which allowed it to survive French, Swiss, Spanish, and, for a little more than seventy years, Austrian rule. Because of this, the Senate enjoyed a certain amount of autonomy in local affairs, allowing it to become quite powerful within the city itself. Difficulties in what had historically been a mutually beneficial relationship between empire and territory, however, began to arise with the arrival of the Habsburgs. And, as Venturi has shown, it was often Gabriele Verri who, in the various roles he played in Milan's governance and administration over the years, spearheaded the resistance against what was viewed by many as Vienna's encroachments on local affairs.[15] This increasing tension between political center and periphery came to a head in the late 1770s precisely over the issue of judicial torture.

On January 2, 1776, in one of her first official acts of the year, Empress Maria Theresa issued a decree that abolished torture and greatly restricted the application of the death penalty in the hereditary lands of the Empire. Along with the Empress's son and eventual heir Joseph, the Austrian chancellor of state and minister of foreign affairs Prince Wenzel Anton Kaunitz had been the principal political voice in favor of abolition in Vienna. Following Maria Theresa's general policy of allowing foreign territories a certain amount of self-governance, the ban on torture did not automatically extend to the Duchy of Milan. This did not mean, however, that Vienna could not apply a bit of political pressure to make the city fall in line. On January 8,

1776, sensing resistance from the Lombard capital, Kaunitz sent a missive to Count Karl Joseph von Firmian, plenipotentiary minister of Lombardy, in which he voiced concern over Milan's frequent use of judicial torture as indicated by its criminal records, and reiterated the Empress's desire to extend the ban on torture to all Habsburg-controlled territories.[16] The message was communicated to the Milanese Senate, which, in turn, formed a committee to examine the request. The committee was led by Gabriele Verri, who, by this point, was one of the longest standing members of the Senate. On April 19, 1776, the committee presented its findings and recommendations to the Senate at large, and it was Gabriele who authored the Senate's *consulta*, its official reply to the Habsburg court. In it, Gabriele outlined the two basic reasons why Milan had chosen not to follow Vienna's directive. It argued first that Vienna did not understand the mindset of criminals in Milan. Torture, or at least the threat of torture, was a necessary deterrent for preventing the city's particularly hardened criminals from wreaking havoc. The Senate's second argument had a decidedly more personal resonance. It rejected calls for torture's abolition, which, in its estimation, were being made primarily by "philosophers" with no practical experience in juridical matters. It is the "philosophers," Gabriele wrote, who "rail against what they define as a most ferocious torment employed with the simple aim of wresting out the truth."[17] Using a strategy common to many of torture's supporters, he then imagined a series of hypothetical scenarios in which torture would be necessary for maintaining public safety, insisting that, in these cases, "even the most compassionate philosophers ... if they want to be true philosophers, will surely understand that test by torture is necessary, when measured with the balance of justice."[18] The Senate's argument was thus both pragmatic and utilitarian, but, given the repeated, disparaging use of the word "philosopher" that peppers it, one has to wonder if its author was not, in fact, arguing with his son as much as with the Habsburg court.

The young philosophers of the *Accademia dei pugni* knew that writing about judicial reform and Milan's use of torture would cause them no shortage of problems with the city's political authorities, to say nothing of their own families. As we saw, Verri never released the *Panegyrical Oration on Milanese Jurisprudence* and had only anonymously published *The Pain of the Spleen* with its riddle on torture. He must therefore have received the news of Maria Theresa's 1776 decree banning torture with a great deal of satisfaction, and he must have been even more pleased to learn that Vienna was pressing Milan to follow suit. The debate on judicial torture that was playing out between the Habsburg court and the Milanese Senate, and between the Habsburg court and his father, seems to have spurred him to revisit the issue. In a letter to Alessandro, dated May 22, 1776, he wrote:

In regards to torture, I've amassed enough material to make a book of horror. I had in my hands the *excerpta* of the *Column of Infamy* trial. Oh, dear Alessandro, what an abomination! Cannibals are not as atrocious as were innocent those unfortunate wretches, who perished in the midst of agonies and tortures. This would be the opportunity to examine a point that's of great interest and quite fashionable at the current moment. By bringing together an actual history of that event, which is both so famous and at the same time so little known, with the theory of torture that produced the tragedy, I would write a book that would certainly shock. I've even been invited to do so. But, my friend, the age of wisdom has arrived. For the dazzle of such a small bit of fame, I don't want to antagonize the Senate whose expected favorable opinion in my case was the reason why our father deigned to come to a settlement with me. From one day to the next, I might need these gentlemen, against either our uncle or our mother, and I certainly won't start a fight with people on whom I depend for my bread.[19]

The reference to his settlement with their father concerned a financial dispute about his marriage, and the other reference to his uncle and mother pointed to what he saw as an inevitable battle with them over his inheritance and the eventual, necessary intervention of the Senate to adjudicate.[20] Therefore, in the spring of 1776, newly married, having arrived at the "age of wisdom," as he put it, Pietro chose not to antagonize the Senate by publishing a book on the Mora-Piazza trial that would have cast a spotlight on the institution's role in that dark piece of Milanese history. This did not, however, prevent him from spending the better part of 1776 and 1777 writing it in private.

Still, it seems that someone else did want to see his book on torture published. As Pietro said in his letter to Alessandro, he was explicitly "invited" to do so. We do not know for sure who made this request, but scholars such as Giorgio Panizza and Barbara Costa have suggested, justifiably it seems to me, that it came from Vienna.[21] After all, Prince Kaunitz had been the primary force behind the abolition movement in the Habsburg Empire. In February 1769, when the Empire's new penal code, the *Constitutio Criminalis Theresiana*, went into effect, he immediately wrote a memorandum to the Empress, expressing his opposition to the retention and illustration (in the form of actual engravings) of the officially sanctioned torture techniques to be used in judicial interrogations in the Empire. He was joined in his opposition by Karl Anton Martini, professor of jurisprudence at the University of Vienna and former tutor to Maria Theresa's sons Joseph and Leopold, and by Joseph von Sonnenfels, another jurist and professor at the University of Vienna. Similarly, Joseph von Sperges, who oversaw Italian affairs in Vienna and with whom Pietro was in friendly correspondence for many years, and Milan's plenipotentiary Firmian were actively engaged in the abolitionist effort.[22]

In 1775, Sonnenfels published an anti-torture treatise, *On the Abolition of Torture*, which was almost immediately translated into Italian by the polygraph Carlo Amoretti and published in Milan the following year, right at the time of the Empress's decree and the Senate's *consulta*. Kaunitz's January 8 missive to Firmian, the quick translation and dissemination of Sonnenfels's work in Milan, as well as the mysterious invitation that was extended to Pietro Verri to publish his own text on torture's role in the Mora-Piazza trial, all seem to point to a campaign to promote the abolitionist cause in Habsburg Lombardy that was organized, in all likelihood, by Kaunitz himself. And here we see the complex interactions between politicians who considered themselves philosophers and philosophers who acted as politicians in the development of the debate on torture in Habsburg Lombardy. As historian Franz Szabo has shown, Kaunitz's opposition to torture was, in fact, largely informed by his reading of Beccaria's *Essay On Crimes and Punishments*. Additionally, notes Szabo, "Kaunitz was not only familiar with the outpourings of the *Il Caffè* group [the journal put out by the *Accademia dei pugni*], but often much influenced by their thought. Many of its most prominent members found service in the Austrian administration of Milan, or were granted academic engagements thanks to Kaunitz."[23] When, for example, Catherine II invited Beccaria to St. Petersburg in 1767, Kaunitz worked with Firmian to keep him in Habsburg territory by creating a chair in economics at the Palatine School in Milan specifically for him. For his part, Pietro Verri, with support from Vienna, occupied increasingly important positions within Milan's economic institutions, first as vice president of the *Supremo consiglio per l'economia* and later as president of the *Consiglio camerale*. In 1770, Verri himself recommended his close friend and ally from the *Accademia dei pugni* days, Luigi Lambertenghi, to Sperges for a position in the empire's Department of Italy.[24] The Viennese court thus knew Verri as both the animating force behind Milan's philosophical movement and as an able public administrator. It is therefore not unreasonable to think that in 1776 Kaunitz, through Sperges or even Lambertenghi, may have reached out to Verri in the campaign to abolish torture in the entire Habsburg Empire.

As we know, however, Milan refused to abandon judicial torture, and the fact that Verri's father Gabriele penned the Senate's official response must have must have pushed Pietro to return to the topic, devoting particular attention to the Mora-Piazza trial of 1630. The text that resulted, *Observations on Torture*, was Pietro's answer both to his father and to the institution he represented. In response to his father's argument for the necessity of torture in deterring criminality and maintaining public safety, Pietro offered a systematic demonstration of how the Milanese Senate, under Spanish rule and during a time of plague, used judicial torture to obtain confessions of the most fantastical crime from two poor men. Under the duress of torture, Guglielmo Piazza, a low-level public health commissioner, admitted to spreading a plague-infested unguent on the walls of his Milanese neighborhood. In a second round of torture, he named Gian Giacomo Mora, a local barber whom he barely knew, as his accomplice. As Pietro showed, the Senate was never able to determine the two men's motive, nor was it able to explain their apparently magical ability to cook up their plague-infested ooze and spread it throughout the city without contracting the illness themselves. All that mattered was that both men confessed to their crimes, and confession was the ultimate, irrefutable proof.

Verri did not publish his text in part for the reasons I mentioned earlier and in part because it seemed to him that Milanese society was on the verge of making the book's primary critique obsolete. This, however, did not prove to be the case. Undisturbed by the Senate's refusal to extend the abolition of torture to its city, Maria Theresa did nothing. Never completely convinced by the argument for abolition, leery of anything that smacked of the new philosophy, and more concerned about maintaining order in the Empire than being an agent for something as abstract as social progress, she allowed the status quo to continue.

In the end, the Senate's refusal to adopt Maria Theresa's decree served little practical purpose. Judicial torture and its symbolic vestiges were already disappearing. At the end of August 1778, the Column of Infamy was quietly dismantled under cover of the night—the result of a clever ploy orchestrated by Firmian.[25] When the Empress died a few years later in 1780, so did the general policy of allowing some territories a certain degree of autonomy in their legislative and judicial proceedings. The new ruler of the Empire, Maria Theresa's son Joseph II, was both more progressive in his politics and more despotic in his rule than his mother. On September 11, 1784, he issued a decree that completely banned the use of torture from the entire Empire, Milan included. Pietro, again, welcomed the news. An enlightened ruler had finally come to drag Milan into the age of enlightenment, or so he thought. That same year, he imagined an epigraph that would commemorate Joseph II's equally imaginary reconstruction of Mora's house, which had been destroyed in 1630 to make room for the Column of Infamy.[26] The epigraph as well as the rebuilt house and public ceremony of restitution would remain imaginary. Instead, Joseph II proceeded to level most of Milan's political, juridical, and economic institutions, including the Senate, which Pietro had spent so much time and energy criticizing, and the *Magistrato Camerale*, of which he was president. Joseph II's absolutism ended up cutting both ways for Pietro: on the one hand, it led to the much-anticipated abolition of torture in Milan; on the other hand, it led to the elimination of Pietro's job and to his marginalization from the political, social, and juridical life of his native city.

More than merely concretizing the tension that had existed between Vienna and Milan for most of the eighteenth century, Joseph's radical overhaul of Lombardy underscored the complex relationship that existed at the time between the Empire's capital and its outlying territories, between its center and its periphery. Joseph may have been every bit the pragmatist that his mother was before him, but he differed from her in one important and obvious respect: in addition to his deep-seated belief in social progress, a belief that can be traced to the influence of teachers and advisors such as Sonnenfels, Martini, and most of all Kaunitz, he was also committed to enlightened absolutism. As his abolition of torture demonstrates, he was prepared to impose his vision of an enlightened state on Habsburg-controlled territories, even at the risk of destabilizing the political and social status quo. Like his closest advisor Kaunitz, Joseph II believed that judicial torture was an inhumane practice, the relic of a barbarous past. It was a belief he shared with philosophers such as Pietro Verri and Cesare Beccaria, whose works, as we have seen, were instrumental in influencing Kaunitz himself. Judicial torture, as John Langbein and others have shown, may have been on the wane in most of Western Europe since the seventeenth century, if not earlier, because of changes in legal proof. However, this does not mean that the historians who have connected the abolition of judicial torture to the efforts of philosopher-propagandists are guilty of spreading in a "fairy tale." If anything, the specific history of judicial torture in Habsburg Lombardy shows quite clearly how this was intricately interwoven with the problematic politics of empire, with competing visions of the past and the present, and even, in the case of the Verri household, with the difficult relationship between a father and his son. It shows how torture was used to construct a vision of enlightened social progress in order to combat old ideas, practices, and institutions. And finally, it shows how one autocratic emperor, under the influence of such a vision, could enact a series of reforms that, in one fell swoop, relegated judicial torture to the past and the philosopher who was most actively engaged in its abolition to the margins of the society he had tried so hard to improve.

NOTES

I would like to thank Barbara Costa and Carlo Capra for their help with my ongoing research on Pietro Verri and the Milanese enlightenment, and I would like to dedicate this article to Pier Luigi Porta whose untimely death has not extinguished the memory of his warmth, humor, and intelligence.

1. As examples of the conventional account of torture's abolition, Langbein cites studies by Carl Joseph Anton Mittermaier, John Gilissen, and Piero Fiorelli. However, his representation of Fiorelli's monumental two-volume *La tortura giudiziaria nel diritto comune* (Milan: Giuffrè, 1953–54), in particular, seems somewhat disingenuous. Fiorelli's depiction of the history of judicial torture is far more nuanced than Langbein would have his readers believe. At the very least, it cannot be dismissed as peddling a "fairy tale." See John Langbein, *Torture and the Law of Proof: Europe and England in the Ancien Régime* (Chicago and London: Univ. of Chicago Press, 1977), 64–69.

2. See Franco Venturi, *Settecento riformatore. Da Muratori a Beccaria*, 5 vols (Turin: Einaudi, 1969), I: 647. This and all subsequent translations are mine.

3. Founded in 1466, the *Società dei protettori dei carcerati* was composed of young Milanese noblemen intending to pursue a career in law. Its primary purpose was to serve the city's most indigent imprisoned population by studying their cases and ensuring that their rights were upheld.

4. C.R.D. Miller, "Three Verri Letters to Isidoro Bianchi," *The Romanic Review* 25 (1934): 33–35. The letter has also been reproduced in Cesare Beccaria, *Dei delitti e delle pene*, ed. Franco Venturi (Turin: Einaudi, 1970): 124–26.

5. Miller, "Three Letters," 34.

6. Miller, "Three Letters," 34.

7. See the *Memorie sincere* in Gennaro Barbarisi, ed. *Edizione nazionale delle opere di Pietro Verri. Scritti di argomento familiare e autobiografico*, 8 vols. (Milan: Fondazione Raffaele Mattioli, 2003), V: 138–39.

8. The form of torture described in the riddle, the same to which Mora and Piazza were subjected, is also known in English as "strappado," a modification of the Italian word "strappata." The riddle is reproduced in Carlo Capra's *I Progressi della ragione* (Bologna: Società editrice Il Mulino, 2002), 202, as well as in Gennaro Barbarisi, *Nota introduttiva* in Pietro Verri, *Edizione nazionale delle Opere di Pietro Verri. Scritti politici della maturità*, ed. Carlo Capra, 1st ser., 6 vols. (Milan: Fondazione Raffaele Mattioli, 2010), VI: 6.

9. "little pamphlets from beyond the Alps."

10. This text has been republished in Pietro Verri, *Osservazioni sulla tortura*, ed. Sergio Cusani (Milan: Claudio Gallone, 1997), 116.

11. Verri, *Osservazioni,* ed. Cusani, 116.

12. "a villain remains always a villain."

13. Cesare Beccaria, *Dei delitti e delle pene* (Harlem [Paris]: Dal Molini, 1780), 54.

14. This is how Verri described the *Column* in his *Historical Memoirs on the Public Economy in the State of Milan*, which were written in 1768, but, like to the *Observations on Torture*, not published until 1804, seven years after his death. Cited in Barbarisi, *Nota introduttiva*, 9.

15. For more on Gabriele Verri's battles to defend Milan's autonomy, see Franco Venturi, *Settecento riformatore. Da Muratori a Beccaria* 5 vols. (Torino: Giulio Einaudi Editore, 1969), I: 649–53.

16. The concerns that Kaunitz expressed in his missive suggest that Milan might have represented something of an anomaly in the overall decrease in instances of judicial torture seen throughout Europe. His letter is cited in Sergio Di Noto, "Documenti del dibattito su tortura e pena capitale nella Lombardia austriaca," *Studi parmensi* XIX (1977): 346.

17. The "consulta," with an accompanying Italian translation, is reproduced in Pietro Verri, *Osservazioni sulla tortura*, ed. Gennaro Barbarisi (Milan: Serra e Riva, 1985), 219.

18. Verri, *Osservazioni sulla tortura*, ed. Barbarisi, 229.

19. See Alessandro Giulini, Emanuele Greppi, Francesco Novati, and Giovanni Seregni, eds. *Carteggio di Pietro e Alessandro Verri, dal 1766 al 1797*, 12 vols. (Milan: Cogliati; 1910–42), VIII: 102.

20. For more on the dispute over the inheritance, see Capra, *I Progressi della ragione* (Bologna: Società editrice Il Mulino, 2002), 478–94. Capra himself draws extensively on Gigliola di Renzo Villata's article "« *Sembra che ... in genere ... il mondo vada migliorando* ». Pietro Verri e la famiglia tra tradizione giuridica e innovazione," in Carlo Capra, ed., *Pietro Verri e il suo tempo. Atti del convegno (Milano, 9–11 ottobre 1997)*, 2 vols. (Bologna: Cisalpino, 1999), I: 147–270.

21. See Giorgio Panizza and Barbara Costa, *L'Archivio Verri* (Milan: Fondazione Raffaele Mattioli, 2000), II: 144. Barbarisi, for his part, rejects the idea that the invitation came from Vienna, but provides no rationale as to why. See note 31 of Barbarisi, *Nota introduttiva*, 19.

22. On Sperges's and Firmian's attitudes toward torture, see Cesare Cantù, *Beccaria e il diritto penale: saggio* (Florence: G. Barbera, 1862), 162–164.

23. See Franz A.J. Szabo, *Kaunitz and Enlightened Absolutism 1753–1780* (New York: Cambridge Univ. Press, 1993), 34 and 184.

24. See Capra, *I Progressi della Ragione*, 323–24.

25. For a summary of the story behind the Column's dismantling, see note 12 of Carlo Annoni's "Le passioni fanno traviare: Parini, Manzoni e la 'Colonna infame'," in Enrico Elli and Giuseppe Langelle, ed., *Studi di letteratura italiana in onore di Francesco Mattesini* (Milan: Vita e Pensiero, 2000): 105–06.

26. For the actual transcription of Verri's imagined Latin epigraph, see Barbarisi, *Nota introduttiva*, 33.

Open Competition in Botany and Diplomacy: The Habsburg Expedition of 1783

HEATHER MORRISON

Narratives about enlightenment science and global empires of the late eighteenth century pay scant attention to the Habsburg Monarchy. Eighteenth-century scholars often write of empire solely in connection with the global reach of colonial powers. Yet in 1783, when Europeans at home and abroad spoke of an emperor, they meant the one residing in Vienna. Though the Habsburg monarchy did not have colonies, it did have centuries of other kinds of imperial achievement on display: art collections, libraries, palace architecture, the natural history cabinet, and botanical gardens all made a show of the dynasty's international power.

One might think that the modernization of knowledge and power on the global stage skipped a state whose center was far from oceanic trade and whose extensive European holdings remained its chief preoccupation. Yet that multinational empire advanced colonial science, global exploration, and overseas markets. One plant-collecting mission in particular, organized from Vienna, came to influence the international pursuit of economic botany, or the study of useful and profitable plants, and led other European states rapidly to develop their own plans for exploring the Pacific Northwest. By pursuing its interests in science and trade through this key event, the Habsburg monarchy excited direct competition from Britain, France, Spain, Russia, and the

United States. Viennese plans, developed by scientists and an enlightened absolutist state, inspired others to shift their interests in plant collecting from the ornamental to the useful and profitable. Indeed, the work of Austrian botanists on this voyage inspired scholars across the world to collect and publish their findings about plants native to the Americas and Africa. The Habsburg presence in colonial science is significant precisely because the state had no overseas empire. Hapsburg influence, I contend, reflects the transition to the modern world in ways explorer narratives or histories of colonizing states obscure. It illuminates the extent to which interconnected political and intellectual spheres during the late enlightenment drove states and people toward the modern ideal of public knowledge freely shared and national interests divergently pursued.

Imperial patronage for a scientific expedition was expected to produce an increase in the empire's prestige through both the expansion of its collection and its ability to support such an international endeavor. In the late 1760s through late 1770s, Captain James Cook's voyages created an international fascination with expeditions to parts of the world remote from Europe. The resulting public good, as opposed to the ornament of courts, had become the primary goal of several state-sponsored explorations in this age of enlightenment. States came to believe in the pursuit of knowledge for practical gains such as in the field of botany, including finding and cultivating useful plants to improve agriculture, develop industry, and enhance the health and consumer choices of the populace. Competition over the grandeur of courtly displays in botanical collections previously had occupied the diplomatic sphere; however, with the new emphasis on rational inquiry for national advancement, states watched warily for others' competitive advancement in knowledge, dispatched hunters of economic goods, and engaged occasionally in direct aggression in trade.

The Habsburg commitment to enlightenment values in botany catapulted to new prominence one winter night in 1782 when an apprentice gardener accidentally neglected the greenhouse stoves in Schönbrunn and then overheated the building to unfreeze the plants; the resulting devastation to the exotic plant collection commanded the court's attention.[1] Over the following decade, this loss was more than redressed by a global endeavor to bring the emperor new specimens. A collecting expedition left Vienna in the spring of 1783, and its initial plans and ultimate course reflect the intersection of international science and Habsburg global political ambitions.

The initial planning for this mission reveals the degree to which the international community paid attention to the plans of Joseph II, the Holy Roman Emperor. The newly established Asiatic Company of Trieste sought to develop Habsburg trade with the east.[2] The group chose as its director

Captain Wilhelm Bolts, whose overseas mercantilist activities in the late 1770s resulted in a rare Habsburg foray into colonial possessions when he purchased islands in India and established two forts in Africa, efforts that shortly proved to be ineffectual.[3] By 1781, Bolts plotted something grander. He hoped to establish a fur trade in the Pacific Northwest to exchange pelts in Japan and China for desirable porcelains, tea, and silks. The loaded ships would continue to ports in south Asia, journey around the Cape of Good Hope, stop in Constantinople to trade with the Ottoman Porte, and then take the final leg back to Trieste carrying truly global goods.[4] Through this journey, the Asiatic Company hoped to establish lasting trade networks bringing great profits and global reach. The plan itself was a novel one because knowledge of the potential wealth in the Pacific Northwest became public only after the 1785 official release of records from the final Cook journey.

These Habsburg overseas ambitions—coalescing around Bolts and radiating from Trieste, Vienna, and the Habsburg Netherlands—may surprise those familiar with world history. But the American Revolution introduced a temporary vacuum in colonial trade and power expansion. War for some meant opportunity for others, and Joseph II used it to reconsider his hereditary state's policy of avoiding overseas commitments in favor of focusing on, expanding, or exchanging its extensive European holdings. Bolts arrived in Vienna in May of 1782 for a meeting about his circumnavigation scheme with an emperor experiencing his first spring without exotic palms in Schönbrunn. The timing could not have been better, for Bolts not only sought wealth through trade but also dreamed of organizing a Cook-style expedition. He hired four men involved in those journeys and chose as his North Pacific destination Vancouver Island where Cook had spent time.[5] Joseph II voiced the desire to have naturalists travel aboard Bolts' ship to collect material for his gardens, menagerie, and natural history collection.[6] The captain eagerly agreed to the emperor's patronage not least to rouse the excitement of potential subscribers eager for signs that this endeavor would be as prestigious as Cook's.

From Bolts' perspective, working for the Holy Roman emperor and Habsburg monarch provided unique advantages when planning a combined trade and natural science mission. Joseph II was not at war, and his hereditary lands never competed for colonies. The emperor's support would allow Bolts' ship to sail through otherwise closed or contentious territories so long as he guaranteed not to infringe on preexisting Habsburg agreements and trade treaties. The emperor also agreed to provide military protection for the merchant ships. Bolts and the Company's investors would profit in exchange for financing. Potentially, this impressive journey would establish for the monarchy a trade presence in areas with little pre-existing colonial activity, without major investment from the state, at a time of minimal British and French competition. Ignaz von Born, the director of the natural history collection (and former mining official), also sought to further Habsburg trading interests while helping defray expenses. He suggested that Bolts carry a large quantity of quicksilver, for they would travel, he wrote, "folglich in eine Gegend, wo wir bis her keine Verschleiß haben, und da wir in der österreichischen Monarchie so ein Menge von diesem Metalle haben, so ist jeder Ausweg solches abzuschazen, schon an sich selbst ein realler Gewinn."[7] The mercury trade, dominated by Spain, could bring the Habsburg monarchy great profit. As a mineralogist, self-proclaimed "enlightener," and court advisor, Born hoped that the work of the naturalists involved would advance knowledge and the state. He fought to have Franz Joseph Märter, a professor of economic botany, head the expedition. Born also hoped to send an expert in mineralogy—an even more potentially lucrative, useful science. The vice chancellor planning the voyage, Prince Philipp von Cobenzl, similarly connected exploration, trade, plant collecting, and economic advancement. As a result of their planning, the practical collecting voyage ordered by Joseph II would be guided by broader enlightenment ideals of the expansion, application, and diffusion of knowledge. Joseph II's involvement with Bolts' schemes also reflected a modernizing economy, one that shifted away from state financing toward public capital investment. With state investment (and potential losses) limited to the naturalists' fare and arming the ship, Bolts needed to solicit private subscriptions, which required advertising both the voyage and Habsburg support. This public endeavor depended on an open exchange of information.

By midsummer 1782, Bolts and the Viennese court had a plan, ship, staff, departure date, and a general consensus about the purpose and destination of the expedition. But given the potential radical shift in global trade and empires that this expedition could usher in, news of these plans did not stay within the confines of the Hofburg for long. Historian Robert King documents how the news spread to the international community. Bolts' imperial voyage rightfully roused suspicion of Austria's economic and colonial intentions, and the British ambassador reported immediately on these matters of competitive national interest. He described the plan as "for the very liberal Purpose of making the Tour of the World, in imitation of Captain Cooke's Voyage." That an Englishman who had journeyed to the Pacific with Cook joined the crew reinforced this connection. The report to London also stated, "Persons of Learning & Curiosity are to carry the Emperor's Orders into Execution." More details followed on July 8, when the ambassador reported on the quicksilver plans, the addition of a second member of Cook's crew, and their intended route through the Magellan Straits. He warned that a well-armed ship was accompanying them and that they would pursue trade with the Spanish colonies.[8] These dispatches reveal competitive national interest in an expedition pursuing profitable trade and natural and geographic knowledge, defended by the emperor's military, and informed by experienced Cook sailors. While political leaders concerned themselves with the sudden threat of a new competitor in global trade, the international public was more interested in what this imperial voyage portended for the advancement of knowledge. Press reports on the voyage dwelled on references to the Cook voyagers or associated locations like Tahiti. Periodicals from Florence to Lisbon reported on the naturalists the Habsburg court chose to accompany this "voyage round the world." The northern German press praised the emperor for supporting scientific discovery and linked this voyage to his other reforms to "abolish abuses."[9] Despite anticipation that the Emperor's illustrious scientific endeavor would contribute to enlightenment, the Bolts plan never came to fruition. Captain Bolts and his fleet of Habsburg-named ships, and even the Asiatic Company of Trieste and the major Antwerp financial houses backing it, were exposed as chimeras.[10] With the first signs of financial collapse, Bolts lost Joseph II's support.[11]

Despite this setback, Bolts used the positive international press and reports about the emperor's patronage to seek more subscribers and a new royal patron for the voyage. Though Bolts ultimately would fail, his plans would not. After being approached by the captain and declining his overtures, the French mounted an expedition in 1785 with a remarkably similar route and agenda. A group sailing from England in the same year also sought to establish trading facilities on the northwest coast of America after learning of Bolts' ideas, and they mentioned the captain in their correspondence with the Royal Society. Although Bolts approached Catherine II, who rebuffed him, the Russian state nevertheless planned an excursion for 1787 to retain supremacy in the north Pacific since all these discussions of combined economic and natural history expeditions suggested other European states would soon descend on the region.[12] Indeed, a Spanish expedition carrying three naturalists also explored this region beginning in 1789.[13] Because of Captain Bolts' effective advertising and the international fascination with the emperor's support of a scientific mission, all of Europe shored up their connections and interests overseas and watched for Habsburg encroachment into their trade zones.

Habsburg plans for a collecting mission did not end with the collapse of Bolts' plans. The next stage in planning for the botanical voyage relied on conventions of open cooperation within international diplomatic and scientific networks. The emperor and vice chancellor crafted a plan to send their collectors to find their own transportation as private passengers. This scheme had the advantage of costing less that the original plan and giving the travellers more flexibility to travel inland, but it made them dependent on ship availability, common travel destinations, and captains' willingness and ability to tolerate their materials and the potential volume of their shipments. The five chosen for the task were Franz Joseph Märter, a second botanist and medical doctor, a plant and landscape painter, and two experienced gardeners. Moving from port to port as the director saw fit, the five would send back shipments along the way.[14] As with other plant-collecting travelers like Carl Linnaeus or John Bartram, free exchange of information through the republic of letters was central to their work; yet, unlike private collectors, this group relied on the state's international political power to request even more sharing of knowledge and natural goods. The vice chancellor's office in Vienna sent out diplomatic letters to ambassadors and colonial governors across the world, reporting on the forthcoming collecting mission and the protocol and financial conventions that should greet them. Underlying these missives was an expectation of global cooperation. A voyage for the sole purpose of enhancing the emperor's gardens, menagerie, and natural history collection (rather than a voyage explicitly seeking information for economic or military gain), commencing from a state yet to indulge in colonial ambitions, could rely on the culture of diplomatic generosity between states.[15] Nevertheless, while the other European monarchies acted to aid the Emperor, competitive national interest ensured states would consider developing their own public gardens in response to the news of Joseph II's plans. Achievement in the natural sciences and natural history collections were, after all, a proving ground for the comparative prestige of nations.

After the court gave notice through international diplomatic networks, the five men finally left Vienna in April of 1783 to make their way to Atlantic ports. While traveling across Europe, they sought to build upon their knowledge of botanical gardens and collecting practices to aid their work overseas. Märter's crew benefited not only from the access granted them as representatives of the emperor but also from an international culture of open access for scientists to notable gardens and natural history collections.[16] They told their international audiences of their practical collecting mission and accompanying idealistic goals of adding to botanical and mineralogical knowledge through their travels.

The group took a detour to Paris, where the prestigious natural historian Jean-Louis Leclerc, the Comte de Buffon welcomed them into the royal gardens and where they also met Benjamin Franklin, who prepared them for their trip to Philadelphia and offered letters of recommendation.[17] Later events suggest that the group's time in Paris initiated and furthered regional rivalries in the field of botany and royal gardens. First, Märter's published travelogue from the newly formed United States reported that animals there were in no way smaller or worse than their European counterparts except those that had been ill tended.[18] This seemingly odd statement makes sense given the context of the contemporary debate over Buffon's published theories of American degeneration. Franklin explicitly campaigned against the theories of leading Parisian natural scientists that stated the natural inferiority of all American species. Franklin used his own stature as proof, and Thomas Jefferson sought a moose to send to Paris to represent the large animal scale typical of North America. While this intellectual debate may seem silly today, it was important to the newly formed nation, and Franklin was in Paris to establish the legitimacy of both America's natural world and government.[19] Märter's publication, siding with the Americans, thus directly inserted itself in a natural history dispute of diplomatic importance to the new nation.

The other link between the group's work and that of the French royal gardens concerned European importation of American plants. In letters and instructions, the vice chancellor, Prince Johann Phillip von Cobenzl, advocated for destinations where the voyagers could collect plants easily naturalized in central Europe. Though tropical plants had been the focus of an earlier generation of imperial garden collectors and planners, by the 1780s, developments in botany and state sciences inspired Cobenzl's push for a new focus on collecting for palace gardens. Instead of concentrating on appearance and exoticism as a measure of a plant's worth, economic botanists argued that plants of a similar latitude from other regions of the world, when imported to Europe, would be easier to grow and expand the natural products available for food, medicine, livestock, and other areas of the economy. Yet these arguments, coalescing around the newly distinct field of economic botany, had yet to affect the gardens displaying monarchical dominion over nature in capitals across Europe.[20] By appointing a professor of economic botany to lead the expedition and leaving the planning in the hands of Cobenzl, a garden enthusiast who embraced cameralist ideas of utility, Joseph II ensured his collecting mission would be innovative. This was a key reason why the voyagers chose the newly formed United States as their first destination. After months traveling and collecting in the northern states, they ultimately made Charleston, South Carolina a base of operations. Märter also set up trade ties for the monarchy with seed collectors who promised to keep the Emperor supplied in American flora.

Competition in garden display between two of the largest courts in Europe almost immediately produced rival plant-collecting missions. Learning of the voyagers' elaborate plans to enrich Schönbrunn's gardens, the French state also determined to populate their royal gardens with North American trees easily naturalized to their climate.[21] The collector chosen for this mission also made Charleston his base, but André Michaux's methods differed slightly from the Austrian group's, for he bought land ten miles from town and established a staging garden for acclimating transplanted trees and cultivating plants for the production of seeds for annual supply to Paris. As a result, he surpassed Märter's record for healthy plant shipments across the Atlantic. Though Michaux's royal plant mission did not encompass the circumnavigation that the Habsburg one did, he traveled regionally throughout the American territories, Spanish Florida, and the Bahamas— all areas that Märter's Austrian expedition had just visited.[22] In this direct competition over the discovery of plants, as with the ideological debate over degeneration theory, openness in international scientific dialogue engendered French and Habsburg competition. That America could be a realm of competition between European nations over scientific exploration, botanical knowledge, and plant imports owed to its recent status as an independent state. No longer a colony of one European nation, it was open to competition from all scientific interests. Yet, the United States was also a new nation that sought to prove itself as it emerged from the chaos of war. The Habsburg collecting mission, and the Michaux one following in its footsteps, thus also came to affect early American botany. Thomas Jefferson supported hiring Michaux for an expedition to the American West, which suggests European plant collecting voyages influenced the new nation's desires to support naturalists on behalf of the state.[23]

Public developments in the study of nature in the United States show even more of a Habsburg impact than in Europe. While America had abundant natural resources, it was not abundant in academic naturalists. Prior to Märter's sojourn in Pennsylvania and South Carolina, no American work of botany had been published. As a result, Märter dismissed the most prominent early American experts on plants as mere seed collectors gardeners. He also found no hope for future American endeavors, for, as he complained in a letter to Vienna, no copy of Linnaeus was to be had.[24] Just after Märter and his crew left Philadelphia, however, some progress was made. The first book published in America on American plants by a permanent resident of North America appeared in that city in 1785. Yet this work was still supplanted in international botanical circles by a French publication.[25] Charleston, South Carolina had even fewer scientific resources than Philadelphia, but botany had its followers in this southern slave port. One planter who cultivated interests in botany was Thomas Walter, an English-born American. He made the acquaintance of Märter as well as other traveling European botanists in the mid-1780s. Märter recommended Walter to the vice chancellor as a correspondent and resource for future seed shipments. In this letter, Märter described him as "eines sehr verständigen und gefäligen Edelmannes."[26] Given Märter's frequent statements that suggest that he was lonely for intellectual company, one can presume he spent considerable time with Walter and told stories of his own experiences and travels. The two botany enthusiasts no doubt discussed the botanical gardens that Märter visited across Europe and the professor's university studies in the Netherlands. Soon after befriending Märter and introducing himself by letter to Cobenzl, Walter sent his work *Flora Caroliniana* to London for publication. His introduction directly evoked the world of difference between an American working in the world of plants and those purely academic European naturalists whom he encountered. He wrote in his preface: "When the author of this compendium first undertook his botanical inquiries, there was no help for him beyond that which ... the works of the most distinguished Linnaeus, provided. He investigated no botanical gardens, whence he might have entrusted the appearances of his memory to or recalled them from authors of plants badly described."[27] While this may seem an expression of humility, the preface soon asserted the value provided by direct experience of the growth of plants in a single place over time. Walter's *Flora Caroliniana* was, in the writer's own words, entirely a recent endeavor upon its publication in 1788. His introduction to Märter, seed exchanges with the court of Vienna, and evocation of the traveling botany professor's knowledge in botanical gardens as opposed to his lifelong experience of Carolina plant growth, all indicate that Walter was indebted to the Habsburg voyagers even as he claimed his own authority.[28]

The Habsburg collectors and the French ones that followed them through America's cities disseminated the latest European ideas in natural sciences. But gains from those travelers were mostly to be realized in distant capitals through publications and the physical stripping of resources from the local landscape. Both the republic of letters and American culture emphasized free exchange, much to the advantage of the European experts on trees. Nevertheless, the newly, proudly independent Americans rapidly developed the field of botany in a way unparalleled in the previous era. The line between open sharing versus national competition turned out to be an even finer one when a branch of the collecting voyage went to French territories off the coast of Africa and another went to Spanish territories in South America. The director of the French royal gardens in the Isle de France wrote flattering letters to Joseph II and loaded the Habsburg gardener who traveled there with multiple shipments of economically important plants. The French Captain Nicolas Thomas Baudin then shipped these specimens from the southern hemisphere to Trieste. The value of the resources that these two French subjects brought Vienna, in goods barely developed yet for French profit, with no thought of betraying French national interests, is remarkable and shows how scientific exchange and individual interests could trump national competition in peacetime and at a great distance from the patria.

Where the French may have done better to cultivate suspicion and protect their botanical wealth, Spain had long practiced protectionism in colonial resources. The South American branch of the collecting voyage similarly encountered problems with the fine line between the open travel allowed a Habsburg scientific expedition versus the usual restrictions on foreigners' movement that fears of military spying and colonial competition brought. Spanish colonial administrators knew European courts valued plant collecting because they continually received instructions from Madrid on the need to send plants, how to choose them, and how to pack them for shipping.[29] In turn, officials in Caracas had certain expectations of the men sent to collect the plants. A visit from a representative of the Habsburg Monarchy required diplomatic politeness, but representatives of a European court also had to represent themselves and their court well by not being unpleasant burdens, supporting themselves in style and acting with dignity.

Notably, Joseph II's traveling plant collectors failed to live up to these diplomatic expectations. The director of the expedition sent the gardener Franz Bredemeyer ahead to Venezuela to pursue the collecting mission as he convalesced in Jamaica from a dangerous fever; unfortunately, he sent the wrong passport with him. While the gardener had letters of credit requesting colonial authorities advance money to Bredemeyer (with the assurance the Emperor's coffer would reimburse them with speed and interest), his identification papers claimed that he was Franz Boos. Märter had also arranged for a backup moneylender, but this contact turned out to be unreliable because of undisclosed, extensive debts. With no proof of identity or access to money, Bredemeyer's possession of ornate letters of credit from the Holy Roman emperor himself, when juxtaposed with his low status, roused suspicion of military or political espionage. His letters begging for help were not received in either Vienna or Jamaica for months, by which point his dire situation forced him to turn to the Spanish colonial administration for help. Though threatened with arrest, he and his traveling companion achieved some relief as one official lent them enough money for sustenance after conceding that their story was too preposterous to be false. Finally, six months after the situation began, their rescue came through Cobenzl in the form of credit arranged through Madrid; the official who had helped them received a chest full of Viennese sheet music and Hungarian wine. Though the two returned to Vienna with the desired plants and animals, the diplomatic event remained a major embarrassment for the court, advertised as it was across Spain and Latin America through reams of diplomatic correspondence. The Habsburg state's special historic relationship with Spain and their lack of overseas colonies had allowed their access to Spanish resources, yet their bumbling organization reflected poorly on Vienna and the imperial expedition.

Diplomatic dispatches about the voyage, combined with the interactions of the actual voyagers with others as they crossed Europe and the Americas, carried out a low-stakes diplomacy in a time of nascent peace; because the Habsburg Monarchy had not been involved in the latest international war, the emperor's voyagers were politely granted access everywhere. Also, the international news blast connected to Cobenzl's letters had an unanticipated effect. Suddenly every diplomat and anyone with connections to international flora and fauna exchanges became aware that the emperor desired new plants and animals; consequently, the court was inundated with gifts.

Custom dictated cooperation between states and scientists in developing plant, animal, and mineral collections. Yet the collections themselves and the naturalists' adventures inspired international competition. Despite the limited goals of repopulating Vienna's gardens, the imperial expedition raised the international attention of naturalists and diplomats. This interest accelerated in the 1780s, when European states, and, slowly, the United States, began to view the work of natural scientists as a source of potential economic and colonial development. Economic botany was, after all, for the good of the public and not the benefit of the court. This botanical voyage's greatest effect was thus in inspiring competing botanical pursuits and publications from not-so-rival nations and their publics. The French arborist Michaux's activities in South Carolina, the Russian expedition following Bolts' plans, and the landmark publication of the American Walter all unfolded through the customary exchange of knowledge among naturalists and the customary competition for resources and prestige among states. Märter's small plant-collecting mission affected the exploring, trade interests, and botanical voyages of ensuing decades because it relied on publicity. Sharing of information was required for the mission's success. Whether it was Bolts advertising for investors, vice chancellor Cobenzl sending out official notices through diplomats and trade houses to ensure that ports the world over knew to expect the travelers, or the voyagers themselves discussing their goals and methods, publicity engendered immediate consideration from other states and natural scientists. Enlightened competition thus straddled old dynastic rivalries over imperial display and patronage and more modern, protonationalist desire that one's countrymen be the ones to advance knowledge or gain from trade. In the atmosphere of diplomatic instability, an ever-expanding public sphere, and general transition in the wake of the American Revolution, competition trumped the cooperation that had been the scientific and diplomatic rule.

NOTES

1. "Short Account of the Imperial Botanic Garden at Schönbrunn, near Vienna," *Annals of Botany* 2 (1806): 384.

2. P.G.M. Dickson, *Finance and Government under Maria Theresia 1740–1780* Vol.1. *Society and Government* (Oxford: Clarendon Press, 1987), 200. Robert J. King, "Heinrich Zimmermann and the Proposed Voyage of the Imperial and Royal Ship *Cobenzell* to the North West Coast in 1782–1783" in *The Northern Mariner/ le marin du nord* 21:3 (July 2011).

3. Alexander Randa, *Österreich im Übersee* (Vienna: Verlag Herold, 1966), 75–77.

4. "Extrait d'un rapport du Chancelier de Cour et dÉtat sur différentes propositions et demandes du Sieur Bolts." Vienna, June 20, 1782, in Haus-, Hof- und Staats-Archiv, Obersthofmeisters Amt, Sonderreihe 176, Kouv 7/1, fol 2–3.

5. King, "Heinrich Zimmerman," 236.

6. "Extrait d'un rapport," fol 2–3.

7. "An area where we have until now had no sales, and because we in the Austrian Monarchy have such a quantity of this metal, therefore every means to increase its value is already in itself a tangible benefit." Author's translation. "Allerunterthänigstens Promemoria." June 15, 1782. Ignaz von Born, HHStA, OeMA, Kouvert 2, fol 7–8.

8. King, "Heinrich Zimmermann," 240–3. Quotes from Sir Robert Keith to Charles James Fox, June 26, 1782, 240.

9. On the use of the terms "voyages" and "voyagers" for explorations and collecting trips of this sort, see Marie-Noëlle Bourguet, "The Explorer," in *Enlightenment Portraits,* ed. Michel Vovelle, trans. Lydia G. Cochrane (Chicago: Univ. of Chicago Press, 1997) 258.

10. Dickson, *Finance and Government*, 200–201.

11. Kaunitz, "Rapport de 24 June 1782", in Ostindische Compagnie-Triest-Antwerp (OIC) Karton 2, Konvulut 1781–1784, HHStA, Staatskanzlei, Staatenabteilung.

12. King, "Heinrich Zimmermann," 247–254.

13. Daniela Bleichmar, *Visible Empire: Botanical Expeditions & Visual Culture in the Hispanic Enlightenment* (Chicago: Univ. of Chicago Press, 2012) 20.

14. Instructions. Fol. 1–8, Cod. Ser. N. 3517, ÖNB Handschriftensammlung.

15. On diplomatic generosity, see Michael Yonan, "Portable Dynasties: Imperial Gift-Giving at the Eighteenth-Century Habsburg Court in Vienna," *The Court Historian*, 14, no. 2 (2009): 177–188, and *Empress Maria Theresa and the Politics of Habsburg Imperial Art* (University Park: Pennsylvania State Univ. Press, 2011).

16. Journal of Mathias Stupicz, ÖNB Handschriftensammlung, Cod. Ser. N. 3794, folder 3, folio 82–87.

17. Märter to Cobenzl, July 21, 1783 In ÖNB Handschriftensammlung, Cod. Ser. N. 3517, folio 13–4.

18. Herren Professor Märter, "Nachrichten über die natürlichen Geschichte

Pennsylvaniens, an Herrn Hofrath von Born" in *Physikalische Arbeiten der einträchtigen Freunde in Wien* 1.3 (1785): 24.

19. Lee Alan Dugatkin, *Mr. Jefferson and the Giant Moose: Natural History in Early America* (Chicago: Univ. of Chicago Press, 2009).

20. Private collectors in Great Britain did more to import American plants; see Andrea Wulf, *The Brother Gardeners: Botany, Empire, and the Birth of an Obsession* (New York: Alfred A. Knopf, 2009).

21. Lisa Ford, "The 'naturalisation' of François André Michaux's 'North American sylva'" in ed. Laura Auricchio, Elizabeth Heckendorn Cook, and Giulia Pacini, *Invaluable Trees: Cultures of Nature, 1660–1830* (Oxford: Voltaire Foundation, 2012).

22. J.P.F. Deleuze, *Memoirs of the Life and Botanical Travels of André Michaux*, ed. Charlie Williams. (Charlotte, NC: Fourbears Press, 2002).

23. Deleuze, *Memoirs,* 79–81.

24. On American botany, see Märter to Born, Sept. 12, 1783, Philadelphia. Folio 17–8. Though they saw John Bartram as a gardener rather than a botanist, the Royal Society in London published some of his essays. Ed. Edmund Berkeley and Dorothy Smith Berkeley, *The Correspondence of John Bartram, 1734–1777* (Gainesville: Univ. Press of Florida, 1992).

25. Ford, "The 'Naturalisation'," 201–204.

26. "A very sensible and likable gentleman." Author's translation. Märter to Cobenzl, February 8, 1785, Charlestown, SC. ÖNB Handschriftensammlung, Cod. Ser. N. 3517, Fol 70, 84.

27. "Thomas Walter from *Flora Caroliniana*," trans. Ward W. Briggs, in ed. David Taylor, *South Carolina Naturalists: An Anthology, 1700–1860* (Columbia: Univ. of South Carolina Press, 1998) 62–3.

28. Letters between Walter and the court in HHStA, Vienna, OeMA, Sonderreihe 176.

29. Bleichmar, *Visible Empire,* 26.

INDIVIDUAL ESSAYS

Northern Designs: British Science, Imperialism, and Improvement at the Dawn of the Anthropocene

MICHAEL B. GUENTHER

In late October, Captain James Cook and the naturalist Joseph Banks arrived to study the curious features of an island they would inhabit over the coming weeks. Banks spent much of his time examining the exotic plants and animals while Cook turned his sights to astronomical matters, recording an important eclipse to send back to colleagues at the Royal Society in London. Both men found the island an ideal setting in which to work on their larger mission of expanding the frontiers of knowledge and empire through scientific exploration. By diligently cataloguing the precise location and resources of these distant lands, figures like Captain Cook and Joseph Banks were helping to launch a second age of European discovery, commercial expansion, and colonization that would fundamentally shape the course of the nineteenth century.[1]

Yet this episode did not take place in Tahiti or some other Pacific island, as one might expect, during the famed voyage of the *Endeavor* (1768–1771), rather it occurred earlier, in Newfoundland, when Cook and Banks both found themselves stationed in the maritime provinces of Canada pursuing scientific missions on behalf of the British government. Following the Seven Year's War, Cook served as a marine surveyor in eastern Canada, producing some of the most detailed hydrographic charts that the British government had ever commissioned while Banks was travelling aboard the HMS *Niger* with his close friend, and future arctic explorer, Constantine Phipps. These northern waters, in fact, became an important training ground for a rising generation of navigators, surveyors, and scientists working to stake out the strategic trading routes and natural resources of the North Atlantic that were increasingly central to the imperial rivalry between Britain and France.[2] Indeed, at the very moment that Cook and Banks were in Newfoundland, the French were sending out some of their most talented scientists and cartographers to Iceland in hopes of developing a new base of influence, and new fishing grounds, in the North Atlantic to compensate for the loss of Canada—a prospect that led some officials in Paris to consider trading the colony of Louisiana to the Danish crown in return for Iceland.[3]

Such ideas reflected a broader transformation unfolding during the middle decades of the eighteenth century, as ideas about scientific exploration, enlightened improvement, and industrial expansion fueled a pointed reappraisal of the economic potential of this sub-arctic world. From the eastern reaches of the Barents Sea to the western shores of Hudson's Bay, contemporaries began to focus on an enticing list of northern commodities, ranging from incredibly valuable fishing and whaling grounds to key supplies of naval stores, pelts, industrial chemicals, minerals, and energy sources like coal, peat, or train oil. In Britain, boosters even tried to rebrand the region as the "Northern Indies," hoping to convince the public that the vast archipelagos of the North Atlantic—stretching from Canada's Maritime Provinces to the North Sea and beyond—could yield the same wealth and naval power that had flowed from the tropics, which they pointed out, had also been deemed uninhabitable in the past because of misguided beliefs about the "torrid" zone.[4] Nowhere was this shift in geo-political perspective more visible than in the popular maps that emerged at mid-century depicting the globe from a polar vantage point—a simple projection technique that nonetheless brought the expansionary gaze of Europeans into sharp focus (fig. 1).

Unfortunately, this northern perspective, and the historical forces animating it, has been largely overshadowed by the subsequent age of Pacific exploration, associated with the epic voyages of Bougainville, Lapérouse, Willis, Cook, and Vancouver.[5] Without disputing the latter's importance, or the vibrant scholarship surrounding it, this article reconstructs the earlier intellectual and political climate that fueled European fascination with the subarctic during this turbulent period when international warfare, economic dislocations, and imperial jockeying made the north Atlantic emerge as an appealing zone of European expansion.[6] These northern campaigns crystalized a new set of relationships between science and imperial power, between the culture of improvement and visions of unlimited economic

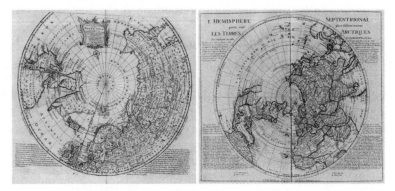

Figure 1. (Left) Emmanuel Bowen, *A new & accurate map of the North Pole* (London, 1747). (Right) Guillaume de L'Isle, *L'Hemisphere Septentrional pour voir plus distinctement les Terres Arctiques.* (Amsterdam, 1742). Courtesy of David Rumsey Historical Map Collection / www.davidrumsey.com.

development, and ultimately between extractive markets and environmental resources that proved to be transformative. Individuals like Cook and Banks may have gained international fame for their exploits in the Pacific, but much of their mission and their worldview had been forged in the icy crucible of the North Atlantic.

This study focuses on the period from the 1730s to the 1770s, analyzing the British campaigns to develop the northern reaches of its Atlantic empire. While the activities of other European nations are important to this story, the British experience is worth exploring in detail because their blend of scientific exploration, improvement, and imperialism blazed a path toward the aggressive development of resources and regions that other nations would follow. In this "age of projects," as Daniel Defoe famously called it, British scientists, merchants, and politicians spawned an array of enterprising schemes—some fanciful, others quite successful—that sought to harness the rich mineral and marine resources of the North to fuel a new age of British prosperity and power. Indeed, as both an imaginative project and a more complicated reality, the Northern Indies helped crystalize an emerging vision of enlightened progress that combined the aggressive development of natural resources, the growing confidence and authority of scientific improvers, and new conceptions of economic development and imperial power. This therefore proved an important moment in creating the constellation of values that came to define our relationship to the natural world at the dawn of the Anthropocene.

Scientific Improvement and the Knowledge Economy

When the naturalist, Johann Reinhold Forster, surveyed the history of northern exploration in 1786, he emphasized that one of the principle "discoveries" had been that nature was no less bountiful here than in other parts of the globe. Indeed, one could "perceive in all parts the traces of the providence, goodness, and wisdom of a supreme being, who dispenses his benefits over the whole" of creation. While plants appeared "dwarfish" and sparse, Forster marveled at their nutritious qualities capable of fattening the largest animals, such as reindeer. Seemingly frigid oceans were teeming with life, including prodigious fish, seals, walruses, and whales. If the environment was incapable of supporting agriculture, it seemed to compensate by offering rich mineral deposits, furs, and marine resources for the benefit of humankind.[7] Such resources, he argued, were capable of endless "improvement" at the hands of inventive and scientifically-minded people. Mosses and lichen, for example, could be turned into valuable dyes; whale oil could be used to improve woolen manufacturing; seaweed could be roasted into alkali-rich ashes for industry, and so forth. "An attentive mind will readily conceive," another observer proclaimed, "how much farther and more extensively useful, every branch of nature's kingdom may yet prove in the oeconomy of human life."[8]

This re-evaluation of the North, and of its commercial prospects, was rooted in an Enlightenment blend of providentialism, science, and improvement. Few captured this vision better than James Sterling, an Irish poet and booster of northern expansion, whose poems depicted the bright future of Britain's subarctic empire:

> Declare what Treasures Snow-sunk Rocks produce
> How dreary Deserts howl for human Use
> Tell Industry; 'twill find, while Ocean rolls,
> Branda, Sainte Barbe, and Guinea in the Poles
> Do Eastern Barriers cramp a Briton's Soul
> Is West deny'd then elevate the Pole!
> Subdue th' astonish'd Globe! 'tis God's Command
> Who never made unvisitable Land!
> Bid utmost North his Treasury display
> Bask in the Warmth of semi-annual Day.[9]

Here was a world of abundant resources waiting for those with the industry, innovation, and knowledge to unlock nature's true potential. The fact that Linnaeus was preaching the same message in Sweden—a message embraced by many of the cameralist regimes in northern Europe—only made it seem more convincing to British audiences.[10]

But it was Britain's extensive scientific networks, along with its associational world of improvement, that helped translate such ideals into a concrete movement for northern expansion. Over the course of the eighteenth century, growing segments of Georgian society became involved in the pursuits of science—attending lectures, conducting experiments, and cultivating "useful knowledge" for the practical benefit of everyday life.[11] Particularly important, in this respect, was the emergence of numerous improvement societies that aimed to promote useful research and experimentation into key areas of public concern, ranging from agriculture and industry to transportation and medicine. Combining aspects of a philosophical society, a social club, and a subscription campaign, these eighteenth-century improvement societies offered contemporaries a powerful tool for generating a range of ambitious projects.[12]

Not surprisingly, groups in northern Britain tended to lead the way in applying the tools of scientific improvement to the northern reaches of the empire. In Ireland, for example, the Dublin Society for Improving Husbandry, Manufactures, and other Useful Arts and Sciences, which emerged in the 1730s, worked to establish much stronger ties between Ireland and the North Sea zone—envisioning a world in which coal, salt, fish, and whale oil would jump-start the local economy and Britain's flagging northern empire.[13] The "Dublin Society," as it was commonly known, sought to spur this sort of economic development through a coordinated campaign of premiums, subsidized experiments, and the dissemination of useful discoveries.[14] Their tendency to focus on particular industries—and to devote the kind of attention and resources needed to address key technical challenges facing producers—reflected a kind of "industrial enlightenment" that made public science integral to Britain's economic transformations in the eighteenth century, as the recent work of Joel Mokyr has shown.[15]

Commercial fishing offers a revealing window into this industrial enlightenment at work, underscoring how the joint efforts of scientific improvers, merchants, and projectors transformed contemporary perceptions of North Atlantic resources. The lucrative cod and herring fisheries became a subject of intense public focus in Britain during the middle decades of the eighteenth century as observers increasingly bemoaned the nation's small share of this vital industry, estimated to be worth more than £10,000,000 sterling per year.[16] Groups worked accordingly to promote new fisheries off the coast of Scotland, Ireland, Labrador, Greenland, Iceland, and throughout the Barents Sea. Even small islands, such as Cherry Island off Spitzbergen, attracted the attention of British projectors, who saw in its rich coal deposits and fishing grounds a promising commercial base in these northern waters.[17] But improvers did more than canvas maps and travel accounts to pin-point areas of commercial promise.[18] They also mobilized the scientific community to study the life cycle and migration habits of North Atlantic fish so as to improve the success of British fishing fleets. Local groups worked to compile natural histories of important species such as cod, herring, salmon, and ling. Even the navy supported this research program, as evident from the instructions to naturalists aboard Constantine Phipps' polar expedition in 1773.[19]

Yet, if wresting control of northern territories and fishing grounds was an appealing prospect, contemporaries recognized that its success would also depend upon technical advances in salt production and the curing process that had proven elusive in the past.[20] Calls for expanding the fisheries would remain idle talk, as one observer noted, "unless we cou'd shew, that we were as capable of curing, as we are of catching the Fish, which is a thing impossible without Salt proper for the Purpose."[21] Forced to buy more powerful salts from the continent, the British fishing industry had to absorb a considerable surcharge that put them at a competitive disadvantage, not to mention the disruptions caused when wars cut off access to this resource. That was a recurring theme throughout the period: it was one thing to propose a new industry, or to suggest that the empire become more self-sufficient through import substitutions, but it was actually quite difficult to succeed in the technical details that often determined the success or failure of such projects.[22]

In the case of the fisheries and salt, improvers were able to mobilize the networks of science to bring collective resources and attention to bear on this problem. In England, for example, the Royal Society helped publicize the work of William Brownrigg, a noted chemist, who had conducted wide-ranging investigations into the techniques of salt-making. Brownrigg discovered that high temperatures and boiling conditions resulted in the formation of hydrochloric acids that undermined the curing power of domestic salt.[23] But perhaps more interesting than the finding itself was the way such research mobilized a vast network of collaborators, which according to one contemporary, ranged from "judicious Salt-Officers" to "inquisitive Navigators, Merchants, and Travellers" to the experimental work of "many learned Physicians, Chemists, and Philosophers."[24] Further north, the Dublin Society was offering premiums and public trials to encourage innovation among salt producers, while Scottish circles, led by the Society for Improvers in the Knowledge of Agriculture as well as the Board of Trustees for Fisheries, Manufactures and Improvements, funded promising experiments with different forms of rock, brine, and bay-salts.[25] At times, it seemed like no aspect of the fishing industry was too insignificant to warrant attention from improvers. In Scotland, for instance, groups experimented with using cheaper types of wood as barrel staves in packing cured fish, suggesting that British producers could reduce their costs by 80% if they switched from oak staves to larch ones (larch being an under-utilized staple of the northern boreal forests).[26]

Equipped with the resources of the scientific community and the social capital of improvers, various groups collaborated on a wide-ranging agenda for the economic development of the Northern Indies that focused on promising fields such as the tanning industry, linen production, naval stores, whaling, deep-sea fishing, coal and copper mining, salt-works, and industrial chemicals and dyes. If Britons were relatively familiar with many of these activities, northern improvers also tried to introduce more exotic branches of trade. The Canadian ginseng "boom," for example, began when scientific accounts and engravings of the prized Chinese plant were circulated among colonists in Quebec and British North America, inspiring locals to "discover" large caches of domestic ginseng that would bring enormous profits in Asian markets. By 1750, ginseng could make up as much as 20% of the value of northern cargoes arriving at European trading depots. Members of the Royal Society not only helped establish this branch of trade in British colonies but also conducted experiments on domestication and the curing process that observers hoped would transform ginseng into a full-blown cash crop.[27] In a similar vein, the swift rise of the kelp industry underscored how new resources and trades could be discovered throughout the northern reaches of the empire. By harvesting and burning sea weed, coastal communities learned to produce ashes rich in alkalis and sodas desperately needed by the growing textile industry, soap-makers, glass-makers, alum producers, and the like. The coastline of the Orkneys, Hebrides, and other islands became sites of a bustling kelp industry, as improving landlords organized the trade into a consolidated business that yielded nearly 20,000 metric tons of ash per year by the end of the century.[28] For their part, scientific improvers conducted experiments and corresponded with experts to identify the types of seaweed that yielded the most sodium rich ashes, new types of kilns to increase purity, and improvements in aquaculture to boost yields.[29] Yet these scientific networks did more than provide intellectual capital in the form of useful knowledge or technical know-how. The involvement of well-connected merchants, aristocrats, and officials also provided access to social and political capital that could be equally decisive in launching challenging projects.

In fact, the political dimensions of this story are worth underscoring since these campaigns to redeem the subarctic forced contemporaries to wrestle with questions about the nature of resources: who should have access to them; whose expertise and authority should guide their use; and to what larger ends or purpose? Northern improvement, in other words, evinced a new "political ecology" of empire as various civic groups used their expertise of the natural world to position themselves as the gatekeepers of progress and patriotism.[30] The institutional world of improvement, after all, helped carve out a new sphere of civil society in which members of the public could work together to advance the welfare of the nation—at times even acting like a government agency in the way it promoted economic development or imperial projects. At a time when the government appeared hamstrung by party politics and factionalism, this associational world of improvement offered Britons an attractive arena for civic action and leadership.[31] As a result, the political ecology of northern expansion helped legitimate the centrality of science and enterprise to the imperial mission and the aggressive development of natural resources ordained by providence for the "improvement" of the world.

The Trials of Exploration

Within this context, British improvers seized upon exploration as a vital tool in opening new avenues of trade in the North Atlantic and beyond as a series of dramatic campaigns to discover the Northwest Passage helped generate new levels of public interest and support. This renewed push for northern exploration began in Ireland in the 1730s with the inveterate improver Arthur Dobbs, who convinced the British navy in 1741 to send a small expedition to search for the passage in Hudson's Bay. Afterwards, Dobbs and his supporters changed tactics, organizing a privately funded expedition in 1746, which attracted subscriptions from merchants and gentlemanly investors to the tune of £10,000. Like many of the northern projectors of this era, Dobbs showed a canny ability to rally scientists, merchants, and high officials to his cause while courting public support through a steady stream of pamphlets and newspaper articles. By mid-century, these activities had created a noticeable shift in public opinion about the merits of scientific exploration, the prospects of a Passage, and the commercial potential of these northern waters.[32]

If such quests appear almost quixotic with the benefits of hindsight, contemporaries believed they were precisely the kind of bold initiatives the nation sorely needed. With the intense commercial pressures wrought by closing markets in Europe and aggressive competition abroad, Britons had to begin actively searching for any and every opportunity to open new branches of trade—a view that expressed itself in a pervasive nostalgia for the exploits of the Elizabethan age, when England's appetite for discovery and expansion knew no bounds. "We cannot think so meanly of our

Countrymen," the Scottish authority John Campbell complained, "as to suppose that either their Courage, their Judgment, or their Spirit, is inferior to that of their Ancestors." Instead, he and others blamed Britain's current complacency on a public culture that had allowed "quick wits ... to ridicule Voyages to cold, barren, desert Countries; and to represent that as Folly and Madness, which is in truth a most noble kind of Public Spirit"—the kind which invariably opened up new spheres of commercial opportunity for the nation.[33] As a result, the period witnessed a proliferation of ambitious schemes which championed exploration as a way to extend the frontiers of both knowledge and imperial trade. The excitement even swept Parliament in 1745, when it issued a £20,000 reward to anyone discovering a Northwest Passage, along with subsequent prizes for navigators who reached certain polar latitudes—a conspicuous endorsement of the aspirations of scientific projectors like Dobbs and his associates.[34]

Throughout the empire, groups vied to launch similar expeditions to the subarctic during this period. In the American colonies, for example, Benjamin Franklin helped organize a subscription campaign in Philadelphia, Boston, and New York to send a schooner, the *Argo*, in search of a northern passage in 1753, demonstrating the "public spirit of this people."[35] Yet like a competing scheme backed by London investors, Franklin's expedition also sought to produce more tangible, and private, gain by exploring the coast of Labrador to stake out potential sites for fishing, whaling, mining, or trade with the indigenous population.[36] As one authority noted, Labrador had recently yielded £50,000 of such commodities in a single season—striking "proof ... [that] it is not always the Beauty or the Fertility of a distant Country that should recommend it to a trading Nation" like Britain.[37]

Exploration and discovery, however, required significant amounts of financial and intellectual capital that the growing authority of scientific improvement helped underwrite. Even short expeditions could cost thousands of pounds, given the need for proper ships along with the skilled captains, crews, and scientific observers necessary for such journeys. A burgeoning culture of exploration also required access to key information and intelligence. Before launching their expedition, for example, Franklin and his associates were busy acquiring a rich collection of maps, sea charts, and traveler's accounts, including material from Dobbs' recent expedition.[38] The mobilization of these transatlantic networks of science turned Philadelphia into a "center of calculation" where knowledge about distant places could be transcribed and aggregated in ways that encouraged scientific projecting.[39] And when the *Argo* returned after failing to locate a passage to the Pacific, Franklin and his associates took comfort in the fact that its crew managed to create "a very good Chart, and have a better Account of the Country, its

Soil, Produce, &c than has hitherto been published"—information which Franklin promised to dutifully transmit to other scientists and gentlemen back in England.[40]

Zeal for northern exploration also reflected a growing suspicion of the Hudson's Bay Company (HBC) and its gloomy portrayal of the region. Critics complained that the common image of the North as an icy and desolate landscape was really a self-serving canard that the HBC encouraged to protect its monopoly over vast territories that it had little appetite to explore, develop, or improve.[41] The respected commercial writer Malachy Postlethwayt was part of a growing chorus of observers who wondered how this company could control an entire continent and yet only employ 3 ships a year and 300 men, all to "enrich 9 or 10 merchants at their country's expense."[42] Knowing that it had many enemies, the company's directors had insisted on absolute secrecy among its employees, preventing anyone from keeping personal records, journals, maps, or collections. Detractors never tired of using this secrecy, along with damaging "revelations" from disgruntled employees, to turn public opinion against the HBC and its depiction of the region's commercial prospects.[43] It would be fair to say, in fact, that a major reason why Arthur Dobbs and his associates were able to raise thousands of pounds to finance their expedition was that a large community of merchants and gentlemanly capitalists were interested in demonstrating the true potentials of the region, with an eye towards breaking up the HBC's monopoly. The role of Henry Ellis, the scientific observer attached to the Dobbs expedition, was seen as crucial in this respect since he was charged with making detailed maps, tidal records, meteorological observations, and an analysis of "the different natures of the soil." Moreover, the sponsors insisted that Ellis spare no effort in collecting "metals, minerals, and all kinds of natural curiosities," which could document the region's potential for mining, especially with regards to copper which seemed to be abundant in in the northern reaches of the Bay.[44] Thus, even if explorers failed to find the Northwest Passage, they might still discover valuable evidence of the untapped resources waiting to be cultivated by private enterprise. Indeed, the popular campaign to divest the Hudson's Bay Company of its monopoly privileges reached its zenith only two years after the ships returned in the summer of 1747, when Parliament ordered a full-scale investigation of the matter in response to an outburst of petitions—drawn from nearly 30 different manufacturing towns and ports—stressing the need to open the imperial playing field to worthy improvers.[45] For their part, Dobbs' circle insisted that the voyage had already revealed the true potential of "these Countries for Furs, Peltry, Fish, Whale-fin, and oil; as well as for Minerals, Pitch, Tar, and other Valuable commodities."[46]

Henry Ellis emerged as one of the most articulate champions of this emerging cult of exploration as his popular work *A Voyage to Hudson's-Bay* (1748) made its way through multiple editions and excerpts in the press.[47] Part travel account, part adventure tale, and part enlightenment manifesto, Ellis's work made the case for a robust program of exploration that would "awaken us from that slothful and drowsy State into which ... we are visibly fallen." Geographic and scientific discovery, he argued, would provide the means by which "the Exportation of our commodities and Manufactures may be vastly increased, that several branches of Foreign Trade may be highly improved, that Navigation in general ... be greatly extended, and our Shipping increased." To skeptics who doubted the commercial opportunities of the icy North Atlantic, Ellis responded that a similar lack of vision could be found in earlier periods, when naysayers belittled the possible benefits of colonization in tropical climes. Experience had proven them wrong. And with the proper encouragement, Ellis declared, future Britons would one day celebrate the great wealth and power generated by "these Northern Indies."[48]

If the particulars of Ellis' prophecy seem fanciful in hindsight, his broader vision of a British Empire that embraced scientific exploration as a tool of commercial and imperial expansion did become a reality in the nineteenth century.[49] And here, I argue, lies the deeper historical significance of the mid-century quest for the Northwest Passage, which sparked a formative public dialogue about the nature of discovery, the merits of expansion, the management of resources, and even the value of "projecting" itself. The proponents of northern exploration also had to forge support among and across the various communities of scientists, navigators, merchants, and state officials who were drawn into these campaigns. Through such efforts, they helped make exploration a cornerstone of the growing alliance among science, empire, and enterprise that flourished in the nineteenth century.

The Rise of the Extractive Economy

In making the case for the Northern Indies, proponents also articulated a vision of empire that revolved around the single-minded extraction of resources, a policy that diverged markedly from existing forms of colonialism. The economic climate of the mid-eighteenth century was pivotal in shaping these new ideas about the political economy of empire. In particular, the rising tide of aggressive mercantilism on the continent, combined with the disruptive effects of frequent warfare, had made British access to European markets and raw materials increasingly precarious.[50] One of the more glaring examples centered on the Baltic Trade, where British merchants ran up a trade deficit of a million and a half pounds a year purchasing timber, naval stores,

ores, and chemicals that were central to British industry and navigation.[51] In response, scientific improvers sought to transform the northern reaches of the empire into a focused zone of extraction, where key resources and commodities could be harvested to fuel the imperial economy.

The dramatic rise of the Society of Arts in 1754 exemplified this new spirit of resource "mining." Members of the London-based organization (officially entitled the Society for the Encouragement of Arts, Manufactures, and Commerce) met in specialized committees that created annual lists of premiums to encourage experimentation and production of key staples, commodities, or industrial techniques that would free the imperial economy from reliance upon foreign markets.[52] Within a decade, the society had expanded enormously, drawing more than two thousand members from diverse professions, and building a vast network of correspondents throughout the empire that allowed it to function as an effective sounding board for the nation's mercantilist needs.[53] Indeed, the society's annual schedule of premiums often reads like an industrial shopping list, singling out items such as cobalt, borax, copperas, alum, vitriol (sulphates), bismuth, madder, alkalis (in both mineral and vegetable forms), bleaching chemicals, colorful dyes, edulcorated train oil, saltpeter, and various metal ores. In addition to identifying these resources, and providing monetary incentives, the society offered crucial technical advice that improved the chances of actually discovering such items.[54] Part of this effort centered on publishing inexpensive books or manuals that instructed non-specialists on how to identify particular resources, how to assess their quality, and how to process them (according to the latest scientific understanding). In the case of cobalt and alkalis—to highlight two prominent examples—the standing committee on chemistry oversaw the creation and publication of manuals for the would-be prospector or improver working with these key industrial materials.[55] Yet the society also provided more tailored advice by agreeing to analyze specimens that correspondents sent to London. One of their early initiatives, in fact, was to build a sophisticated "assaying furnace" to conduct metallurgical and chemical analysis of samples—a service that helped northern improvers determine the value of particular deposits of minerals they discovered.[56] These tools were also used to evaluate new industrial techniques, such as the analysis the society conducted during the late 1750s of iron samples that had been smelted with northern energy sources (peat turf and coal) instead of the traditional, but increasingly scarce, charcoal.[57]

Armed with their lists of priorities, imperial projectors fostered a regime of single-minded extraction in the North that sought to harvest key mineral and marine resources rather than creating cohesive societies overseas. Proponents of the fisheries and whaling, for instance, often emphasized the fact that these industries did not require permanent settlements along with the expensive infrastructure and administrative burdens they entailed. Seen from this perspective, a desolate colony like Newfoundland had not failed to evolve into a mature, populous society; rather it represented a successful example of an extractive zone that yielded valuable commodities with few responsibilities or costs.[58] Such attitudes cast the Northern Indies in a very different light, as boosters of commercial expansion argued that the inhospitable landscape of places like Labrador, Greenland, or Hudson's Bay should not prevent British crews from harvesting their resources.[59] This theme resurfaced again and again in the Parliamentary hearings over the Hudson's Bay Company, as rival British merchants attacked the company's languid management while still embracing the "factory" model of imperial commerce associated with it. Indeed, what they found objectionable was not the HBC's failure to develop settler colonies, which they too rejected, but its failure to develop an expanding chain of small trading houses and factories that could exploit the region's fishing, whaling, and mining potentials.[60] Like similar proposals for Greenland, these ventures emphasized a light "footprint," with temporary crews extracting commodities from the sea and land, while relying on the hunting prowess of indigenous populations whenever possible.[61]

This northern vision of empire and its political economy would revolve around sailors and fleets, rather than settlers or plantations, and would prioritize the kind of bulky commodities that sustained a merchant marine. The commercial authority Malachy Postlethwayt insisted that too much attention had been paid to luxury staples at the expense of "those gross and bulky commodities that are the chief and principle sources of navigation," and consequently "more profitable to a nation than the mines of Mexico and Peru."[62] While no one suggested that Britain give up its sugar colonies or its share of valuable goods like tobacco, wine and silks, they argued that bulky northern commodities such as fish, timber, hemp, iron, and coal could generate as much benefit as tropical luxuries—but this wealth and power would be measured in terms of fleets and sailors rather than the private balance sheets of planters. In other words, developing the Northern Indies was particularly suited to the kind of maritime empire that Britain aspired to be.[63] As one poet of northern expansion succinctly put it, "While our great Monarch doubling his Command,/Shall count more Subjects on the Waves than Land."[64]

The British economy's growing appetite for key resources helped sharpen this vision of northern extraction. If industry needed vast quantities of alkalis, then scientific improvers would find the necessary kelp beds, forests, or mineral deposits in the North Atlantic that could supply the requisite chemical ashes. As sulphuric acid became the workhorse of industry—due in part to Scottish improvement societies, which had promoted its use as a bleaching agent in the textile trades—improvers looked to the volcanic islands of the North Atlantic to replace Italian sulphur. By the 1780s, for example, imperial boosters were demanding that Britain annex Iceland, or purchase it from the Danes, so that its rich sulphur deposits could be incorporated into the British fold.[65] To some contemporaries, it seemed like a *fait accompli*, with Londoners quizzing one bemused gentleman about whether the island had indeed become a British colony already, while Sir Joseph Banks was lecturing cabinet officials on Iceland's destiny (along with the Faeroe islands) as part of the greater British "archipelago ... eminently fitted for the establishment of a Naval Empire."[66] As contemporaries catalogued the rich deposits of iron, copper, lead, and minerals scattered throughout the North Atlantic basin, it seemed to confirm "the design of providence," as John Campbell put it, that "every Island, Holm [i.e. inlet], and Rock" in these icy waters "would be applied to some useful purpose."[67] But it was the expanding British economy, more than providential design, that determined what "useful purpose" these distant shores would serve.[68]

This point is underscored by the heavy emphasis that contemporaries placed on the rich energy sources of the North Atlantic world, reflecting the more prominent role they were assuming in the British economy and consciousness. Marine oils, derived largely from whales and seals, were high on the wish-list of British projectors who valued them as an important lighting fuel as well as industrial ingredient. But it was the immense coal reserves of the Northern Indies—stretching from Scotland through the Faeroe Islands and Greenland to Canada's Maritime Provinces—that transformed the region's economic potential in the eyes of many Britons. The "rich coal mines of *Newfoundland* as well as *Cape Breton*," Captain Cook boasted, "would be sufficient to supply all Europe and America abundantly with this commodity."[69] Some of this northern coal might be imported into Britain because of special properties—such as the anthracite coal found on the Faeroe Islands, which was tried in Scotland because its chemical composition seemed ideal for smelting metals.[70] But given Britain's own abundance of coal, most contemporaries perceived the fossil fuels of the North Atlantic as a necessary foundation for establishing extractive industries in these northern zones. Coal deposits, for example, would allow mining operations to smelt iron, lead, and copper ores on-site, before sending these metals off to Britain. The energy from coal was also needed to fuel salt-works for fisheries, try-works for marine oils, and many forms of chemical manufacturing, including the production of valuable coal tar. And as British observers pointed out, the French had already demonstrated how these northern coal fields could supply the energy needs of colonial industries to the south, by sending coal from Cape Breton to the Caribbean where it fueled sugar production.[71] Not unlike today, the "Northern Indies" of the eighteenth century was to be a fundamentally extractive zone where minerals, energy, and supplies were mined to feed the growing appetites of distant economies.

Coda: Lessons from the North

British trade and colonization evolved in markedly different ways throughout the globe, as recent scholarship has shown. Engagement with different cultures, commercial systems, and environmental realities forged distinct modes of imperialism that reflected the unique dynamics of their time and place.[72] Nowhere was this point more evident than in the mid-century campaigns to expand imperial trade and development throughout the northern reaches of the Atlantic world. Previous patterns of empire—whether from North America, the Caribbean, or the East Indies—were set aside as projectors embraced a world of fleets, factories and transient workers who targeted resources with the tools and efficiency of the industrial enlightenment. Indeed, looking back at these northern schemes from our current vantage point, we can see how they embodied a fundamental transition taking place in Great Britain, as the nation shifted from an economy based upon organic energy and materials to a "mineral-intensive industrialization" that staked out a key path on the road to our modern world (both in terms of ecology and economy).[73]

In other parts of the world, British experiences could lead to strikingly different outcomes and outlooks. On tropical islands, for example, many scientists and officials came to embrace an *ethos* of conservation in response to the rapid environmental deterioration at the hands of European trade and settlement—a phenomenon particularly visible in such confined settings.[74] Likewise, Scottish improvers working to transform the agriculture and economy of the Highlands began to develop new ideas about the carrying capacity of the land, emphasizing the concrete limits of nature to support larger settlements or growth.[75] In each case, the convergence of science, improvement and empire led to dramatically different lessons than the ones northern projectors had drawn from their experiences, which tended to celebrate nature's abundance and the virtues of extracting a "useful purpose" from every island and rock, as John Campbell had put it. Such differences help underscore the fact that there was nothing inevitable about the worldview that emerged from these northern campaigns. Their ideological vision, in other words, was not the expression of some general *zeitgeist*, but instead represented a new amalgam of ideas about science, natural resources, energy, and global development that were forged in this northern crucible of trial and debate. It was with good reason, therefore, that Mary Shelley's famous tale of the dangers of scientific hubris and the drive to dominate nature revolved so centrally around characters, scenery, and dialogue pertaining to arctic exploration. This backdrop provides the perfect foil for Shelly's critique in *Frankenstein* precisely because it was the advocates of northern imperialism who had worked so tirelessly to link scientific discovery, the control of nature, and the quest for imperial glory in the minds of the public.[76]

Beyond ideology, however, these northern campaigns helped forge institutional relationships and careers that would influence the patterns of imperial and economic expansion in the decades to come. One important example can be seen in the cluster of lasting ties that formed among scientists, navigators, and officials during these formative years when projects for northern exploration created partnerships among key figures such as Sir Joseph Banks, Capt. James Cook, Constantine Phipps, the Earl of Sandwich, Sir John Barrow, and Daines Barrington.[77] Over time, these shared interests would lead to a tightly-knit "Arctic Lobby," as one historian has called it, which carried the banner of science, improvement and imperial expansion throughout much of the nineteenth century.[78] Other parts of the empire would feel these impacts too. Sir John Barrow, for instance, was not only a powerful advocate of Arctic exploration but also promoted numerous campaigns linking scientific discovery and commercial expansion throughout Africa and Asia during his nearly half-century term as Secretary of the Admiralty and founding member of the Royal Geographic Society.[79] Joseph Bank's role in cultivating imperial botany around the world is perhaps well known, although the link between this career and his formative experiences in the world of northern improvement are less so.[80] In a similar vein, Sir Roderick Murchison—dubbed the "scientist of empire," for making geology central to the way British industry mined resources on nearly every continent in the nineteenth century—actually received his training in geology alongside the explorers John Franklin, John Richardson, and George Bach as these men prepared for their arctic expeditions in 1818. It is fitting that the man who systematically inventoried the mineral and energy resources of the empire, was himself schooled in such practices as they were being honed in the northern reaches of the Atlantic.[81]

Ironically, nothing would have pleased these men more than our current notions of an Anthropocene, vindicating their prophecies in the power of science, innovation, and global markets to utterly transform the natural world.[82] Yet looking back at this forgotten eighteenth-century moment, with its schemes for imperial power and wealth in the subarctic, can help illuminate the emerging relationship between science, industrial capitalism, imperial expansion, and environmental change that came to define our modern world. In many ways, we are still reckoning with the consequences today.

NOTES

1. A. M. Lysaght, *Joseph Banks in Newfoundland and Labrador, 1766: his diary, manuscripts and collections* (Berkeley, Calif.: University of California Press, 1971); and Victor Suthren, *To Go Upon Discovery: James Cook and Canada, 1758–1767* (London: Dundurn Press Ltd., 1999).

2. Stephen J. Hornsby, *Surveyors of Empire: Samuel Holland, J.W.F. Des Barres, and the making of the Atlantic Neptune* (Canada: McGill-Queen's Univ. Press, 2011); Glyndwr Williams, *Voyages of Delusion: The Quest for the Northwest Passage* (New Haven: Yale Univ. Press, 2003).

3. Anna Agnarsdóttir, "Iceland in the Eighteenth Century: An Island Outpost of Europe?" *Sjuttonhundratal* 10 (2013): 19–22.

4. On the "Northern Indies" trope, see for example Henry Ellis, *A Voyage to Hudson's-Bay, by the Dobbs Galley and California, in the years 1746 and 1747, for Discovering a North West Passage* ... (Dublin: George and Alexander Ewing, 1749), ix; John Harris, ed., *Navigantium atque Itinerantium Bibliotheca* ..., revised and enlarged by John Campbell, 2 vols. (London: T. Woodward, et al., 1744–8), II:398; James Sterling, *An Epistle to Arthur Dobbs* ... (London: R. Dodsley, 1752), 28; and William Doyle's discussion (and map) in *Some Account of the British Dominions Beyond the Atlantic* ... (London: J. Browne, 1770).

5. While the literature in this field is vast, David Mackay's *In the Wake of Cook: Exploration, Science, and Empire, 1780–1801* (Wellington: Victoria Univ. Press, 1985), provides a focused entrée into this view of the Pacific voyages as a watershed moment in the relationship between science and empire.

6. Bob Harris, *Politics and the Nation: Britain in the Mid-Eighteenth Century* (Oxford: Oxford Univ. Press, 2002); Kathleen Wilson, *The Sense of the People: Politics, Culture and Imperialism in England, 1715–1785* (Cambridge: Cambridge Univ. Press, 1995).

7. Forster, *History of the Voyages and Discoveries Made in the North* (London: J. Robinson, 1786), 488–9.

8. "An Historical Memoir Concerning a Genus of Plants Called Lichen, by Micheli, Haller, and Linnaeus ...," *Philosophical Transactions* 50 (1757): 687–8.

9. Sterling, *Epistle to Arthur Dobbs*, 27–8.

10. Lisbet Koerner, *Linnaeus: Nature and Nation* (Cambridge, MA: Harvard Univ. Press, 1999), esp. ch. 3. See also the positive coverage of Linnaeus' northern "prospecting" in [Anon.], Article XII, *Literary Journal* 1746): 192–7.

11. Larry Stewart, *The Rise of Public Science: Rhetoric, Technology, and Natural Philosophy in Newtonian Britain, 1660–1750* (Cambridge: Cambridge Univ. Press, 1992); Richard Drayton, *Nature's Government: Science, Imperial Britain, and the 'Improvement' of the World* (New Haven: Yale Univ. Press, 2000); Jan Golinski, *Science as Public Culture: Chemistry and Enlightenment in Britain, 1760–1820* (Cambridge: Cambridge Univ. Press, 1992); John Gascoigne, *Joseph Banks and the English Enlightenment: Useful Knowledge and Polite Culture* (Cambridge: Cambridge Univ. Press, 1994).

12. D.C.G. Allan, "The Society of Arts and Government, 1754–1800: Public Encouragement of Arts, Manufactures, and Commerce in Eighteenth-Century England," *Eighteenth-Century Studies* 7 (1974): 434–52; D.G.C. Allan and J. L. Abbott, eds., *'The Virtuoso Tribe of Arts and Sciences': Studies in the eighteenth century work and membership of the London Society of Arts* (London: Univ. of Georgia Press, 1992); James Livesey, "The Dublin Society in Eighteenth-Century Irish Political Thought," *The Historical Journal* 47 (2004): 615–640; Fredrik Albritton Jonsson, *Enlightenment's Frontier: The Scottish Highlands and the Origins of Environmentalism* (New Haven: Yale Univ. Press, 2013); Roy Porter, "Science, Provincial Culture and Public Opinion in Enlightenment England," *British Journal for Eighteenth-Century Studies* 3 (1980): 20–46.

13. Arthur Dobbs, *An Essay on the Trade and Improvement of Ireland* (Dublin: A. Rhames, 1729); Gerard Boate, *A Natural History of Ireland in Three Parts. By Several Hands* ... (Dublin: G. Ewing, 1726); Samuel Madden, *Reflections and Resolutions proper for the Gentlemen of Ireland* ... (Dublin: G. Ewing, 1738); Henry Fitz-Patrick Berry, *A History of the Royal Dublin Society* (London: Longmans, Green and Co., 1915), 8–9.

14. For their wide ranging interests—which included such diverse fields as hydraulics, bee keeping, industrial chemicals, forestry, fishing, and linen production—see *The Dublin Society's Weekly Observations* (Dublin: R. Reilly, 1739); *Essays and Observations on the Following Subjects. Viz. On Trade* ... (Dublin & London: C. Corbett, 1740); Samuel Madden, *A Letter to the Dublin-Society...* (Dublin: G. Ewing, 1739).

15. Joel Mokyr, *The Gifts of Athena: Historical Origins of the Knowledge Economy* (Princeton: Princeton Univ. Press, 2002); and Mokyr, *The Enlightened Economy: An Economic History of Britain 1700–1850* (New Haven: Yale Univ. Press, 2010).

16. Dobbs, *An Essay on Trade and Improvement*, 28; William Doyle, *A Letter to every Well-Wisher of Trade and Navigation* ... (Dublin: R. Reilly, 1739), 1–2. [Anon], *The Wealth of Great Britain in the Ocean Exemplified* ... (London: M. Cooper, 1749); [Anon.], *Some Considerations on the British Fisheries* ... (Dublin: P. Wilson, 1750); Edward Vernon, *Considerations upon the White Herring and Cod Fisheries...* (London: M. Cooper, 1749). See also Bob Harris, "Patriotic Commerce and National Revival: The Free British Fishery Society and British Politics, c. 1749–58," *English Historical Review* 114 (1999): 285–313.

17. Harris & Campbell, *Navigantium Bibliotheca*, II: 389–90.

18. See, however, John Campbell's spirited defense of this kind of arm-chair "projecting" in *Navigantium Bibliotheca*, II: 397. Following in the footsteps of Defoe's *A Tour through the Whole Island of Great Britain* (1727), many improvers were inspired to create detailed geographic surveys that would catalogue the numerous projects for improvement waiting to be implemented in particular places.

19. See, for example, James Dodd, *An Essay Towards a Natural History of the Herring* … (London: T. Vincent, 1752); Thomas Harmer, "Remarks on the …Fecundity of Fishes, with Fresh Observations on That Subject" *Philosophical Transactions* 57 (1767): 280–292; Arthur Edmonston, ed. *A View of the Ancient and Present State of the Zetland Islands*, 2 vols. (Edinburgh: James Ballantyne & Co., 1809), I: 234; "Instructions sent out with Capt. Phipps on his northern Voyage" in Lysaght, *Joseph Banks in Newfoundland*, 258.

20. John Chamberlayne, *Magnæ Britanniæ Notitia: or, the Present state of Great Britain* (London: D. Midwinter, et al., 1735), 362–3; Dobbs, *An Essay on Trade and Improvement*, 123–4; Francis Cawood, *An Essay: or, Scheme Towards Establishing and Improving the Fishery* … (London, 1721), 38; *Wealth of Great Britain in the Ocean*; 53; *The Old England Journal*, 17 Aug. 1745 and 21 Sept. 1745.

21. John Knightley, *Essay toward Proving the Advantages which may Arise from Improvements on Salt Works* … (Dublin: S. Powell, 1733?), n.pag. See also the discussion in *Read's Weekly Journal or British Gazetteer*, 27 Oct. 1750.

22. James Harrison, *Encouraging Innovation in the Eighteenth and Nineteenth Centuries* …. (High View: Gunnislake, Cornwall, UK, 2006).

23. William Brownrigg, *The Art of Making Common Salt…* (London: C. Davis, et al., 1748).

24. Watson, "An Account of a Treatise by Wm. Brownrigg …," *Philosophical Transactions* 45 (1748): 371.

25. Berry, *History of the Dublin Society*, 61–2. The Scottish efforts are reviewed in Archibald Cochrane, *The Present State of the Manufacture of Salt Explained* … (London: W. & A. Strahan, et al., 1785), 43–76; Postlethwayt, *Britain's Commercial Interest Explained* … (London: A. Millar, et al., 1757), 59.

26. James C. Anderson, *An Account of the Present State of the Hebrides* (Edinburgh & London: C. Elliot, 1785), 115–117. Although my focus here is on the fisheries, much the same story occurred in whaling, where scientific improvers sponsored research into new harpoon guns, engines, and refining techniques that would boost this flagging industry. Walter M. Stern, "The Society and the Improvement of Whaling," in Allan and Abbott, eds. *Virtuoso Tribe of Arts and Sciences*, 158–181.

27. John H. Appleby, "Ginseng and the Royal Society," *Notes and Records of the Royal Society of London* 37 (1983): 121–45; Brian L. Evans, "Ginseng: Root of Chinese Canadian Relations," *Canadian Historical Review* 66 (1985): 15; Joseph Banks to Humphrey Marshall, 5 April 1786, in William Darlington, ed. *Memorials of John Bartram and Humphrey Marshall* …, (Philadelphia: Lindsay & Blakiston, 1849), 559–60.

28.   Martin Rackwitz, *Travels to Terra Incognita: The Scottish Highlands and Hebrides in Early Modern Travelers' Accounts, c. 1600–1800* (Munich: Waxman Munster, 2007), 436–52; Martin Rackwitz and Colin A. Russell, ed., *Chemistry, Society and Environment: A New History of the British Chemical Industry* (Cambridge: Royal Society of Chemistry, 2000), 48–9.

29.   *Transactions of the Society of Arts*, 55 vols. (London, 1783–1845), I:174; See also the improvement tracts on the kelp industry by Dr. John Walker, Angus Beaton, and Robert Jameson, reprinted in *Prize Essays and Transactions of the Highland Society*, 1st Ser., 6 vols. (Edinburgh & London: W. Creech, et al., 1799–1824), I:1–49.

30.   Paul Robbins, *Political Ecology: A Critical Introduction*, 2nd ed. (London: Wiley-Blackwell, 2012); Noel Castree, *Making Sense of Nature* (New York: Routledge, 2014). On the political ecology of improvement, more specifically, see Michael Guenther, "Tapping Nature's Bounty: Science and Sugar Maples in the Age of Improvement," in Laura Auricchio, Elizabeth Heckendorn Cook and Giulia Pacini, eds. *Invaluable Trees: Cultures of Nature, 1660–1830*, (Oxford: Voltaire Foundation, 2012), 145–9.

31.   Michael Guenther, "Enlightened Pursuits: Science and Civic Culture in Anglo-America, 1730–1760 (Ph.D diss., Northwestern University, 2008), ch. 1–2.

32.   [Arthur Dobbs?], *A Short Narrative and Justification ... of the Adventurers, to Prosecute the Discovery of the Passage...* (London, 1749).   The historian, Glyndwr Williams, who (for good reason) is dismissive of many of Dobbs' schemes, nevertheless admits that he was quite successful in persuading officials, opinion makers, and the public to embrace his perspective. Williams, *Voyages of Delusion*, ch. 3–5.

33.   Harris & Campbell, *Navigantium Bibliotheca*, II: 198.

34.   18 George II. c. 17; *Gentlemen's Magazine* 15 (1745): 51.   Henry Beaufoy, F.R.S., emphasized the interwoven strands of scientific, commercial, and imperial aspirations driving this push "for northern discoveries" in his recollections printed in the *Annals of Philosophy, Or, Magazine of Chemistry, Mineralogy, Mechanics ...*, 10 (1817): 424–5.

35.   Franklin to Jared Eliot, 19 December 1752, *Papers of Benjamin Franklin*, ed. Leonard W. Labaree, 35 vols. (New Haven: Yale University Press, 1959–), 4:389; The goals and details of the voyage were covered in lengthy pieces in the *Pennsylvania Gazette*, 10 May 1753; 15 and 29 Nov. 1753.

36.   Philadelphia Committee of Merchants, "Petition against patent exclusive rights of trade to Labrador," (Ms) in the Benjamin Franklin Papers, American Philosophical Society Archives, Philadelphia, B F85.96. On the competing schemes of this period, see Bertha Solis-Cohen, "Philadelphia's Expeditions to Labrador," *Pennsylvania History* 19 (1952): 148–162; Edwin Swift Balch, "Arctic Expeditions Sent from the American Colonies," *Pennsylvania Magazine of History and Biography* 31 (1907): 419–28. Captain Swaine, who headed the Philadelphia expedition, recorded that a "Draughtsman & Mineralist" was included as part of the crew, but unfortunately the extant documents do not name who filled these posts.

37. John Campbell, *A Political Survey of Great Britain*, 2 vols. (London: Richardson and Urquhart, et al., 1774), II: 638.

38. James Logan to Franklin, 7 & 9 Nov. 1748; Franklin to Jared Eliot, 19 Dec. 1752, 12 Apr. 1753, *Papers of Benjamin Franklin*, 3:325, 329; 4:387–89; 4:465; Franklin was also asking his colleagues to send "any queries to make concerning that Country, its Productions, &c. or would have any particular observations made there" which he would pass along to the Captain and crew (3:389).

39. Bruno Latour, *Science in Action: How to Follow Scientists and Engineer through Society* (Cambridge: Harvard Univ. Press, 1987), ch. 6.

40. *Pennsylvania Gazette*, 15 Nov. 1753; Peter Collinson to Franklin, 26 Jan. 1754; Franklin to Sir John Pringle, 27 May 1762; and Franklin to Richard Jackson, 6 Dec. 1753, in *Papers of Benjamin Franklin*, 5:190–3; 14:352; 4: 148.

41. Arthur Dobbs, *An Account of the Countries Adjoining to Hudson's Bay* (London: J. Robinson, 1744).

42. Postlethwayt, *Universal Dictionary of Trade and Commerce* ..., 2 vols. (London: W. Strahan, et al., 1773), I: lii. For the broader contexts of these attacks, see Glyndwr Williams, "The Hudson's Bay Company and its critics in the eighteenth century," *Transactions of the Royal Historical Society*, 5th Ser., 20 (1970): 149–171.

43. Anon. *A Short State of the Countries and Trade of North America Claimed by the Hudson's Bay Company* (London: J. Robinson, 1749), 5, 9–10, 28–43.

44. Henry Ellis, *A Voyage to Hudson's-Bay*, 50. On the interest in copper mining, see the "Report from the Committee Appointed to Enquire into Hudson's Bay" reprinted in *Reports from Committees of the House of Commons*, 16 vols. (London, 1803–06), II: 213–86.

45. *Gentlemen's Magazine*, 19 (1749): 100; Williams, *Voyages of Delusion*, ch. 6.

46. Privy Council petition printed in Dobbs, *A Short Narrative and Justification*, 24.

47. On the spread and influence of this work, see Guenther, "Enlightened Pursuits," 175.

48. Ellis, *Voyage to Hudson's Bay*, x: vii, ix.

49. Robert A. Stafford, 'Scientific Exploration and Empire', in Andrew Porter, ed. *The Oxford History of the British Empire, Vol. 3, The Nineteenth Century* (Oxford: Oxford Univ. Press, 1999), 294–319.

50. Harris, *Politics and the Nation*, ch. 6.

51. Postlethwayt, *Universal Dictionary of Trade and Commerce*, 1: xxvi.

52. The discussion in this section about premium lists is based upon research in the Society of Arts archives, which contain not only their own lists but also those from societies in Ireland, Scotland, and the American colonies. Archives of the Royal Society of Arts, London, RSA/PR/GE/110/30/163; RSA/PR/GE/110/12/106; RSA/PR/GE/110/30/145; RSA/PR/GE/110/30/144; RSA/PR/GE/110/12/106; RSA/SC/IM/701/S985; RSA/PR/GE/110/30/156; RSA/PR/GE/110/18/127; and RSA/PR/GE/112/13/6.

53. The weekly lists of elected members, contained in the (ms.) minutes, usually indicate the profession or trade of individuals. RSA Archive, Templeman's Transactions, Vol 1–2; Minutes of the Society, RSA/AD/MA/100/12/01/01–07.

54. On the society's key role as a source of technical advice, see Harrison, *Encouraging Innovation*, esp. xix–xii, 38.

55. Templeman's Transactions, II: f.27–50, 66, 88–9.

56. Templeman's Transactions, II: f. 79. For public discussion of the furnace's potential benefits, see George Cockings, A*rts, Manufactures, and Commerce: A Poem* (London: J. Cooke, et al., 1766), 23.

57. Templeman's Transactions, ff. 94–f.96.

58. Harris & Campbell, *Navigantium Bibliotheca*, II: 198.

59. See, for example, these arguments driving British designs on Iceland during this period, Anna Agnarsdóttir, "Scottish Plans for the Annexation of Iceland, 1785–1813," *Northern Studies* 29 (1992): 86.

60. Their testimony is reprinted in "Report from the Committee Appointed to Enquire into Hudson's Bay," esp. 231–4.

61. Harris & Campbell, *Navigantium Bibliotheca*, II: 385–6, 390.

62. Postlethwayt, *Universal Dictionary of Trade and Commerce*, I: lii.

63. Daniel A. Baugh, "Maritime Strength and Atlantic Commerce: The Uses of 'a Grand Marine Empire'," in Lawrence Stone, ed. A*n Imperial State at War: Britain from* 1689 (London: Routledge, 1994), 185–223.

64. Sterling, *Epistle to Dobbs,* 47.

65. L. Gittins, "Premiums for Vegetable Alkali: The Society and the Supply of Potash, Barilla and Kelp, 1758–1827," *Journal of the Royal Society of Arts* 63 (1963): 577–581; Archibald Clow and Nan Clow, "Vitriol in the Industrial Revolution," *The Economic History Review* 15 (1945): 44–55; Francis Home, *Experiments on bleaching* ... (Edinburgh: Sands, Donaldson, Murray & Cochran, 1756); Agnarsdóttir, "Scottish Plans for the Annexation of Iceland," 84–7.

66. Anecdote and quotation cited in Agnarsdóttir, "Iceland in the Eighteenth Century" 11, 23.

67. Campbell, *Political Survey of Britain*, II: 664.

68. Russell, ed., *A New History of the British Chemical Industry*, ch. 1–5.

69. Cook's assessments were reported in Forster, *Voyages & Discoveries made in the North*, 297. See also, *London Chronicle*, 6 Nov. 1760.

70. These Scottish experiments are recounted in Jørgen Landt, *A Description of the Feroe Islands* ... (London: Longman, Hurst, Rees & Orme, 1810), 73. For British interests in acquiring the Faeroe Islands, see Doyle, *British Dominions Beyond the Atlantic*, 16–31.

71. Harris & Campbell, *Navigantium Bibliotheca*, II: 354–5; Postelthwayt, *Universal Dictionary of Trade and Commerce*, I: n. pag ("France: Remarks Before the Last War").

72. See, in particular, Alison Games' study of different models of colonial engagement that arose from British experiences in the Mediterranean, Atlantic, and Pacific in her Alison Games, *The Web of Empire: English Cosmopolitans in an Age of Expansion, 1560–1660* (Oxford: Oxford Univ. Press, 2008).

73. E.A. Wrigley, *Continuity, Chance and Change: The Character of the Industrial Revolution in England* (Cambridge: Cambridge Univ. Press, 1988); and E.A. Wrigley, "Two Kinds of Capitalism, Two Kinds of Growth," in *Poverty,*

Progress, and Population (Cambridge Univ. Press, 2004).

74. Richard H. Grove, *Green Imperialism: Colonial Expansion, Tropical Island Edens and the Origins of Environmentalism, 1600–1860* (Cambridge: Cambridge Univ. Press, 1996).

75. Jonsson, *Enlightenment's Frontier.*

76. Mary Wollstonecraft Shelley, *Frankenstein; or, The Modern Prometheus*, 3 vols. (London: Lackington, Hughes, Harding, Mavor, & Jones , 1818). For the broader, cultural fascination with the North, see Angela Byrne's *Geographies of the Romantic North: Science, Antiquarianism, and Travel, 1790–1830* (Basingstoke: Palgrave Macmillan, 2013).

77. John Gascoigne, *Science in the Service of Empire: Joseph Banks, the British State and the Uses of Science in the Age of Revolution* (Cambridge: Cambridge Univ. Press, 1998), 36–40.

78. Robert A. Stafford, *"Scientist of Empire": Sir Roderick Murchison, Scientific Exploration and Victorian Imperialism* (Cambridge: Cambridge Univ. Press, 1989), 68.

79. Fergus Fleming, *Barrow's Boys: A Stirring Story of Daring, Fortitude, and Outright Lunacy* (New York: Grove Press, 2001).

80. Drayton, *Nature's Government*; and Gascoigne, *Science in the Service of Empire.* In his early years, Banks not only spent time exploring Newfoundland (1766) and Iceland (1772), but also intended to study northern botany under Linnaeus, and was preparing for a polar expedition he hoped to lead.

81. Stafford, *"Scientist of Empire,"* 68; Stafford, "Geological Surveys, Mineral Discoveries, and British Expansion, 1835–71," *Journal of Imperial and Commonwealth History* 12 (1984): 5–32.

82. Will Steffen, Jacques Grinevald, Paul Crutzen, and John McNeill, "The Anthropocene: conceptual and historical perspectives," *Philosophical Transactions of the Royal Society of London A: Mathematical, Physical and Engineering Sciences* 369 (2011): 842–867. See also the recent collection of essays on the relationship between the Anthropocene and the eighteenth century in "Humans and the Environment," special issue of *Eighteenth-Century Studies* 49 (2016): 117–302.

John Gay's *Polly* (1729), Bernard Mandeville, and the Critique of Empire

RICHARD FROHOCK

When the production of John Gay's *Polly*, sequel to the famous *Beggar's Opera* (1728), was just about to go into rehearsals at Mr. Rich's theater, it suddenly was halted by order from the Lord Chamberlain, who, after reading the script, determined to prohibit the performance. Gay published his play in 1729 instead with a preface and an introduction that offer a defense of his work. The Lord Chamberlain did not state reasons for his decision to ban *Polly*, but Gay tells readers that he had been charged generally with having written many "disaffected libels" and "seditious pamphlets," and that *Polly* in particular contained "immoralities" and "slanders against particular persons," as well as against majesty itself. Gay offers a familiar defense of his satire, claiming that it attacks vice generally, not particular persons, and that only the guilty would have reason to apply its critiques to themselves. Such defenses can be disingenuous, and certainly part of the gleeful irreverence of *The Beggar's Opera* lies in its lampooning of several contemporary persons of note. In the case of *Polly*, however, there is something to Gay's claim; in his banned sequel, Gay moves beyond Jonathan Wild, Lord Charles Townshend, Robert Walpole, and the particulars of law, crime, and politics in London to critique the building of empire in broad terms.[1]

The practice of transporting criminals makes the West Indies a logical setting for Gay's *Polly*, and the contact zone of the Caribbean islands allows Gay to juxtapose familiar and foreign cultural outlooks and practices. Gay's play explores the relationship between imperial center and colonial outpost, suggesting in many ways that planter society, though geographically removed and commonly disparaged as a degenerate simulacrum of the metropole, is culturally and ideologically contiguous with home. Gay also includes two alternative societies that raise possibilities of reconceiving and refashioning social organization in the West Indies. The pirates, led by a disguised Macheath, have abandoned mainstream society and have fashioned a rogue commonwealth with its own laws and protocols, while the indigenous West Indians represent a starkly drawn utopic vision of a virtuous society. The interplay among these cultural groups—their alignments and collisions—allow for an imaginative examination of the essentials of human nature and civil society, both within and beyond the expanse of English empire.

Scholars of Gay's *Polly* have long addressed the play's engagement with empire and offer very diverse—even opposing—opinions concerning the extent to which Gay critiques imperialism in *Polly*. Albert Wertheim and Diana Dugaw were among the first to read Gay's play as a critique of empire; Robert G. Dryden and Peter P. Reed took matters a step further by reading Morano/Macheath as a subversive figure who challenges a colonial ideology built on racial oppression. In contrast, John Richardson counters such arguments by asserting instead that the play encourages the "duplicitous mental habits" that support slavery and empire, and Jochen Petzold aligns with Richardson in opposing those who read *Polly* as an anticolonial play by arguing that its satire is directed primarily at domestic rather than imperial corruptions.[2] In this essay, I offer a new perspective on Gay's engagement with empire by contextualizing it in terms of topical discussions of human nature and civil society stirred up in the 1720s by Bernard Mandeville's notorious *The Fable of the Bees* (1714). Gay, like Mandeville, imagines and thinks through the core philosophical issue of the place of virtue in a fundamentally self-serving world; in *Polly*, he extends Mandeville's domestic social analysis to the realm of Atlantic empire, positing that self-love and self-interest determine how people organize themselves abroad as well as at home. The alternative societies he presents—the pirate commonwealth and the West Indian nation—reinforce in different ways the view that a successful trade economy and the successful expansion of the imperial state must be predicated on, and driven by, base human desires and vice. Gay's Mandevillian outlook defines his critique of English empire and illuminates the play's ambivalent ending, which celebrates Polly's choice of virtue but within a West Indian colonial setting that cannot be reformed or successfully replaced by alternative models.

Mandeville' *Fable of the Bees* began as a short satirical poem titled *The Grumbling Hive* (1705), which Mandeville soon expanded though a series of editions in the subsequent decades, adding lengthy notes and independent essays that transformed his original poem into a substantial philosophical treatise on human nature and the origins of civil society. Over these years, Mandeville's expanding work became the center of considerable intellectual controversy. His *Fable* was presented as a public nuisance before the Grand Jury of Middlesex in 1723, and it was attacked repeatedly and stridently by numerous opponents, including Bishop George Berkeley. In the span of just five years, ten books were published attacking Mandeville and his *Fable*; for the negative attention it garnered, one editor has described Mandeville's work as provoking one of the "most heated controversies of the century."[3]

What made Mandeville's book so objectionable to so many was his core argument that private vices are necessary complements to public virtues. His philosophy, Hobbesian in conception, posits that all people are motivated fundamentally by self-interest and private desires. With these assertions, Mandeville sharply contradicted the views of many moralists, most notably the third Earl of Shaftesbury, whose benevolism Mandeville specifically cites and rejects.[4] Mandeville places human selfishness at the center of his economic theories by reasoning that vices, such as profligacy and pride, result in a demand for luxury goods of all sorts; this demand drives the economy by supplying jobs for laborers and merchants. With this argument, Mandeville also contradicted the prevailing viewpoint of many economic theorists who insisted that resisting foreign imports and luxurious consumption was key to a favorable national trade balance and economic prosperity. In his *Fable*, Mandeville additionally considers the origin of civil governance, determining that because people are by nature selfish and asocial, they can only be brought together in a productive civil society when their vices are harnessed to create public benefits.[5] Accordingly, he argues that if acts of altruism are artificially endowed with high social esteem, then prideful individuals will seek to be distinguished for benevolence not because they want to help their fellows but because they receive public applause and praise for such actions. For Mandeville, hypocrisy is omnipresent because human selfishness is always at odds with the cultural capital attached to outward goodness; because human nature is fundamentally self-interested, people can only be tricked by what he calls "skillful politicians" into rising above their natural self-serving condition.[6] Perhaps most infuriatingly for his opponents, Mandeville does not seem particularly bothered by his conclusions about the uncharitable condition of human nature and the omnipresence of vice in a prosperous society. For him, the failings of human nature cannot be corrected but only managed, and vice cannot be eradicated but only channeled in productive ways. Mandeville goes so far as to assert the indispensible benefit of vice, for without it, a society could not flourish economically and the state could not become prominent or powerful. Mandeville theorizes that a society made up of truly virtuous individuals, were it to exist, must necessarily be a small, vulnerable, and isolated one.[7]

Gay's Mandevillian exploration of vice and virtue in West Indian society begins in his opening scene, which depicts a dialogue between Mrs. Trapes, a bawd, and Mr. Ducat, a wealthy creole planter. Gay's satirical method is to have these characters talk openly and unabashedly about the base motives that inform their actions; in the world of inverted values that Mrs. Trapes and Mr. Ducat articulate, terms of honor and virtue always function ironically, and all their acts of apparent benevolence are mere calculated pretense. Mrs. Trapes tells Polly, whose chest was "broke open" on the journey to the West Indies, that she will help her out of her destitute condition by securing her employment in a reputable household when in fact she sells her to Mr. Ducat for a concubine. Mr. Ducat uses similarly misleading rhetoric when he insists that he has purchased Polly to serve as his wife's maid, although Mrs. Ducat sees through the ruse and declares that Mr. Ducat only wants to add a "trollop" to his house. Mr. Ducat at once explains the way of the world and exemplifies it when he urges Polly to be content with her role as his mistress by exhorting her to "consult her own self-interest, as every body now-a-days does." Polly is an exception who proves the rule by not embracing the philosophy that Mr. Ducat and Mrs. Trapes tout.[8]

The dialogue between Mr. Ducat and Mrs. Trapes also illustrates the Mandevillian principle that self-interested people covet luxury items like fine clothes, rich foods, and grand properties not only for the direct enjoyment of such material goods but also to gratify pride and vanity. Mandeville argues that virtuous people, wishing to have basic needs met, would only ever purchase simple articles of clothing designed to provide warmth and protection against the elements. Due to the essential vanity of human kind, however, clothing takes on the additional social function of "Ornament;" people seek social recognition by means of fashion, and members of each class purchase more than they need or can easily afford in an attempt to dress in the style of their social superiors, which prompts each higher class to elevate its dress in turn to preserve the visible social distinctions on which vanity depend.[9] The West Indian colonists in Gay's play embrace the principles of conspicuous consumption in characteristically open terms. Mrs. Trapes insists that indulgence in luxury is a marker of a cultured, respected gentleman, and she urges Mr. Ducat to mimic this practice. Mr. Ducat counters that he already is among the most profligate of the planters: "I have a fine library of books I never read; I have a fine stable of horses that I never ride; I build, I buy plate, jewels, pictures, or any thing that is valuable and curious, as your great men do, merely out of ostentation."[10] Because of their fixation on social rank and reward systems, use value hardly figures into Mr. Ducat's and Mrs. Trapes's estimations of worth.

Mrs. Trapes views women as "cargo" for sale, and the main transaction she wants to conduct—selling Polly to Mr. Ducat as a servant and concubine— also follows the cultural logic of consumption rather than merely serving the gratification of appetites. Mr. Ducat initially reacts to Mrs. Trapes's proposal by stating that he has no sexual desire for a lover, but Mrs. Trapes scoffs at this objection and convinces him that as with other goods, taking a mistress is a manner of indexing social distinction. Mrs. Trapes wants Mr. Ducat to be "a fine gentleman in every thing," and she convinces him on these grounds to purchase Polly because he "would fain make a fashionable figure in life." For semiotic reasons, people seek to accumulate more goods than they can use or comfortably afford; as Trapes counsels Mr. Ducat, "'Tis genteel to be in debt. Your luxury should distinguish you from the vulgar." Polly herself recognizes that wealth and luxury—like charitable acts—are not ends in themselves but rather social markers, and she once again proves to be the exception when she defiantly declares that "tho' I was born and bred in England, I can dare to be poor, which is the only thing now-a-days men are asham'd of." The English have created a value system grounded in material wealth; Polly understands this way of the world but rejects it in spite of the advantages it could create for her, just as she did in the *Beggar's Opera* when her parents attempt to convince her to betray Macheath and have him hanged so she can receive a jointure and become a rich widow.[11]

If the motive to wealth is vanity, a principal means to wealth is treachery. In his *Fable*, Mandeville describes legal, accepted trade practices as built on deceit. In an anecdote about a West Indian trader and a buyer in London negotiating over a cargo of sugar, Mandeville makes his point that buyers and sellers deceive each other as a matter of course in order to gain the best deal for themselves. Although buyer and seller treat each other in a friendly and civil manner, they each withhold crucial information and take advantage as well as they are able; as Mandeville sees it, the Golden Rule is neither applicable nor expected in trade negotiation. The West Indian world of Gay's play operates on these terms, too, and although Mr. Ducat and Mrs. Trapes generally conspire together, Mr. Ducat remarks that Mrs. Trapes has "the conscience of other trades-people" and will drive up Polly's price by any effective means. Mrs. Trapes and Mr. Ducat have no scruples about acting dishonestly to gain excess wealth and prestige, and Mrs. Trapes generalizes the point succinctly when she comments, "If we could content our selves with the necessaries of Life, no man alive ever need be dishonest."[12]

In arguing that Gay's *Polly* should not be viewed as a radical critique of empire, scholar Jochen Petzold emphasizes how Gay uses his West Indian setting to direct satire back at England. Gay does this, for instance, when Mrs. Trapes compares her professional practices as a bawd to those of statesmen who "betray and ruine provinces and countries" and when she likens pimps and politicians in a song, declaring that "Each a secret commerce drives,/ First corrupts and then connives,/ And by his neighbours vices thrives,/ For they are all his own."[13] Petzold concludes from such examples that the play is primarily concerned with corruption in England rather than in its West Indian colonies.[14] However, it is possible to view the play's depictions of vice as equally relevant to colonial society and to England—one satirical target need not exclude or diminish the other. To be sure, Mrs. Trapes' remarks may well have evoked Robert Walpole specifically for readers, but Gay's satire goes beyond this particular figure to illustrate the ubiquity of vice across social strata and geographical space. As Polly remarks about Trapes, "Climates that change constitutions have no effect upon manners"; relocation to the colonies does not reduce human vice, and the same corruptions that are commonplace at the metropolis also characterize society in its furthest colonial outposts.[15] Gay's satirical linking of England and its colonies gets added fuel from the common cultural perception of the colonies as centers of corruption populated by the dregs of society; Gay draws parallels where many assume absolute difference, just as he does when connecting upper and lower classes.[16]

To take matters a step further, Gay's play represents imperial expansion as necessarily predicated on, and inextricable from, vice. Trapes remarks that "If the necessaries of life would have satisfied such a poor body as me, to be sure I had never come to mend my fortune in the Plantations."[17] In other words, the plantations are a place where one goes to create a superfluity of wealth, which one does to gratify vanity and pride; one might say that the plantations exist only for the sake of human vice, and that they are necessitated by the nearly insuperable compulsion for self-enrichment and aggrandizement. In the course of their dialogue, Mr. Ducat and Mrs. Trapes agree that social prominence in the West Indies requires conspicuous consumption, that morals need not curb the indulgence of desires, and that dishonesty is a chief means for achieving great wealth. *Polly*'s colonial characters are thoroughly Mandevillian in that they position vice as an indispensible, systemic component of economic robustness and political and social empowerment in a colonizing nation, both at home and abroad.

The play's pirates and the roguish society they form allows for further reflection on the place of virtue and vice in civil government. Beginning with Caribbean buccaneering narratives of the seventeenth century, writers frequently credited pirate communities with constructing alternative societies founded on a high degree of liberty and equality for all members. By the 1720s, the idea that pirates fashioned articles of governance that established rights of the common men and limited the power of the captains was widespread. In the first part of the eighteenth century, the idea of progressive pirate governance was advanced through the legend of Captain Avery, who, according to many fictionalized biographies, created a pirate republic on the island of Madagascar.[18] The pirates in Gay's play tap into these tropes when they refer to their articles of governance, the voting rights of the men, and the limited power of the captain as components of their equitable social organization.[19]

The idea of pirates maintaining well-run contractual governments grounded in democratic principles was also heavily satirized in the period, however. Captain Charles Johnson's *A General History of the Pyrates* (1724), the chief compendium of pirate lore in the period, provides numerous examples of self-serving pirates who, while declaring noble, republican sentiments, prove very willing to abandon their principles and betray their closest fellows for private advantage. Gay's *Polly*, too, relentlessly satirizes the idea of pirates creating progressive rogue commonwealths. In spite of their references to pirate brotherhood, these pirates clearly are driven by individualist self-interest rather than a commitment to the common welfare of their community. In their first appearance in the play, pirates Capstern, Hacker, Culverin, and Laguerre discuss their plan to keep for themselves any booty they find while reconnoitering, and in their first song, they proclaim that deception is the surest way to secure wealth. The idea of a democratically organized West Indian piracy is further undermined by these pirates' heated argument over who will become the proprietor of the rich kingdom of Mexico and who will be awarded control of inferior locations like Cuba and Cartagena after the completion of their heroic conquest of the West Indies. Each is so insistent on his arbitrary claim to the largest prize that they draw swords and come to blows.[20] Captain Macheath, who, pardoned at the end of the *Beggar's Opera*, disguises himself in blackface and leads the pirates under the assumed name of Morano, proves to be no more public-minded than the crew. He is easily persuaded to put self-interest above that of the community when he, Vanderbluff, and Jenny conspire to abscond with the ships and plundered treasure while the other pirates are in battle. Laguerre encapsulates the pirates' Mandevellian notion of equality when he declares, "Every man for himself, say I. There is no being even with mankind, without that universal maxim."[21]

Through her interactions with the pirates, Polly also exposes the emptiness of the pirates' declarations of honor and brotherhood. When

Polly stumbles upon Capstern, Hacker, Culverin, and Laguerre, she flatters them by reinforcing their self-image and adopting their heroic discourse. Embracing pirate clichés in order to ingratiate herself with these dangerous rogues, Polly sings a song that declares that pirates, unlike those who rise to power through trickery and deceit, fight openly and therefore heroically and honestly for their plunder. The pirates are flattered, but Polly's song is deeply ironic because the pirates earlier in this same scene have declared their readiness to cheat and deceive their fellows. Polly expands on pirate clichés later, characterizing herself as a youth who has been victimized by an unjust world and who seeks to join the pirates in order to engage in an honorable war of retaliation. Her portrait of the pirates' fighting for social justice creates a satiric disjunction in the context of Macheath and his men, whose individualism and petty personal ambitions are rife.[22]

The play also reveals ironies beyond the pirates' individual hypocrisies. The pirates position their rogue commonwealth as a contrast to the exploitive and corrupt mainstream world, but Gay's play continually draws parallels between piracy and state-sanctioned imperialism. The planters in the play have formed an alliance with the Indians to fend off the pirate attack, but the pirates can imagine replacing the colonists as the Indians' allies; as Hacker quips, "Who knows but [the Indians] may side with us? May-hap they may like our tyranny better." The pirates also draw on familiar heroic tropes to rationalize their criminal plundering, describing their activities as epic in nature and representing themselves not as marauders but as conquerors who will topple empires and establish vast new domains. Macheath terms his piratical attack on West Indian colonies his "great design," an appellation that may still have suggested to English audiences Oliver Cromwell's Western Design, a grand initiative to wrest the Americas away from the Spanish.[23] The pirates' base criminality undermines their ennobling self-representations while simultaneously pointing to the piracy that lurks behind familiar official justifications for violent acquisition.

Gay additionally uses his pirate characters to disrupt the common rationalization that the English were more virtuous colonizers than other European nations. In establishing English imperial virtue, apologists frequently emphasized Spanish cruelty in particular, often depicting in graphic details the torturing of Indian bodies. John Philips famously made use of such images to promote Cromwell's imperial ambitions, for instance, in his preface to *Tears of the Indians* (1656), the title he gave to his translation of Las Casas' influential *Brief History of the Destruction of the Indies* (1552). In *Polly*, Gay draws on this well-established motif but renders it in inverted, satirical form. Gay perhaps had Dryden's *Indian Emperour* (1665) in mind when he composed the scene in which his pirates threaten to torture Cawwawkee, the captured Indian prince, in order to compel him to disclose the location of his hidden gold. Like Montezuma in Dryden's play, Cawwawkee wonders at the Europeans' lack of virtue, accuses them of coveting and invading "the properties of another," and stoically resolves to meet his death rather than to betray his countrymen by assisting their persecutors. The English pirates take on the role of Pizarro in Gay's parodic adaptation of the scene, and the substitution implies that in the colonial world, the English can match the notorious cruelty of the Spanish. Moreover, the capacity for extreme violence is not limited to English pirates. Macheath has become notorious in the West Indies for his "rapine and barbarities," as an Indian reports, but as the pirate Culverin observes, Macheath "had never been the man he is, had he not been train'd up in *England*."[24] Gay presents the violence of piracy as a national attribute, a prominent trait of official and unofficial English empire.

Gay's play evokes the motifs of progressive buccaneer self-governance only to show its failure. Rather than constituting a genuinely alternative social organization, Macheath's rogue commonwealth mirrors the corruptions of mainstream imperialism and illustrates that selfish desire motivates individual behavior and structures society from its origin. The pirates ultimately are put down militarily, but, more importantly, they fail ideologically because their ostensibly alternative society is predicated on the same Mandevillian vices—avarice, vainglory, hypocrisy—as the society they wage war against.

The indigenous West Indian nation depicted in *Polly* allows Gay to present an ideological challenge to English culture from a different angle by showing what a society built on virtue might look like. The Indians, commanded by King Pohetohee and Prince Cawwawkee, provide the antithesis to the ideological outlook of the pirates and planters, and they articulate their noble principles in uncompromising terms.[25] When he is held captive, Prince Cawwawkee meets the pirates' demands with steadfast stoicism; he holds to his principles of bravery, honesty, and loyalty to his people, declaring "With dishonor life is nothing worth." King Pohetohee similarly espouses the preeminence of an unwavering adherence to virtue in a conversation with Mr. Ducat and again at the end of the play when Jenny and Macheath attempt to convince him to act other than justice would dictate in their cases. For King Pohetohee, "virtue, honour, and courage [are] as essential to man as his limbs, or senses."[26]

In sharp contrast to the English characters in the play, the Indians also practice the virtues they profess. Cawwawkee bravely determines to undergo torture rather than betray his fellows, and Pohetohee rejects all Morano's and Jenny's pleas to compromise justice. The Indians insist on a perfect correspondence between their principles and actions, and they do not tolerate contractions between a person's interior thought and exterior deeds. For the Indians, language is only useful when it is mimetic; Cawwawkee concludes that "speech can be of no use" among Europeans because they do not invariably practice truth. In representing native West Indians, Gay evokes tropes of noble savagery, playing with parodic reversals of civility and barbarity. Morano calls Cawwawkee and his people "Barbarians" because they practice "our notional honor," and Vanderbluff concludes that the pirates must "beat civilizing into 'em."[27]

Although the Indians' purely virtuous society exposes faults and vices, Gay indicates that it does not—and cannot—serve as a model for reforming corrupted English empire. Individually, the pirates and planters alike incredulously reject and mock the Indians' principles, recognizing that adopting virtuous practices would thwart their ambitions and ruin their plans for enrichment and self-gratification. More fundamentally, Gay's play indicates that the practice of pure virtue is incompatible with the aspirations of a wealthy, colonizing state. In the conclusion of *The Grumbling Hive*, Mandeville imagines that an angry Jove, fed up with the bees' constant complaints about the vices of their neighbors, transforms all the bees into virtuous beings. The transformation reduces everyone's needs to the simplest terms and makes all human interactions transparent and honest; the consequences of these changes include the end of professions, like law; the collapse of whole industries, such as the manufacture of luxury items; and the cessation of wars of aggression and imperial expansion. With the end of "Pride and Luxury," the incentive for overseas trade vanishes because everyone is content with the humble products they can get at home. Mandeville also posits that a purely virtuous society would become vulnerable to attack by less virtuous neighboring nations; a righteous war of self-defense would engage the members of this shrinking community, and they would fight bravely to protect their country. Mandeville further imagines that this virtuous hive would succeed in defending itself but that it would be able to exist as a small, isolated community only—"Blest with Content and Honesty," but taking up residence in a "hollow tree" and living in a self-contained way, largely cut off from the rest of the world that does not share its values.[28]

In many ways, Gay's imaginary Indian society parallels Mandeville's virtuous hive. The Indians are committed to the theory and practice of pure virtue, are unjustly assailed by an outside community, and show strong resolve in defending their community. Due to their skill and bravery, they are able to stave off the pirate attack and administer swift justice to the aggressors, but the future of the Indian society appears to be one of isolation. Although allied with the planters, they share no common ideological ground with the colonists, and the interactions between the two groups seem therefore limited to their *ad hoc* military union. The Indians can best protect their values by defending their borders, being self-contained, and minimizing intercourse with the rest of the world.

For Gay, as for Mandeville, the purely virtuous society serves as a theoretical device, shedding light on how European society functions at its most fundamental level, but it provides no model for a prosperous and wealthy nation. It sets a utopic standard, and, as such, an utterly impracticable one.[29] In the final song of the play, the Indians celebrate that virtue and justice always win out in the end: "Virtue subduing,/ Humbles in ruin/ All the proud wicked race. /Truth, never failing, /Must be prevailing,/ Falsehood shall find disgrace." Because of this conclusion, Gay's readers and critics have sometimes complained of an overly moralistic end—and indeed the Poet promises in the play's introduction not to "give up my moral for a joke" as he had been accused of doing in the *Beggar's Opera* by reprieving Macheath. *Polly* holds true to the poet's promise in that this time the order for Macheath's reprieve arrives too late, and he hangs on the gallows along with other pirate leaders for their crimes; Indian justice wins out, and the villains' rapine and brutalities are brought to a halt.[30]

In spite of this triumph, however, the Indians' concluding song conveys considerable irony because the defeat of the pirates and the collapse of their rogue commonwealth leaves extensive vice unpunished and unreformed. The whole colonial machinery, exposed and critiqued for its vices and piratical orientation throughout the play, continues unaffected. The corrupt planter society remains unchanged at the play's conclusion; the Indians deny Mr. Ducat's claim to Polly, but they return the other revolted slaves who fought with the pirates, and the exploitive colonial system remains firmly in place.[31] As Mandeville argues, states can and should punish individuals who are caught practicing egregious vice or committing crimes, but it does not follow that systemic vice can (or should) be eradicated from society. Indian virtue triumphs, but only in a limited sphere, while English vices continue unabated at home and in the colonies. As in *The Beggar's Opera*, Gay crafts an ending that in spite of Macheath's hanging illustrates the failure of justice to be enacted on a broad scale.

In addition to the many philosophical parallels, Gay and Mandeville differ in a key matter. As a satirist, Mandeville exposes follies and vices but offers a genuine argument for the beneficial role of these moral shortcomings in a powerful state economy. Gay's satire also exposes follies and vices but makes no claim for their secondary benefits to society. For both writers, though, a world without vice is an unobtainable fantasy. Mandeville urges the benefit of resigning to and embracing this reality, while Gay's satire laments the incorrigible immoral state of imperial society. Gay suggests that just as a few crooks can be brought to justice without reforming a corrupted civilization, a few exceptional individuals may choose virtuous paths without suggesting a more widespread social amelioration. Polly is unique within the play because she bridges worlds. The daughter of the immoral Mr. and Mrs. Peachum, she comes from a world of vice, and she understands the use and power of deception. In the course of the play, she uses disguise, flattery, and bribery to protect herself and aid the Indians; she and Prince Cawwawkee escape captivity only because the savvy Polly recognizes and exploits the pirates' self-interest and secures their release with a pay-off. Yet Polly, who distances herself from the vice of her family and others, becomes increasingly enamored with Indian virtues and the possibilities of adopting them for herself. At the conclusion of the play, she faces a Mandevillian choice: to compete for position and power in a corrupt English world or to be virtuous and withdraw. The play ends without her making a definitive decision, as she will take time to mourn Macheath's death and perhaps also her connection to an English way of being in the world.[32] Gay presents Polly's hopeful choice against a backdrop of an imperial world that has no viable means of wholesale reform.

In his introduction to *Polly*, Gay has a character complain that "A Sequel to a Play is like more last words … in a thing of this kind I am afraid I shall hardly be pardon'd for imitating my-self."[33] In his sequel to the *Beggar's Opera*, Gay reasserts but also extends his satirical vision, moving beyond London society and its particular characters and corruptions to consider the expanding empire and the possibilities for remaking civil governance in a New World setting. His play *Polly* concludes that familiar human failures prevent the English from realizing any reform potential that the Americas might offer. The examples of a progressive rogue commonwealth and a virtuous utopia collapse or retreat in the face of an encroaching colonial culture that exemplifies Mandeville's point that vice is an essential aspect of enlarging state power and wealth.[34] Gay's play is not an abolitionist appeal, nor does it offer an enlightened perspective on slavery or race relations. *Polly*, however, is bitingly critical of English empire as a manifestation of human vice and folly. Like Mandeville, Gay sees vice as engrained in colonial society at all levels, from the transported criminals to the ruling planter class to governing statesmen. For Gay, the thief-catcher is a thief, the prime minister is a crook, and creole planters are piratical, though with superior protections in place to prevent them from sharing the fate of Macheath. Moreover, Gay confirms the Mandevillian viewpoint that colonial expansion is necessarily predicated on vice—without a culture of avarice, luxury, and pride, the English would not be encroaching in the West Indies in the first place. Virtuous imperial expansion is an impossible contradiction because, as the Indians know, "covet[ing] and invad[ing] the properties of another" is fundamentally unjust.[35] Although virtue is admirable, and perhaps achievable by some individuals or even small societies, *Polly* teaches that the power and wealth of empire can only come about through the robust practice of private vice.

NOTES

1. See John Gay, preface to *Polly* in *Dramatic Works*, ed. John Fuller 2 vols. (Oxford: Clarendon, 1983), 2:70, for Gay's defense of his satire. *Polly* was not staged until it was adapted and produced by George Colman; see George Colman and John Gay, *Polly: An Opera, Being the Sequel of the Beggar's Opera* (London: Printed for T. Evans, 1777). For discussion of Colman's adaptation, see Peter Reed, "Conquer or Die: Staging Circum-Atlantic Revolt in *Polly* and *Three-Finger'd Jack*," *Theatre Journal* 59 (2007): 245–6. C. F. Burgess, "John Gay and Polly and a Letter to the King," *Philological Quarterly* 47 (1968): 596–98, describes how Catherine Douglas, the Duchess of Queensberry, sold subscriptions for Gay's banned play and was banished from court as a result. See John Sutherland, "'Polly' Among the Pirates," *The Modern Language Review* 37 (1942): 291–303, for discussion of editions, especially pirated editions, of the play. John Fuller, "Cibber, the Rehearsal at Goatham, and the Suppression of *Polly*," *Review of English Studies: A Quarterly Journal of English Literature and the English Language* (1962): 125–34, takes on the question of Colly Cibber's possible involvement in the suppression of *Polly*. Several critics have found *Polly* to be less politically topical than the *Beggar's Opera*. Albert Wertheim, "Captain Macheath and Polly Peachum in the New World: John Gay and Peter Hacks," *Maske und Kothurn: Internationale Beitrage zur Theaterwissenschaft* 27 (1981): 176–84, describes *Polly* as less directly "anti-Walpole" than *The Beggar's Opera* (177). Fuller, "Cibber, the Rehearsal at Goatham," also states that *Polly* is less directed at Walpole than *Beggar's Opera* (125). Reed, "Conquer or Die," remarks that Polly does not deliver pointed political critique (246).

2. Albert Wertheim, "*Polly*: John Gay's Image of the West," in *Theatre West: Image and Impact*, ed. Dunbar H. Ogden, Douglas McDermott, and Robert Károly Sarlós (Amsterdam; Atlanta, GA: Rodopi, 1990), 195–206, and Dianne Dugaw, "The Anatomy of Heroism: Gender, Politics, and Empire in Gay's *Polly*," in *History, Gender, and Eighteenth-Century Literature*, ed. Beth Fowkes Tobin (Athens: Univ. of Georgia Press, 1994). Robert G. Dryden, "John Gay's *Polly*: Unmasking Pirates and Fortune Hunters in the West Indies," *Eighteenth-Century Studies* 34 (2001): 539–57, and Reed, "Conquer or Die." John Richardson, "John Gay and Slavery,"

The *Modern Language Review* 97 (2002): 15–25, quotation on 17. See also John Richardson, *Slavery and Augustan Literature: Swift, Pope, and Gay*, (New York: Routledge, 2004) and Jochen Petzold, "John Gay's *Polly* and the Politics of 'Colonial Pastoral,'" *Zeitschrift fur Anglistik und Amerikanistik* 60 (2012): 107–120.

3. See Phillip Harth, introduction to *The Fable of the Bees* (London: Penguin, 1970), 7–43, for discussion of various editions and the controversy Mandeville's work triggered (quotations on 11, 12, 13).

4. Mandeville, *Fable of the Bees*, 329.

5. These ideas are explored particularly in the essay "An Enquiry into the Origin of Moral Virtue," included in *Fable of the Bees*, 80–92.

6. Mandeville, *Fable of the Bees*, 85.

7. See John Sekora, *Luxury: The Concept in Western Thought, Eden to Smollett* (Baltimore: Johns Hopkins Univ. Press, 1977), especially 63–135, for a description of Mandeville's challenge to dominant views of luxury in the early eighteenth century. Laura Brown, *Ends of Empire: Women and Ideology in Early Eighteenth-Century English Literature* (Ithaca: Cornell Univ. Press, 1993), argues that many writers including Mandeville portray chiefly women as driving the demand foreign luxury goods, thereby making them responsible for empire (114–116, 134). I find Mandeville to be less gender-specific than Brown does in how he articulates the demands for luxurious consumption. For a succinct but informative overview of the moralists and economists that Mandeville opposed, see Harth's introduction to Mandeville's *The Fable of the Bees*, particularly 15–34.

8. Gay, *Polly*, 1.5.77–80, 1.6.1–56, 1.8.67, 1.11.2–3.

9. Mandeville, *Fable of the Bees*, 151.

10. Gay, *Polly*, 1.1.54–57.

11. Gay, *Polly*, 1.1.62, 1.1.67, 1.1.116–17, 1.1.10–11, 1.11.52–54. Gay, *The Beggar's Opera*, in *Dramatic Works*, vol. 2,1.10.16–71.

12. Mandeville, *Fable of the Bees*, 96–97; Gay, *Polly*, 1.6.16, 1.1.32–33.

13. Gay, *Polly*, 1.4.24–27.

14. Petzold argues, "it needs to be emphasised that the main thrust of Gay's satire is not colonial expansion, but the political elites in London" in Jochen Petzold, "John Gay's *Polly*," 112.

15. Gay, *Polly*, 1.11.61–62.

16. See Jack Greene, "Outposts of 'Loose Vagrant People': The Language of Alterity in the Construction of Empire," in his *Evaluating Empire and Confronting Colonialism in Eighteenth-Century Britain* (Cambridge Univ. Press, 2013), 50–83, for discussion of the tendency to disparage colonists and the culture that they created abroad.

17. Gay, *Polly*, 1.1.26–28.

18. Early Avery narratives include Adrian van Broeck, *The Life and Adventures of Capt. John Avery, the Famous English Pirate* (London, 1709); Charles Johnson, *The Successful Pyrate* (London, 1713); and the anonymous *The King of Pirates* (London, 1719). Scholars have emphasized this aspect of pirate history, with some accepting pirate claims to have created well functioning sailing republics with advanced rights for all members. See for example Marcus Rediker, "Hydrarchy

and Libertalia: The Utopian Dimensions of Atlantic Piracy in the Early Eighteenth Century," in David J. Starkey, E. S. van Eyck van Heslinga, and J. A. de Moor, eds. *Pirates and Privateers: New Perspectives on the War on Trade in the Eighteenth and Nineteenth Centuries* (Exeter: Univ. of Exeter Press, 1997), 29–46.

19. Gay, *Polly*, 3.5.15–25.

20. See Richard Frohock, "Satire and Civil Governance in *A General History of the Pirates* (1724, 1726)," *The Eighteenth Century: Theory and Interpretation* 56 (2015): 467–83, for discussion of the satirical treatment of pirates in *A General History*. Wertheim, "Captain Macheath and Polly Peachum in the New World: John Gay and Peter Hacks," reads the pirates in *Polly* as mock-heroic figures who undermine progressive ideals with their shallow individualism. Gay, *Polly*, 2.2.6–9; 2.2.12–18. Robert G. Dryden, "John Gay's *Polly*," 547, misreads the pirates' argument when he claims that Culvern desires the governorship of Cartagena for himself.

21. Gay, *Polly*, 2.9.34–88, 2.12.26–27.

22. Gay, *Polly*, 2.2.129–41, 2.5.18–23.

23. Gay, *Polly*, 2.2.146–48, 2.9.71.

24. Gay, *Polly*, 2.8.22–23, 1.12.49, 2.2.61–62.

25. For an opposing viewpoint, see Noelle Chao, "Music and Indians and John Gay's *Polly*," in *Ballads and Broadsides in Britain, 1500–1800*, ed. Patricia Fumerton (Burlington, VT: Ashgate, 2010), 297–316. Chao argues that the Indians are characterized by ethical shortcomings, and she reads them as as complicit with the planters and implicated in the exploitive colonial system that Gay condemns in his play.

26. Gay, *Polly*, 2.8.118, 3.1.29–30.

27. Gay, *Polly*, 2.11.6, 2.8.36–39.

28. Mandeville, *Fable of the Bees*, 70, 75.

29. Wertheim, "Captain Macheath and Polly Peachum in the New World," 179, 184, argues that the Indian society is an unrealistic model, and he notes that in the conclusion of Peter Hack's German adaptation of *Polly*, the "ill-fated" Indians are destined to be driven from the land by the encroaching English planters.

30. Gay, *Polly*, 3.15.63–69; Gay, *Beggar's Opera*, introduction, lines 31–32. At the beginning of *Polly*, 1.5.39–40, readers learn that Mr. Peachum has also been hanged for his crimes.

31. Gay, *Polly*, 3.15.5–24. The play makes almost no references to enslaved Africans, and it uses the word "slave" several times to refer to white indentured servants (1.5.53, 1.11.56, 3.13.64). It is therefore unclear if the revolted slaves who are returned to their masters should be understood to include Africans, Europeans, or a mixture of both. Rob Canfield, "Something's Mizzen: Anne Bonny, Mary Read, Polly, and Female Counter-Roles on the Imperialist Stage," *South Atlantic Review* 66 (2001): 45–63, contests Dugaw's reading of the play as a critique of empire by arguing that while Polly escapes bourgeois capitalism by choosing virtue, the return of the slaves to the plantations at the end reaffirms colonial discourse and the exploitation upon which the imperialism depends.

32. For further views on Polly's choice and her position in relation to virtue,

see Joan H. Owen, "Polly and the Choice of Virtue," *Bulletin of the New York Public Library (Stony Brook, NY)* 77 (1974): 393–406, who reads the play as a straightforward allegory about choosing virtue over pleasure that resolves the moral ambiguities of the *Beggar's Opera*, and Jochen Petzold, "Polly Peachum, a 'Model of Virtue'? Questions of Morality in John Gay's *Polly*," *Journal for Eighteenth-Century Studies* 35 (2012): 343–57, who challenges the view that Polly is a moral corrective to the *Beggar's Opera* and argues that the ethical practices of Polly and the Indians are flawed, even Machiavellian. Gregory Timmons, "Gay's Retreatment of *The Beggar's Opera* in *Polly*," in Debra Taylor Bourdeau and Elizabeth Kraft, eds. *On Second Thought: Updating the Eighteenth-Century Text* (Newark, DE: Univ. of Delaware Press, 2007), 112–22, argues that Polly's integrity is not absolute and that her virtue should be viewed as relative to the more corrupt characters in the play (120–21).

33. Gay, *Polly*, introduction, lines 13–15.

34. Wertheim, "*Polly*: John Gay's Image of the West," 206, argues that "the failure of redemption in the New World is, finally, part of Gay's recognition that acquisitiveness and economic determination are part and parcel of the human condition." Norman Simms, "War and Peace in John Gay's *Polly*: Literal, Figurative and Cynical," in Paul-Gabriel Boucé, ed. *Guerres et paix: La Grande-Bretagne au XVIIIe siècle, I–II,* (Paris, France; Univ. de la Sorbonne Nouvelle, 1998), 281–91, applies Hobbesian and Machiavellian philosophy to the play and argues that the Leviathan that is the state remains in place in spite of the alternative societies that are presented to it.

35. Gay, *Polly*, 2.8.22–23.

Pity, Gratitude, and the Poor
in Rousseau and Adam Smith

ADAM POTKAY

Pity and gratitude are moral emotions—or "moral sentiments," as Adam Smith calls them—because they respond to perceived goods or ills. Pity recognizes that an undeserved ill has befallen another, or simply that another is in pain. Conversely, the sentiment of gratitude affirms as good something given to us, as well as the agent who grants it. These two emotions are often conjoined in eighteenth-century narratives: I take pity on someone, often someone who is acutely or chronically poor; I seek to alleviate his suffering or privation through word or alms; my feelings or actions are met with a feeling and/or expression of gratitude. Take, for example, the following episode from Henry Mackenzie's sentimental novel, *The Man of Feeling* (1771), in which the protagonist Harley takes pity on an impoverished prostitute who faints from hunger in his presence:

> "I am sorry, sir," said she, "that I should have given you so much trouble; but you will pity me when I tell you that till now I have not tasted a morsel these two days past."—He fixed his eyes on hers—every circumstance but the last was forgotten; and he took her hand with as much respect as if she had been a duchess. It was ever the privilege of misfortune to be revered by him .... He had one half-guinea left. "I am sorry," he said, "that at present I

should be able to make you an offer of no more than this paltry
sum."—She burst into tears: "Your generosity, sir, is abused; to
bestow it on me is to take it from the virtuous ... " "No more of
that," answered Harley; "there is virtue in these tears; let the fruit
of them be virtue."—He rung, and ordered a chair.—"Though
I am the vilest of beings," said she, "I have not forgotten every
virtue; gratitude, I hope, I shall still have left, did I but know who
is my benefactor."—"My name is Harley."[1]

In this exchange, pity or compassion motivates Harley to treat a socially
degraded woman with respect, indeed reverence; in his eyes, suffering
ennobles her. She responds with a verbal sophistication indicative of the
relative gentility from which she has fallen, and she responds with gratitude
for the relief he offers.

The sentimental narrative of well-placed pity met with virtuous gratitude
is not so simple for Rousseau or for his Scottish interlocutor, Adam Smith.
Yet the complexity of their attitudes towards pity, gratitude, and the poor
has not been fully appreciated. Each author seems, at first glance, more
sentimental than he is. Rousseau presents pity as the ur-virtue in his highly
influential *Discourse on the Origin and the Foundations of Inequality
among Men* (1755), and Smith in turn appears to endorse it at the outset
of *The Theory of Moral Sentiments* (1759, 6th ed. 1790). Smith's apparent
endorsement of pity leads one critic to link Smith's work to Mackenzie's:
"Smith's first paragraph ... urges (what Mackenzie's novel dramatizes) the
moral import of one man's 'pity or compassion' for another man, and allies
it with the dynamics of sympathetic reading: 'By the imagination, we place
ourselves in his situation, we conceive ourselves enduring the same torments,
we enter as it were into his body and become in some measure him ...'"[2]
Upon closer inspection, however, neither Smith nor Rousseau treats pity—or
gratitude—as an unqualified ethical or political good. Both teach us, rather,
to be suspicious of the type of scenario illustrated in Mackenzie's novel,
and in similar examples throughout eighteenth-century British and French
sentimental literature.[3] For Rousseau, pity is as apt to avoid suffering as to
alleviate it, and in his ideal, relatively egalitarian society, pitiable poverty
would be eliminated. For Smith, pity is not only generally inefficacious,
but potentially unjust—indeed, we're most apt to pity those, including
criminals and the majority of the poor, who do not (Smith argues) deserve
pity or relief. Conversely, for Smith as for Rousseau, not all benefactors
deserve gratitude. Gratitude is rightly bestowed, and for Smith properly
sympathized with, only when beneficence is given freely, without any self-
interested motive in the giver. And when is that? For Smith, anticipating

Kant, a moral act requires a moral motive, but motives are not always, or perhaps ever, empirically evident.

In Rousseau's second *Discourse*, pity appears to be the natural root of social virtues, though recent criticism suggests just how marginal pity is in the larger body of Rousseau's ethical and political thought, in which virtuous bonds are established not by interpersonal compassion but rather by independence from other individuals and dependence on the political community as a whole.[4] In *The Social Contract* (1762), Rousseau's goal is to make every citizen independent "with respect to all the others," and dependent "with respect to the city."[5] His goal is also, implicitly, to lessen the material inequalities of Europe's ancien régime: as he maintains in the concluding footnote of Book One: "the social state is advantageous for men only insofar as they all have something and as none of them has too much."[6] Neither destitution nor opulence has a place in Rousseau's projected society. "Do you, then, want to give the state stability? Bring the extremes together as close as possible. Tolerate neither extremely rich people nor beggars" (Book 2, Chapter 11).[7]

Gratitude, in the ancien régime, binds the beneficiary through indebtedness, and the benefactor through expectation of future assistance. Ideally, a benefactor should not expect a return or recompense for the good he does for others, and those others should not come to expect that good as their continual due: these ethical points will be familiar to the reader of Rousseau's *Reveries of the Solitary Walker* (1780). In the "Sixth Walk," when the pleasure of giving to a crippled boy he passes on a familiar route becomes "a habit" and "a kind of duty" (*une espèce de devoir*), Rousseau thereafter avoids that route.[8]

One way to understand Rousseau's ideal society is through its preclusion of the very sorts of pity and gratitude that thrive in the rank-bound world of sentimental narrative. Pity shines forth as a natural good in the second *Discourse* but grows more problematic as Rousseau recurs to it in subsequent writing. Similarly, Rousseau's early focus on pity inspires in Adam Smith a certain tentative faith in the virtue of moral sentiment that dwindles as he progresses with *The Theory of Moral Sentiments*. Smith published in 1756 an appreciative review of the *Discourse on Inequality*, in which he notes the foundational moral role that Rousseau there assigns to pity: "Mr. Rousseau ... criticises upon Dr. Mandeville: he observes that *pity*, the only amiable principle which the English author allows to be natural to man, is capable of producing all those virtues [generosity, humanity], whose reality Dr. Mandeville denies."[9] Smith's *The Theory of Moral Sentiments* has been read as a reply to Rousseau's second *Discourse*,[10] and with good reason: Smith begins his work with a tribute to Rousseau, remarking that "pity or compassion, the emotion which we feel for the misery of others," is by its very nature a refutation to any "selfish" system of morals (Smith refers here to Bernard Mandeville, author of *The Fable of the Bees* [1705–1733], whose ethics Smith later critiques in his 1790 additions to his text[11]).

This first chapter of *The Theory of Moral Sentiments*, taken out of the context of the work as a whole, has sometimes led literary scholars to take Smith for a sentimental philosopher, a proponent of "sympathy" understood as a culture of feeling and fellow feeling, predicated on the natural goodness of humanity.[12] Smith's use of pity, however, does not extend very far into *The Theory of Moral Sentiments*, where, along with benevolence, it is subordinated to considerations of justice.[13] Smith applauds the rational self-command of the person who refuses to be pitied, and, by the end of Smith's treatise, it is not clear if anyone—least of all the poor—deserves pity. As I suggest below, if pity derives its presumptive moral force from the Christian gospels, the critique of pity—in particular, Smith's—is informed by the ancient Stoic analysis of pity as a mistaken assessment of what constitutes privation.[14]

Smith accepts gratitude as a valuable social emotion, though not an unproblematic one. More systematically than Rousseau, Smith questions the *motives* of apparent benefactors, and makes the accurate discernment of those motives crucial to the assessment of whether gratitude is or is not appropriate in a given circumstance. He particularly questions the motives of the great in bestowing favors as they do. Like Rousseau, Smith satirizes social deference to superiors, especially kings, courtiers, and aristocrats.[15] In courts and drawing rooms, "success and preferment depend ... upon the fanciful and foolish favour of ignorant, presumptuous, and proud superiors."[16] Should one ever feel grateful to the great for the favors they bestow? The approbation a disinterested spectator feels for an apparent act of kindness depends on a judgment about the motives of the benefactor. Yet Smith offers no assurance that we can ascertain the motives of those with whom we enter into contact—even as he assumes the ill motives of some or all of the great. Thus gratitude, no less than pity, becomes a moral problem.

Rousseau

When Rousseau, in his *Discourse on Inequality*, presents pity as the ur-virtue, he implicitly follows Christianity's positive evaluation of the emotion. In the Gospels, Jesus is repeatedly moved with pity or compassion (variant translations of the Greek verb, *splagchnizomai*) for the suffering of others, especially the poor and humble: for example, "when he saw the multitudes, he was moved with compassion on them, because they fainted, and were scattered abroad, as sheep having no shepherd."[17] Jesus then miraculously alleviates their sufferings. The poor feature in the Gospels as an intractable problem (until the coming kingdom of God)—"ye have the poor always with you"[18]—and, in Jesus's ethics, they make an infinite demand on the pity and alms of the rich: "If thou wilt be perfect, go and sell that thou hast, and give to the poor, and thou shalt have treasure in heaven."[19]

In the seventeenth century, compassion as a motive to moral action was stressed, in Christological terms, on both sides of the Channel. The Oratorian priest Jean-François Senault, whom Rousseau read in the 1730s under the guidance of Madame de Warens,[20] writes in his anti-Stoic treatise *De l'Usage des Passions* (1641):

> *Car l'homme est si desreglé par l'amour propre, qu'il a falu que la Providence divine l'ait rendu miserable par la pitié, pour l'interesser dans la misere d'autruy; si elle ne le touchoit pas, il n'en chercheroit point le remede, & ne se mettroit pas en peine de guerir un mal qui luy seroit indifferent.* [21]

"*La compassion*" and "*la misericorde*" (mercy), Senault continues, comprise "*une vertu, que Jesus-Christ a voulu consacrer en sa personne.*"[22]

Senault's moral defense of pity reappears, in ostensibly secularized form, in Jean-Jacques Rousseau's influential account of the state of nature. His *Discourse on Inequality* presents mankind's pre-social state as one in which pre-moral individuals roam open terrains, almost entirely independent of one another (aside from a child's dependency on its mother, a period oddly truncated in Rousseau's account). The first moral or proto-moral relations are established by pity (*la pitié*), "a virtue all the more universal and all the more useful to man as it precedes the use of all reflection in him, and so natural that the beasts themselves sometimes show perceptible signs of it."[23] Rousseau assumes that pity at least sometimes issues in efforts to alleviate distress, and thus in the rudiments of moral behavior. He claims that "from this single attribute [pity] flow all the social virtues ... Indeed, what are generosity, clemency, humanity except pity applied to the weak, the guilty, or the human species in general? Benevolence and even friendship are, properly understood, products of a constant pity focused on a particular object."[24] It bears remarking that this list of virtues is a limited and limiting one; for example, its exclusion of justice is striking. Rousseau turns away from the classical virtues (wisdom, justice, courage, prudence or temperance) that, in ancient ethics, are generally associated with men in the higher orders of society.

For Rousseau, the morality stemming from pity obtains not only in the state of nature but also among "savages" and, more importantly, among the lower orders of European society. Pity, natural to man, appears wherever the civilizing process—and, as in Senault, *l'amour propre*—has not corrupted human personality. Pity is the moral passion of the humble and the poor. Rousseau asserts: "Savage man ... is always seen heedlessly yielding to the first feeling of humanity. In riots, in street fights, the populace assembles, the prudent man moves away. It is the rabble, it is the marketwomen, who [through pity] separate the combatants and keep decent people from slitting one another's throats."[25] Here pity is socially effective, if only in the negative way of preventing violence. Rousseau's satire on "decent people" (*les honnêtes gens*) is clear, as is his paradox: truly decent people are not those of social rank.[26]

Pity plays a clear role in Rousseau's speculative anthropology and anti-hierarchical satire. It is the virtue of savages and the poor, and its practical effect, in Rousseau's example, that sometimes spares people from mutual slaughter. Within Rousseau's larger corpus, however, pity does not clearly or consistently motivate persons (or animals) to assuage the suffering of others. On the contrary, as Richard Boyd argues, Rousseau believes that pity is as apt to make us *avoid* others in pain in order, instinctively, to preserve ourselves. "At its best," Boyd writes, "pity may awaken our natural repugnance to seeing human misery. But ... this need not incline us to do anything much about remedying it."[27] Rather, we recoil from the sight and sound of misery, as in a passage Boyd quotes from Rousseau's *Émile* (1762): Émile, in the course of his maturation, "will begin to have gut reactions at the sounds of complaints and cries, the sight of blood flowing will make him avert his eyes: the convulsions of a dying animal will cause him an ineffable distress."[28] But Émile must be taught the pleasure pity affords the detached spectator. Rousseau maintains (recalling the opening lines of Lucretius, *De Rerum Natura*, Book 2), "Pity is sweet because, in putting ourselves in the place of the one who suffers, we nonetheless feel the pleasure of not suffering as he does."[29] Boyd concludes, "human suffering" is "attended to not so much out of a desire to relieve those who suffer, but instead for the development of Emile's character."[30] Finally, in *The Social Contract*, "Rousseau's ideal of democratic citizenship ... does not rest on compassion for others," but rests instead on the independence of citizens from personal bonds and their incorporation through impersonal, political ones.[31]

Rousseau admits pity into his pre-rational state of nature but not into the political society envisioned in *The Social Contract*. Into neither state does he admit interpersonal gratitude. The omission is salient because, as Patrick Coleman notes, gratitude was accounted a good in seventeenth-century natural jurisprudence from Thomas Hobbes to Samuel Pufendorf, as something necessary for peace and sociality.[32] Rousseau does not condemn gratitude *per se*, but seeks to disentangle it from obligation and dependence— to carve an imaginative space in which it can be, as Coleman notes, "a free response to a freely given favor" rather than "a formal obligation, the failure to fulfill which brings justified reprobation, and which may even provoke anger in the benefactor."[33] In *Émile*, Part IV, Rousseau explains why "ingratitude" may be justified in a society in which gifts are rarely free:

> Ingratitude would be rarer if kindness were less often the investment of a usurer .... If you sell me your gifts, I will haggle over the price; but if you pretend to give, in order to sell later on at your own price, you are guilty of fraud; it is the free gift which is beyond price. The heart is a law to itself (*le coeur ne reçoit de loix que de lui-même*); if you try to bind it, you lose it; give it its liberty, and you make it your own.[34]

In *Reveries of the Solitary Walker*, Rousseau recoils from the "kind of contract" that arises "between benefactor and beneficiary," that is, the assumption that "if the beneficiary tacitly promises his gratitude, the benefactor tacitly promises to keep showing the other ... the same kindness."[35] A favor at first freely given thus becomes a duty, and the benefactor becomes the servant of the beneficiary who depends on him.

Rousseau can escape gratitude's shackle only through a theological turn: "If I had remained free, unknown, and isolated, as I was meant to be, I would have done only good .... If I had been invisible and omnipotent like God, I would have been beneficent and good like him."[36] True gratitude, Rousseau implies, can be felt only to a superior being who neither expects a return for, nor is constrained by, the good he does others. As in his praise of pity, Rousseau's suspicion of gratitude to other human beings harkens back to the gospels. Jesus preached the giving of free gifts with no expectation of earthly return: "When thou makest a dinner or a supper, call not thy friends, nor thy brethren, neither thy kinsmen, nor thy rich neighbors; lest they bid thee again [invite you in return], and a recompense be made thee. But when thou makest a feast, call the poor, the maimed, the lame, the blind; and thou shalt be blessed, for they cannot recompense thee: for thou shalt be recompensed at the resurrection of the just."[37] The Rousseau of the "Sixth Walk" would concur with this injunction—at least up to its final, eschatological sentence. Theologian Peter Leithart writes: "Christianity freed people from onerous personal bonds by defining gratitude as *right use* of the gift rather than gratitude as *return* [of service or goods to the benefactor]."[38] Rousseau sought a similar liberation through a similar re-definition of true gratitude.

Rousseau himself was, in his private life, notorious as an "ingrate," especially in the years leading up to his 1766 quarrel with David Hume. Hume, who arranged for Rousseau's safe haven in England, and procured him the offer of a pension from George III, was warned by Baron d'Holbach of Rousseau's "unfair proceedings, printed imputations, ungratefulness." Later, when Rousseau turned against Hume allegedly for patronizing and conspiring to dishonor him, Voltaire in a public letter summarized Rousseau's conduct as "the proceeding of ingratitude against generosity."[39] Critical opinion typically sides with Hume, who "conspired" with associates in England only to perform services for Rousseau, over Rousseau, who jealously guarded against any service, any gift, that might compromise his independence. Rousseau's ultimate accusation of Hume as the presumptive "blackest of men" is undoubtedly unfair and paranoiac.[40] Yet Rousseau's commitment to independence, apart from the dubious means by which he pursued it, retains its nobility and power to surprise: here was a man who rejected patronage from three monarchs—Louis XV, Frederick the Great, and George III. Conversely, Hume, in his recriminatory letter (written to Hugh Blair) about his affair with Rousseau, half-acknowledges that gratitude can be a humiliating bond. Hume suspects "that he [Rousseau] had only picked a quarrel with me in order to free himself from the humiliating burden of gratitude towards me."[41] Did Hume mean for his reader to understand "humiliating" ironically? Perhaps, but perhaps not; to my ear, Hume's adjective sounds matter of fact, a rapid and unpursued concession that dependency has its ills. Be that as it may, Hume's next sentence treats Rousseau's avoidance of humiliation not as extenuating but as exacerbating his misdeeds: "His motives, therefore, were much blacker than many seem to apprehend them."

Smith

In the first chapter of *The Theory of Moral Sentiments*, Hume's friend Adam Smith approves of both gratitude and pity, which compose, along with joy, grief, and resentment, the first and central group of what he considers to be "moral sentiments."[42] Identifying "pity or compassion" in his treatise's second sentence as the ur-moral emotion might lead a learned reader, especially in 1759, to think that Smith's project was Rousseauvian, or indeed Christian. But for Smith pity quickly turns into a more intellectual event than it is in either Rousseau's *Discourse on Inequality* or in the Gospels. Whereas Rousseau insists that pity "is the pure movement of nature prior to all reflection," Smith makes it, and every moral sentiment, fundamentally reflective, the product of an imaginative self-doubling. (Rousseau himself will do the same in writings subsequent to the *Discourse on Inequality*.[43]) When we see another suffer, Smith writes, "it is by the imagination only that we can form any conception of what are his sensations"; "by the imagination we place ourselves in his situation."[44] Smith then asserts that it is only through specular and imaginative participation that we concern ourselves with others in any way at all:

> Whatever is the passion which arises from any object in the person principally concerned, an analogous emotion springs up, at the thought of his situation, in the breast of every attentive spectator. Our joy for the deliverance of those heroes of tragedy or romance who interest us, is as sincere as our grief for their distress, and our fellow-feeling with their misery is not more real than that with their happiness. We enter into their gratitude towards those faithful friends who did not desert them in their difficulties; and we heartily go along with their resentment against those perfidious traitors who injured, abandoned, or deceived them.[45]

The type of fellow-feeling that Smith describes differs from Rousseau's in his second *Discourse* not only in its reflective nature —an imaginative projection of oneself into another situation—but also because it is based on the type of clear knowledge about character that is, Smith implies, most readily available in "tragedy or romance." Smith's implication is the later Rousseauvian (and proto-Proustian) one that the only characters whose motives we can readily know, or sympathize with, are fictive ones. Rousseau, for his part, writes in middle age (in *Confessions*, Book 9) of his disillusionment with actual friends and lovers, and of the ideal world he had created in their stead. Parts 1 and 2 of *Julie, ou la Nouvelle Héloïse* sprang, he writes, from "an ideal world which my creative imagination soon peopled with beings after my own heart ... Altogether ignoring the human race, I created for myself societies of perfect creatures, celestial in their virtue and in their beauty; and of reliable, tender, and faithful friends such as I had never found here below."[46]

Fictive beings can not only be perfect, but also can be *known* to be perfect. In this, they differ markedly from actual persons, who can be opaque or misleading. Nonetheless, the basis of Smith's ethics lies in knowing and then approving or disapproving the presumed motives of other moral agents. Nicholas Phillipson notes that Smith follows his teacher Francis Hutcheson in basing moral approval or disapproval on the inquiry into an agent's motives, a basis that leads to the question, as Phillipson phrases it: "How could we ever be sure that we interpreted another person's motives correctly?"[47] Smith's first chapter maintains: "our sympathy with the grief or joy of another, before we are informed of the causes of either, is always extremely imperfect … The first question which we ask is, What has befallen you?" We "perfectly" pity, and should only pity, those in a clearly defined and innocent "situation."[48] How did they come to their misfortune? Was it deserved or undeserved? Moral emotion thus blurs into informed moral judgment.

As Smith proceeds from descriptive psychology to normative ethics, he variously ties his project back to the living philosophical tradition of Stoicism. First, his ethical focus becomes Stoic self-command: "that degree of self-command which astonishes us by its amazing superiority over the most ungovernable passions of human nature."[49] Smith argues that one ought to display—and, ideally, feel—no more emotion (particularly fear, anger, or distress) than an impartial spectator might readily sympathize with, and this, it turns out, is not very much: "We are generally most disposed to sympathize with small joys and great sorrows."[50] These are, then, the only emotions it is prudent to display, though the magnanimous man will not even feel great sorrows. In Stoic fashion, he rises above "sudden changes of fortune," impervious to all that lies outside his benevolent intentions or designs.[51] Pain and suffering are not, for the Stoic, absolute evils, because they are not moral evils; conversely, pleasure and the favors of fortune are not absolute goods, because they are not moral goods. Yet Smith, unlike the ancient Stoics, tends not only to the absolute value of things but also to their appearance to a spectator of limited sympathy, whose approval must be courted by self-command: "It is on account of … [the impartial spectator's] dull sensibility to the afflictions of others, that magnanimity amidst great distress appears always so divinely graceful."[52]

A second feature of Smith's normative ethics is caution against undue ambition because it will excite envy in others, and because social pre-eminence and wealth are not inherent goods. In the first edition of *The Theory of Moral Sentiments*, Smith introduces Stoicism as a correction of our tendency, which he satirizes, to admire the rich and scramble for "place" (in Johnson's sense of "precedence, priority").[53] "According to the stoical philosophy," Smith counters, "to a wise man all the different conditions of life were equal."[54] One can exercise the virtues (wisdom, courage, justice) under any circumstances, even the most unenviable. If nothing except for reason and virtue are valuable, then any accidents of fortune another person might be suffering—such as undeserved public shame, illness, or poverty—are not really evils. As impediments to potentially virtuous activity, they are conditions the benevolent person should seek to alleviate. But as accidents of fortune they are not fundamentally detractions from a flourishing which involves only the things an individual can control: her state of mind, assessment of things, and benevolent will. Moreover, individual suffering was viewed by the Stoic in relation to the causal necessity and providential arrangement of all things. As Smith puts it:

> He [the Stoic] enters ... into the sentiments of that Divine Being, and considers himself as an atom, a particle, of an immense and infinite system, which must, and ought to be disposed of, according to the conveniency of the whole. Assured of the wisdom of which directs all the events of human life, whatever lot befalls him, he accepts it with joy, satisfied that, if he had known all the connexions and dependencies of the different parts of the universe, it is the very lot which he himself would have wished for.[55]

The Stoic world view leaves little if any room for pity. Most Stoics disapproved of pity as "unnatural," in this special sense: it is unnecessary suffering for him who pities, grounded in a mistaken assessment of what constitutes the individual's good, and in ignorance of the greater good to which all events (somehow) contribute.[56] These Stoic criteria partly account for Smith's disinclination to pity the poor, unfortunate, or criminal. Indeed, a reader of *The Theory of Moral Sentiments* searching for objects worthy of pity will be disappointed. People often pity those sentenced to death, Smith observes, but such pity is misplaced. The malefactor who comes to a bad end should not be pitied, because nothing transcends justice and the moral order: there is no forgiveness, and little clemency, in Smith's world-view. "Mercy to the guilty," he concludes, "is cruelty to the innocent."[57]

Smith's pitilessness is also due, in part, to his proclivity to view poverty as a moral failing. When Smith turns to the poor of society—we must assume that these are the unphilosophical poor, as opposed to Stoics flourishing in rags—he shows little if any compassion. He divides the poor into two groups, those born poor and those who have fallen from material comfort into poverty. Of this first group, Smith declares as an empirical fact: "The mere want of fortune, mere poverty, excites little compassion. We despise a beggar; and, though his importunities may extort an alms from us, he is scarce ever the object of any serious commiseration."[58] With regard to the second group, those who fall into poverty, Smith largely disapproves of the commiseration a spectator is apt to feel, because "in the present state of society, this misfortune can seldom happen without some misconduct, and some very considerable misconduct, too, in the sufferer." The materially unfortunate, Smith contends, are rarely innocent.

Still, despite the suspicion and austerity Smith exercises whenever he imagines particular social interactions, he nonetheless maintains that people do act generously towards others, and that their acts are met with just gratitude. This general principle is restated through his final, 1790 additions to the text;[59] however, curiously, it is a principle that he never illustrates. (By contrast, Smith vividly illustrates, with a novelist's eye, scenes of crime and remorse.[60]) If a sufferer's distress is alleviated or his fortune advanced by another's freely-given favor, he ought to feel gratitude: on this point, Smith never wavers.[61]

He does, however, complicate the situation by making gratitude a right action only in response to benefaction that is judicious and properly motivated. If the benefactor has good and judicious motives with which we as a third party can sympathize, then we can sympathize with the gratitude of a recipient; otherwise, his gratitude is, and strikes us as, misplaced: "Our heart must adopt the principles of the agent ... before it can entirely sympathize with, and beat time to, the gratitude of the person who has been benefited by his actions. If in the conduct of the benefactor there appears to have been no propriety, how beneficial soever its effect, it does not seem to demand, or necessarily to require, any proportionable recompense."[62] Gratitude is thus, for Smith, a hermeneutic as well as an ethical problem, involving a correct or incorrect assessment of motives and contexts.

We have no surety that we have ever interpreted another person's motives correctly. Thus, it is never clear in Smith's *The Theory of Moral Sentiments* if anyone outside of "tragedy or romance" deserves either gratitude or pity. Has a real-life benefactor acted from judicious and unselfish motives? Is there anyone not at least partly to blame for his fall into poverty or crime? Rousseau's criticism of modern society in the *Discourse on Inequality* left intact Christian pieties about the virtuous poor and the primal bond of pity. Smith's vision of society appears at once more idealistic than Rousseau's, where it looks to ancient Stoic virtues, and also more disillusioned, where it surveys a social landscape in which no appropriate sentimental bond among real people has perhaps ever existed.

Conclusions

For both Rousseau and Smith, pity and gratitude have limited usefulness in ethical and political life. In Rousseau's second *Discourse*, pity may sometimes be able to stave off a massacre, and it underwrites humanity and benevolence, but its very linkage to "savages" and the poor disqualify it, in *The Social Contract*, from the creation of political structures that might transcend poverty and the independence of Rousseau's state of nature. Gratitude, for Rousseau, is a form of personal dependency unknown in nature, one that his ideal state of civic equality would diminish, if not render unnecessary. Smith does not, of course, share Rousseau's political theory; indeed, we have no clear evidence that he read any work of Rousseau's after the second *Discourse* except for a portion of the *Dictionnaire de Musique*.[63] Smith's own reservations about pity and about gratitude arise from his primary address to the mercantile and professional interests of Britain, and particularly Scotland, an audience he cautions both against admiring their aristocratic betters (who, he implies, rarely if ever deserve gratitude for their supposed favors), and against pitying the poor. We despise beggars, Smith claims, and he implies that we ought to do so. And such is the orderliness of society, Smith maintains (however misguidedly), that those who have fallen into poverty have probably done so through their own fault. However, contempt for the poor would be more perfect were the poor characters in a romance, because both for Smith and for Rousseau after the *Discourses*, perfect sympathy with moral sentiments, including pity and contempt, gratitude and resentment, is best suited to fiction, where we can understand contexts and motives clearly, and virtues and vices unambiguously.

In conclusion, I would like to suggest two avenues for further inquiry, one in political theory and one in literary history. First, in relation to political economy, Rousseau and Smith suggest two divergent answers to the question, why are poor people poor?[64] Rousseau seems to imply that the poor are poor because others are rich at their expense. This idea goes back, as does much in Rousseau's thought, to Biblical culture: see, for example, the prophet Isaiah, who upbraids the rich ("princes") that "the spoil of the poor is in your houses," asking "What mean ye that ye ... grind the faces of the poor?"[65] William Blake, who saw himself in the prophetic line, updated Isaiah for the radical 1790s: "Pity would be no more, / If we did not make somebody Poor."[66] The notion that the poor are *made* poor has, as its converse, the policy that poverty can be undone through redistribution of goods, and this is what Rousseau recommends in *The Social Contract*, a text that links the Bible to modern socialism: "It is precisely because the force of things always tends to destroy equality [of possessions] that the force of legislation should always tend towards maintaining it."[67] Smith, by contrast, pioneers the classic liberal state, where freedom is freedom from coercion or undue intervention in personal and mercantile life. His conflicting answer to the question of why the poor are poor is that poverty is due to intractable conditions or poor choices. The poor do not, as a group, deserve pity, any more than criminals do, but rather indifference, contempt, or perhaps, in exceptional situations, compassion.

In addition to raising broad questions about poverty and modern political theory, my essay on Rousseau and Smith's complex attitudes towards moral emotions—in particular pity, the moral emotion most often associated with them—might lead to further literary-historical inquiry into the role of emotions, affect, and feeling in what has been long been known as the age of sensibility. Setting Rousseau's corpus alongside Smith's *The Theory of Moral Sentiments* affords an insight into the dialectical constitution of modernity, in which the aim of reshaping community through sympathy and moral sentiment interacts with an equally strong distrust of feeling and interiority. Indeed, even a work as apparently sentimental as Mackenzie's *The Man of Feeling*, is at least half satirical, a critique of the affectations and aristocratic anachronism of sentimentality.[68] We have yet fully to understand the degree to which the age of sensibility involves the cure or disciplining of the emotions, in part through adaptations of classical ethics, including Stoicism, which remains a living tradition for much longer than is typically recognized; and in part alongside new political and economic formulations, including "general will" democracy, capitalism, and liberalism, that come into being with the waning of Europe's ancien régime and Christian pieties.[69]

NOTES

1. Henry Mackenzie, *The Man of Feeling* (New York: Norton, 1958), 33–34.
2. Susan J. Wolfson, *Romantic Interactions: Social Being and the Turns of Literary Action* (Baltimore: Johns Hopkins Univ. Press, 2010), 118.
3. On that literature, and the ethical problems it raises, see Lynn Festa, *Sentimental Figures of Empire in Eighteenth-Century Britain and France* (Baltimore: Johns Hopkins Univ. Press, 2006), and Vivasvan Soni, *Mourning Happiness: Narrative and the Politics of Modernity* (Ithaca: Cornell Univ. Press, 2010), 290–334.
4. Richard Boyd, "Pity's Pathologies Portrayed: Rousseau and the Limits of Democratic Compassion," *Political Theory* 32.4 (2004): 519–46, discussed below.
5. Jean-Jacques Rousseau, *On the Social Contract* Book 2, Chapter 12, in John T. Scott, ed. *The Major Political Writings of Jean-Jacques Rousseau: The Two Discourses and The Social Contract*, trans. (Chicago: Univ. of Chicago Press, 2012), 202.
6. Jean-Jacques Rousseau, *Major Political Writings*, 178.
7. Jean-Jacques Rousseau, *Major Political Writings*, 200.
8. I quote from Russell Goulbourne's translation, *Reveries of the Solitary Walker* (Oxford: Oxford Univ. Press, 2011), 59, and Jacques Voisine, ed. *Les Rêveries du Promeneur Solitaire* (Paris: Garnier-Flammarion, 1964), 109.

9. Adam Smith, *Letter to the Edinburgh Review*, in W. P. D. Wightman, et al., eds. *Essays on Philosophical Subjects* (Oxford: Oxford Univ. Press, 1980), 242–56, quotation from 251.

10. Ryan Patrick Hanley, *Adam Smith and the Character of Virtue* (Cambridge: Cambridge Univ. Press, 2009), 24–52; Nicholas Phillipson, *Adam Smith: An Enlightened Life* (New Haven: Yale Univ. Press, 2010), 145–57.

11. Adam Smith, *The Theory of Moral Sentiments*, ed. D. D. Raphael and A. L. Macfie (Oxford: Oxford Univ. Press, 1979), 306–14.

12. Scholars advancing this view are reviewed in Hina Nazar, *Enlightened Sentiments: Judgment and Autonomy in the Age of Sensibility* (New York: Fordham Univ. Press, 2012), 17–18. Nazar argues, convincingly, that Smith's sentimentalism—and Enlightenment sentimentalism more generally—is founded in a socially-embedded rationality, centered on the subject's spectatorial judgment of her own sentiments or emotions (19–27, 52–56). Nancy Yousef, in her important book *Romantic Intimacy* (Stanford: Stanford Univ. Press, 2013), detects a disjunction in Smith between "a theory of sympathy" and "the radical limitation of our knowledge of others" (30); while this may be a problem for a certain view of *sympathy*, which is for Smith as earlier for Hume a mechanism for perceptual sharing, it only becomes an ethical problem if we mistakenly conflate *sympathy* and *pity or compassion*, the latter of which, as an emotion, is dependent on, if not reducible to, a judgment about a person or situation. On the cognitive aspect (or core) of emotions, see Martha Nussbaum, *Upheavals of Thought: The Intelligence of Emotions* (Cambridge: Cambridge Univ. Press, 2001), 1–88. As I suggest in this essay, Smith's theory of moral emotions or sentiments, including pity and gratitude, recognizes the limitation of our knowledge of others, even while it makes proper judgment dependent on such knowledge.

13. See especially Part 2, section ii, 78–91.

14. The literature on Smith's debts to (and divergences from) ancient Stoicism is considerable, but it does not grapple with Smith's complex attitudes towards pity or gratitude. On Smith and Stoicism, see Vivienne Brown, *Adam Smith's Discourse: Canonicity, Commerce, and Conscience* (London: Routledge, 1994); Isabel Rivers, *Reason, Grace, and Sentiment: A Study of the Language of Religion and Ethics in England, 1660–1780*, 2 vols. (Cambridge: Cambridge Univ. Press, 2000), 2: 259–64; Gloria Vivenza, *Adam Smith and the Classics: The Classical Heritage in Adam Smith's Thought* (Oxford: Oxford Univ. Press, 2001), 191–212; Thomas Pfau, *Minding the Modern: Human Agency, Intellectual Traditions, and Responsible Knowledge* (Notre Dame: Univ. of Notre Dame Press, 2013), 329–40, 350–54; Ryan P. Hanley, "Adam Smith and Virtue," *The Oxford Handbook of Adam Smith*, ed. Christopher J. Berry et al. (Oxford: Oxford Univ. Press, 2013), 219–40. On Rousseau and Stoicism, see Christopher Brooke, "Rousseau's Political Philosophy: Stoic and Augustinian Origins," in *The Cambridge Companion to Rousseau,* ed. Patrick Riley (Cambridge: Cambridge Univ. Press, 2001), 94–123, and *Philosophic Pride: Stoicism and Political Thought from Lipsius to Rousseau* (Princeton: Princeton Univ. Press, 2012), 188–202. I touch upon Rousseau and Smith in relation to the Stoic/anti-Stoic debate over pity in "Contested Emotions: Pity and Gratitude from the Stoics to Swift and Wordsworth," *PMLA* 130:5 (2015): 1332–46.

15. Smith tended, in the first edition of *The Theory of Moral Sentiments,* to accept deference as a natural reflex, if a moral mistake. In this first edition, Smith satirizes courtly "politeness," particularly in France (54–5), yet maintains, "We consider the condition of the great, in those delusive colors in which the imagination is apt to paint it" (51). Yet Smith does not, in 1759, predict this delusion passing away anytime soon, nor seem particularly troubled by it. It is only in his work's revised, 1790 edition that we find Smith's indignation at unjust deference: here, the "disposition to admire, and almost to worship, the rich and powerful" reveals "the *corruption* of our moral sentiments" (61, emphasis mine).

16. Adam Smith, *Theory of Moral Sentiments*, 63.

17. The Bible, King James Version, Matthew 9:36; cf. 14:14, 15:32, 18:27, 20:34. In the Greek Bible, the verb for Jesus's feeling compassion (*splagchnizomai*) is related to the noun for entrails, *ta splagchna* (Acts 1:18). The text I have consulted is Barbara Aland, et. al, eds. *The Greek New Testament*, fourth revised edition (Stuttgart: Deutsche Bibelgesellschaft, 1998). The bowels, entrails, or inner organs were associated with pity from antiquity through the eighteenth century: the third definition of "bowels" in Samuel Johnson's 1755 *Dictionary of the English Language* is "tenderness, compassion."

18. The Bible, King James Version, Matthew 26:11.

19. Matthew 19:21; cf. 25:31–46.

20. See Robin Douglas, *Rousseau and Hobbes: Nature, Free Will and the Passions* (Oxford: Oxford Univ. Press, 2015), 153–55. On Rousseau and the "French Augustinians" (Jansen, Senault, Pascal), see also Christopher Brooke, *Philosophic Pride*, 76–92.

21. Jean-François Senault, *De l'Usage des Passions* (Paris, 1641), 561. Translated in *The Use of Passions, written in French by J. F. Senault, and put into English by Henry, Earl of Monmouth* (London, 1671), this passage reads: "Because Self love hath put us so much out of order, that divine Providence hath been fain to make us miserable by Pity, so as to interest us in the Miseries of others; did not she touch us, we should not seek out a remedy for them; neither should we ever dream of curing a malady, which were indifferent to us" (508).

22. Jean-François Senault, *De l'Usage des Passions*, 562; in English: "a Vertue, which Jesus Christ hath pleased to consecrate in his own Person," *The Use of Passions*, 508. Compare the English Latitudinarian divine John Tillotson (1630–1694): "*Mercy* and *Pity* are not more welcome to others, than they are delightful and beneficial to our selves; for we do not only gratifie our own Nature and Bowels, by relieving those who are in misery, but we provoke Mankind by our Example to the like Tenderness, and do prudently bespeak the Commiseration of others towards us, when it shall be our Turn to stand in need of it" (Tillotson, *Several Discourses*, 4 vols. [London, 1704], 4:23).

23. Jean-Jacques Rousseau, *Discourse on Inequality* in John Scott, ed. *The Major Political Writings*, 83; my French text is Jacques Roger, ed. *Discours sur les sciences et les arts; Discours sur l'origine et les fondements de l'inégalité parmi les hommes* (Paris: Garnier-Flammarion, 1971), 197.

24. Jean-Jacques Rousseau, *Discourse on Inequality*, 84.

25. Jean-Jacques Rousseau, *Discourse on Inequality*, 84–5; *Discours sur l'origine et les fondements de l'inégalité*, 198.

26. Rousseau's attribution of pity or humanity to the poor aligns with a larger strain of eighteenth-century moralism that includes Henry Fielding's *Joseph Andrews* (1742), in which a poor postilion acts the good Samaritan to the beaten and naked protagonist (Book 1, Chapter 12), and, among lesser known works, Herbert Croft's *A Brother's Advice to His Sisters* (1775), which features "an honest negro" who "stop[s] short, in passing an old sailor, of a different complexion, with but one arm and two wooden legs—It was my fortune, I say, to have the luxury to watch this worthy savage take three halfpence and a farthing, his little all, out of the side pocket of his tattered trowsers … force them into the weeping sailor's retiring hand, with both his; wipe his eyes with the corner of his blue, patched jacket; and walk away so happy, and so fast—that I was obliged to put your friend Spot [a horse] into a Canterbury gallop, to get up to the dog, in order to shake him by the hand" (111–12).

27. Richard Boyd, "Pity's Pathologies Portrayed," 532.

28. Jean-Jacques Rousseau, *Émile*, IV, quoted in Boyd, 529.

29. Jean-Jacques Rousseau, *Émile*, IV, quoted in Boyd, 525.

30. Richard Boyd, "Pity's Pathologies Portrayed," 525. Christopher Brooke sees Emile's development, structurally, as a Stoic *oikeoisis* (a technical term, untranslatable, that concerns the link between self-preservation and ethical relations), *Philosophic Pride*, 192–96, although he concedes that it involves cultivating a pity "the Stoics … would have found … bizarre, for their sharply rationalist ethics denied that pity was a virtue" (196).

31. Richard Boyd, "Pity's Pathologies Portrayed," 539.

32. Patrick Coleman, *Anger, Gratitude, and the Enlightenment Writer* (Oxford: Oxford Univ. Press, 2011), 160–61.

33. Patrick Coleman, 16.

34. Jean-Jacques Rousseau, *Émile*, trans. Barbara Foxley, intro. P. D. Jimack (London: J. M. Dent, 1974), 195; my French text is Rousseau, *Oeuvres Complètes*, gen. eds. Bernard Gagnebin and Marcel Raymond, 5 vols. (Dijon: Gallimard, 1969), 4:521.

35. Jean-Jacques Rousseau, *Reveries*, 62. Rousseau expresses his dislike of obligation in terms that harken back to Montaigne's essay, "Of Vanity": "I find nothing so expensive as that which is given me and for which my will remains mortgaged by the claim of gratitude …. I am so fond of throwing off burdens and obligations that I have sometimes counted as profit the ingratitude, affronts, and indignities that I have received from those to whom, either by nature or by accident, I owed some duty of friendship, taking the occasion of their offense as that much acquittance and discharge of my debt" (*The Complete Essays of Montaigne*, trans. Donald M. Frame [Stanford: Stanford Univ. Press, 1957], 738–9).

36. Jean-Jacques Rousseau, *Reveries*, 66.

37. The Bible, King James Version, Luke 14:12–14.

38. Peter Leithart, *Gratitude: An Intellectual History* (Waco: Baylor Univ. Press, 2014), 7. Leithart's history of gratitude does not address Rousseau.

39. My quotations from d'Holbach and Voltaire are drawn from Robert Zaretsky

and John T. Scott's masterful study, *The Philosophers' Quarrel: Rousseau, Hume, and the Limits of Human Understanding* (New Haven: Yale Univ. Press, 2009), 135 (d'Holbach), 185 (Voltaire).

40. Rousseau's private, accusatory letter to Hume is quoted in Robert Zaretsky and John T. Scott, *The Philosopher's Quarrel*, 151.

41. This sentence is quoted from Hume's letter to Blair—as is Hume's subsequent sentence, below—as that letter appears in Robert Zaretsky and John T. Scott, *The Philosopher's Quarrel*, 195.

42. Adam Smith, *Theory of Moral Sentiments*, 9–11.

43. Rousseau, revisiting pity in *Émile*, Book 4, makes it dependent on imagination: "no one becomes sensitive till his imagination is aroused and begins to carry him outside himself" (184); this apparent contradiction of his position in the *Discourse on Inequality* also appears in Chapter 9 of his *Essay on the Origin of Languages* (published posthumously, 1781). Jacques Derrida deconstructs Rousseau's account of pity (imaginative pity supplements or supplants its natural provenance) in *Of Grammatology*, trans. Gayatri Chakravorty Spivak (Baltimore: Johns Hopkins Univ. Press, 1976), 167–92; see also David Marshall, *The Surprising Effects of Sympathy: Marivaux, Diderot, Rousseau, and Mary Shelley* (Chicago: Univ. of Chicago Press, 1988), 148–51. Ryan Patrick Hanley traces a developmental trajectory between the "natural pity" of the Discourse and the "developed pity" of *Émile* in Chapter 3 of his forthcoming book, *Love's Enlightenment: Rethinking Charity in Modernity* (Cambridge: Cambridge Univ. Press).

44. Adam Smith, *Theory of Moral Sentiments*, 9.

45. Adam Smith, *Theory of Moral Sentiments*, 10.

46. Jean-Jacques Rousseau, *The Confessions*, trans. J. M. Cohen (Harmondsworth: Penguin, 1953), 398; on the origins of *Julie*, see 397–401, 406. Marcel Proust's analysis of narrative art illuminates what is implicit in Smith's comments on romance and tragedy, and Rousseau's on how he came to write *Julie*: "all the feelings we are made to experience by the joy or the misfortune of a real person are produced only through the intermediary of an image of that joy or that misfortune; the ingeniousness of the first novelist consisted in understanding that in the apparatus of our emotions, the image being the only essential element, the simplification that would consist in purely and simply abolishing real people would be a decisive improvement. A real human being, however profoundly we sympathize with him, ... remains opaque to us, presents a dead weight which our sensibility cannot lift" (*Swann's Way*, trans. Lydia Davis [New York: Penguin, 2002], 86).

47. Nicholas Phillipson, *Adam Smith*, 50–52; quotation is from 52.

48. Adam Smith, *Theory of Moral Sentiments*, 11–12. Smith here accords as well with Bernard Mandeville, who writes: "it is impossible to judge of a Man's Performance, unless we are thoroughly acquainted with the Principle and Motive from which he acts. Pity, tho' it is the most gentle and least mischievous of our Passions, is yet as much a Frailty of our Nature, as Anger, Pride, and Fear .... [A] s it is an Impulse of Nature, that consults neither with the publick Interest nor with our own Reason, it may produce Evil as well as Good. It has help'd to destroy the Honour of Virgins, and has corrupted the Integrity of Judges" (*The Fable of the*

Bees, ed. F. B. Kaye, 2 vols. [Oxford: Clarendon Press, 1924], 1:56).

49. Adam Smith, *Theory of Moral Sentiments*, 25. The subjugation of passions is elaborated in Smith's 6th and final edition of *The Theory of Moral Sentiments*, 1790, in the sections "Of Self Command" (Part 6, 237–62), followed by 21 pages (272–93) devoted to Stoicism in his Part 7 review of ethical systems (by comparison, Plato gets 3 pp., Aristotle 2 pp, and Epicurus 5pp). On Smith's "impartial spectator" as a Stoic inheritance, see my essay, "Discursive and Philosophic Prose," in *The Oxford History of Classical Reception in English Literature*, Vol. 3, 1660–1790, ed. David Hopkins and Charles Martindale (Oxford: Oxford Univ. Press, 2012), 593–613; on self-mastery through self-division, from Seneca to Shaftesbury and Smith, see 605–7.

50. Adam Smith, *Theory of Moral Sentiments*, 40.

51. Adam Smith, *Theory of Moral Sentiments*, 41; cf. 93–101.

52. Adam Smith, *Theory of Moral Sentiments*, 47. Julie Ellison comments: "For Smith, the ideal manifestation of moral sentiment involves a dignified upper-class sufferer whose very self-control provokes his friends to vicarious tears," a bond "belong[ing] to the neoclassical scenario of the Roman Stoic surrounded by his sympathetic friends" (*Cato's Tears and the Making of Anglo-American Emotion* [Chicago: Univ. of Chicago Press, 1999], 10). These friends are, moreover, men: as David Marshall notes, Smith's "ethics of self-command ... helps explain the almost total absence of women from the world of *The Theory of Moral Sentiments*" (*The Figure of the Theater: Shaftesbury, Defoe, Adam Smith, and George Eliot* [New York: Columbia Univ. Press, 1986], 184). See also Maureen Harkin, "Adam Smith on Women," in *The Oxford Handbook of Adam Smith*, 501–20. Ryan Patrick Hanley argues that Smith's virtue theory is indebted to and in some ways aligned with Stoicism, but is finally "eclectic": see Hanley, "Adam Smith and Virtue," in *The Oxford Handbook of Adam Smith*, 219–40, quotation from 221.

53. Adam Smith, *Theory of Moral Sentiments*, 57. My definition of "place" is from Samuel Johnson, *A Dictionary of the English Language* (London, 1755).

54. Adam Smith, *Theory of Moral Sentiments*, 58. Smith's original summary and endorsement of Stoicism in the first edition,1.3.3, appears as an extensive footnote in *Theory of Moral Sentiments*, 58–60.

55. Adam Smith, *Theory of Moral Sentiments*, 59.

56. For the Stoic case against pity, see Epictetus, *Encheiridion* (Handbook), section 16; Seneca, *De Clementia*; Martha Nussbaum, *Upheavals of Thought*, Chap. 7, "Compassion: The Philosophical Debate," 354–400.

57. Adam Smith, *Theory of Moral Sentiments*, 88.

58. Adam Smith, *Theory of Moral Sentiments*, 144; the following quotation is also from 144.

59. Adam Smith, *Theory of Moral Sentiments*, 326.

60. Adam Smith, *Theory of Moral Sentiments*, 65, 119, 177.

61. A beneficiary's gratitude, and its approval by an impartial spectator, must come from "the heart": on this point, Smith is in accord with Rousseau's *Emile*, Book 4. Smith later maintains that gratitude expressed out of duty alone is "perhaps" second best to actions motivated by the "sentiment of gratitude"

(*Theory of Moral Sentiments*, 162).

62. Adam Smith, *Theory of Moral Sentiments*, 69–73; quotation from 73.

63. Adam Smith quotes from Rousseau's writings on music in "Of the Imitative Arts," in Essays on *Philosophical Subjects*, 198–99.

64. My model for dividing different schools of economic and political thought in relation to the question, "why are poor people poor?," is Paul Collier's "Wrong for the Poor," *TLS* September 25 (2015), 3–4.

65. The Bible, King James Version, Isaiah 3:14–15.

66. William Blake, "The Human Abstract," lines 1–2, in *Songs of Experience*, The Blake Archive, www.blakearchive.org, accessed March 18, 2016.

67. Jean-Jacques Rousseau, *On the Social Contract* (Chapter 11) in *Major Political Writings*, 200.

68. See William J. Burling, "A 'sickly sort of refinement': The Problem of Sentimentalism in Mackenzie's *The Man of Feeling*," *Studies in Scottish Literature* 23:1 (1988): 136–49; Maureen Harkin, "Mackenzie's *Man of Feeling*: Embalming Sensibility," ELH 61:1 (1994): 317–40; Juliet Shields, *Sentimental Literature and Anglo-Scottish Identity* (Cambridge: Cambridge Univ. Press, 2010), 69–78.

69. This essay began as a paper for Ourida Mostefai's Rousseau Association Panel at the 2015 ASECS Annual Meeting in Los Angeles. The essay's finished form is indebted to comments from my ASECS audience; to Eve Tavor Bannet and my two anonymous readers for *SECC*; and to William Galperin and the Eighteenth- and Nineteenth-Century Reading Group at Rutgers University, where I presented a version of this paper in October, 2015.

Sodomy, Suicide, and the Limits of Legal Reform in Eighteenth-Century France

JEFFREY MERRICK

Foreign critics who described the French as a frivolous people could have cited two humorous treatments of serious subjects, sodomy and suicide, that provoked laughter in Paris in 1781. According to *Le Pot-pourri de Loth*, a comical and musical version of the story of Lot in the book of Genesis,

> In awakening one fine morning,
> The Almighty eyed Sodom
> And swore, with lightning in hand,
> To grill every last one of them,
> For in that place each wretch
> Enjoyed himself as in Berlin,
> And the rogues all took each other
> In the rear as in the front.
> And the rogues all took each other
> In the rear as in the front, from under as from over.[1]

The pleasures of Berlin in the sixth line refer to the "abnormal" sexual interests of Frederick the Great of Prussia, who did not share his days or nights, in the city or at Sans-Souci, with his wife.[2] The first plate in the French text shows the indignant Jehovah, with lightning in hand, ready to smite the Sodomites, including two men hugging and kissing in a classical archway. One of them has a hand around the other's erection, and they are framed by two male couples symmetrically engaged in anal intercourse.[3]

As for suicide, a Parisian shoemaker with a bossy wife, a frisky daughter, and a comely son busied himself with taking measurements and making deliveries, counting the money hidden in his room, and talking literature with his friends, who knew no more about it than he did. When he got home late one night, he found that his wife had run off with his foreman, that his daughter had been arrested for solicitation, that his son had enlisted in the army, and, worst of all, that his money had been stolen. Overwhelmed by these misfortunes, the shoemaker resolved to take his own life. He was about to cut his throat when he recalled that it was customary to leave behind an explanatory note. He put down his knife, took up his quill, and scrawled a few lines:

> Let no one be charged with my death. I myself have killed myself
> in a fit of the most righteous fury, yes, of the most righteous
> sorrow that any bourgeois de Paris has ever felt, for, as Molière
> puts it so well,
> When one has lost everything, when one is without hope,
> Life is a disgrace and death a duty.[4]

Molière, he wondered, or Jean Baptiste Rousseau? Worried about his posthumous reputation as a man of parts, he delayed his demise long enough to consult his literary friends, who attributed the verses to other poets. They gave themselves a week to investigate. During that week the shoemaker realized that his wife did him a favor by leaving him, that his daughter deserved her punishment, that his son had the honor of serving their king, and that he could replace the money he had saved and lost. So much for deadly despair.[5]

Humor aside, sodomy and suicide were not only serious subjects at this time but also criminal offenses that had been widely and loudly stigmatized for many centuries.[6] The revered Greeks and Romans embraced sex between men and endorsed self-destruction, though not without restriction and contention on both counts, but the church condemned and the state punished these marginal practices throughout early modern Europe. As the eighteenth century unfolded, however, both types of transgression seemed more prevalent and visible in major cities such as Paris. During the course of 1781, the police arrested dozens of "pederasts" (by this time they used classical rather than Biblical terminology to categorize males who desired males of any age) for prowling public places in search of sex.[7] They also documented the successful and unsuccessful efforts of dozens of men and women to end their lives by drowning, hanging, stabbing, shooting themselves, cutting their throats, or jumping to their deaths. Ten years later, the National Assembly decriminalized many religious, moral and sexual offenses, not by declaring them legal in so many words but by omitting them from the criminal code promulgated in 1791. The deputies meant to consign what they regarded as savage and useless punishments, such as burning sodomites at the stake and dragging suicides through the streets, to the bad old days. They did not mean to condone sodomy and suicide, any more than the philosophes and reformers whose reflections and rhetoric influenced them did.

Since French magistrates inflicted the statutory penalties only selectively and sporadically during the reign of Louis XV and almost never during the reign of Louis XVI, the routine critiques of the archaic penalties are less instructive than the lively debates about the transgressions themselves. This article analyzes assumptions and arguments about nature and culture in a variety of texts that discussed sodomy and suicide at some length and not just in passing. The sources include the notable treatises on jurisprudence by the more traditional Muyart de Vouglans and the less traditional Jousse, the *Encyclopédie* of Diderot and d'Alembert and the more voluminous *Encyclopédie méthodique*, classic titles by philosophes, and dissertations by lawyers and judges submitted to or at least inspired by the famous contests announced by the Société Economique de Berne in 1777 and the Académie de Châlons-sur-Marne in 1779.[8] The Société directed contestants to address the question of proportionality in crimes and punishments, and the Académie instructed them to explore the methods of reducing the severity, while enhancing the efficacy, of criminal penalties. The men of the law and men of letters who tackled the subject of legal reform exposed tensions in the program of the Enlightenment in their discussions of the two marginal practices that provoked the Almighty and tempted the shoemaker in 1781.[9]

To outline the train of thought that structures both sections of this article, defenders of traditional jurisprudence invoked Scripture and nature, as well as social utility, to condemn sinful individuals who committed sodomy and suicide. Most philosophes, such as Montesquieu, Voltaire, and Rousseau, ignored Scripture but embraced nature and censured sodomy more vehemently than suicide in its name. They specified social causes of both offenses, most notably sexual segregation and perennial poverty, and they criticized selfish individuals who shunned the common human obligations of procreation and community. Materialists such as Diderot, d'Holbach, and Naigeon, who espoused more radical opinions on many subjects, from religion to politics, challenged the normative conception of nature and the large claims about social utility advanced by their more moderate brethren. Most of the reformist lawyers and judges followed the mainstream and endorsed conventional moral standards. They accepted the social causes discussed by Montesquieu and others without suggesting any more practical solutions to the social problems than the philosophes themselves did. Controversialists of all stripes, across the spectrum from traditionalists to materialists, largely agreed about the barbarous penalties, which many of them denounced more stridently than they needed to, but not about the unnatural and antisocial, truly detestable or simply deplorable character of the transgressions. The legal issues resolved in 1791 were less difficult and contentious than the moral issues on the table before, during, and after the eighteenth century.

Sodomy and suicide provoked concern and conflict because they confirmed enduring anxieties about human misconduct and social disorder. Both offenses required and embodied personal agency in a time and place that did not accept modern notions of privacy and liberty, but some differences between the two offenses made some difference in attitudes toward and arguments about these marginalized practices. Sodomy involved more than one person, and sometimes seduction as well, but suicide, except for the rare double cases, did not.[10] A man could have sex with many men over many years, unless deterred from doing so through persuasion or punishment, but, setting aside bungled attempts, an individual could kill him or herself just once. Both crimes were voluntary and therefore punishable, unless the sexual relations involved coercion, which was not common, or the self-destruction involved derangement, which was not uncommon. Younger males corrupted by older males could be represented as victims, but so could desperate men and women driven, reprehensibly but comprehensibly, to take their own lives. Most commentators assumed that sex between men and self-destruction implied surrender to uncontrolled but not uncontrollable passions and therefore weakness of character, though some authors believed that some people who killed themselves displayed courage in doing so. Both offenses seemed unreasonable and irresponsible, but, in the end, violation of sexual taboos inspired more aversion and less sympathy than self-inflicted death.

The police regarded pederasts and suicides alike as dangerous examples for the Parisian populace, but they considered one type of deviance more contagious than the other. By the time of Louis XVI, they worried not about moral issues as such but about private conduct that threatened public order. While opponents and proponents of enlightenment wrangled over the boundaries between liberty and license, the police struggled to control or at least contain sex between men and self-destruction in the crowded urban setting. They discouraged publicity in order to discourage imitation, but they generated hundreds of reports about pederasts and suicides, which I have sampled in the archives and analyzed elsewhere.[11] My objective here is not to catalogue opinions from as many sources as possible but to study the ways in which representative philosophes and reformers rejected and recycled tradition, against the background of published disputes about the ancestral principles of the ancien régime and unpublished evidence of repressive practices during its last decades. I have not only compared discussions of two types of marginal practices that problematized agency but also juxtaposed learned debates with patterns of life and death in the streets of Paris as documented by the police. There was little resemblance between the pederasts they incarcerated, much less the suicides they investigated, and the types profiled in the controversial literature.

Sodomy

The traditional condemnation of sex between persons of the same sex, which Jousse labeled "the most abominable of all the lewd acts," was based on the exemplary devastation of Sodom recounted in Genesis, chapter 19 and the familiar restrictions on sexuality expounded in Leviticus, chapter 18.[12] Sodomy was wrong because God said so and showed that He meant it, with flames, which modeled the appropriate form of capital punishment for the crime. Sodomy was considered more offensive and penalized more severely than other types of sexual misconduct, according to Muyart de Vouglans, because it violated "the rules prescribed by nature for reproduction."[13] Nature intended males and females to mate and propagate, for the benefit of families as well as society, so she injected them with desire and rewarded them with pleasure. The magistrate Boucher d'Argis wondered:

> Can one imagine the madness of a contrary feeling? It exists, however, and it exists in different ways. It has perpetuated itself from age to age down to our time, and this idiotic and crude vice would inevitably bring about the annihilation of society as a whole if it were possible that its contagion became widespread.[14]

Without exploring and explaining issues about class and force, traditionalists noted that even the ancient Greeks and Romans criminalized sodomy in some cases. They assumed that the Biblical prohibition incorporated into Roman law and French law justified a long list of executions, including those of Deschauffours in 1726, Diot and Lenoir in 1750, Pascal in 1783.[15] "Can these examples not stop the most debauched men? Will they always affront the justice of heaven and earth with impunity?"[16] In posing these questions, abbé Meusy implied that human governments enforced or at least should enforce divine commandments. Muyart de Vouglans suggested, more awkwardly, that

> if the examples of punishment are not as common as the crime is, it can be said that it is less as a result of the negligence of the magistrates than as a result of the secret precautions those who fall into it have the habit of taking, to conceal knowledge of it from the public.[17]

By 1790, however, abbé Bergier acknowledged that the attitude of the magistrates toward sodomy had changed: "Unless the scandal is public, it is judged to be better to ignore it than to punish it."[18] Note the use of the passive voice. On the defensive, traditionalists had reason to worry about the future of Scriptural imperatives, but not, as it turned out, about the stigmatization of same-sex relations.

The philosophes, by and large, did not challenge what Montesquieu called "the horror that people have for a crime that religion, morality and politics condemn in turn," as if independently. He declared that "it would be necessary to outlaw it if it did nothing but give to one sex the weaknesses of the other and lead to a disreputable old age through a shameful youth."[19] Regardless of religious principles, in other words, sodomy deserved censure because it feminized and degraded males. It is not clear if this obscure forecast applied to "active" as well as "passive" partners, but it is significant that a philosophe gendered the issue in this way, in the name of personal and collective welfare, in order to condemn sex between men. Montesquieu explained the deviant behavior in the spirit of social science: "The crime against nature will never make great progress in a society if people are not otherwise led to it by some custom," such as exercise in the nude among the Greeks, segregated education among the French, and polygamy among the Asians.[20] Humans created institutions like gymnasia, schools, and seraglios, and humans could presumably restructure them to avoid the unintended consequences. Montesquieu declared: "Let nothing lead to this crime, let it be proscribed, like all transgressions against morals, through strict maintenance of order, and one will immediately see nature either defend her rights or recover them."[21] It is not clear what "maintenance of order" involved, in Montesquieu's mind, since he did not mention punishment, but he suggested that if culture did its part to resolve the problem, nature would somehow do the rest.

Voltaire exposed the tension between nature and culture more explicitly by asking: "[h]ow has it happened that a vice that would destroy the human race if it were widespread, that an infamous vice against nature, is nevertheless so natural?"[22] He did not mean to suggest that some men had a biological motivation or psychological disposition to seek sex with other men in the way that some women, according to ancient and modern lore, had an enlarged clitoris that enabled and encouraged them to seek sex with other women and usurp the "active" role in vaginal intercourse.[23] He meant that boys, raised and schooled separately from girls and not yet fully differentiated from them through secondary sex characteristics, naturally (read understandably) directed their natural (read inborn) instincts to available and desirable but unnatural (read inappropriate) objects.[24] Their confusion was both natural in the loose, descriptive sense of the word, and unnatural in the strict, prescriptive sense of the word, and culture was the culprit.

Montesquieu and Voltaire attributed sodomy not to human sinfulness that could not be remedied but to defective customs that could be corrected, though history suggested that sexual segregation would continue for a long time. They evidently assumed that the majority of males, after experiencing pleasure with other young males, outgrew this phase and turned to females, while a minority of corrupted males continued to seek sex with members of their own sex, which inspired horror and warranted infamy. In viewing sodomy as a social product, they did not relieve individuals of the responsibility for knowing and doing what morality and utility required of them. Montesquieu and Voltaire did not cite Scripture, but they agreed with traditionalists that nature wanted and society needed men, apparently all men, to have sex with women in order to replenish the population.[25] They defended pleasure, including sexual pleasure, in general, but when they addressed the subject of same-sex relations in particular, they restricted pleasure in the name of propriety and procreation. Even if sodomites married and produced children, sodomy remained unnatural as well as offensive and deserved to be denounced, though not punished, as in the past.

Materialists, who rejected the conception of providential order in the physical and human worlds, challenged traditional assumptions more aggressively.[26] Diderot identified natural, physiological as well as cultural, sociological causes for "the antiphysical taste" of American Indians but still identified it as a "depravation."[27] He also suggested, more boldly, that "everything that is cannot be either against nature or outside nature," inasmuch as nature itself enabled "combinations" that might seem "contrary to nature," and that chastity, which deprived the self of pleasure and the state of children, offended nature and society more than same-sex relations did.[28] Diderot's literary executor Naigeon claimed that "pederasty" was not detrimental to society or unnatural in any meaningful sense of the word.[29] Naigeon could not know and of course did not cite the remarkable essay (written around 1785 but not published until 1978) in which Jeremy Bentham systematically reviewed and dismissed all the traditional and philosophic justifications for stigmatizing and penalizing sex between men or women.[30]

Some of the reformist lawyers and judges used negative adjectives like degrading, hideous, horrible, indecent, infamous, odious, revolting, but others did not waste words in this way. Most accepted the philosophic explanation of the conduct and rejected the traditional retribution for the offense. In the spirit of Montesquieu and Voltaire, a self-styled freethinker declared that

> The legislator's constant concern should be to seek remedies for the evils resulting from conventions made by men contrary to the wish of nature. The bodies or classes of men for whom relations with women are forbidden or impossible are necessarily given over to these shameful disorders that make even extreme depravation blush.

Note the term, "necessarily." The men in question had natural instincts that they could not satisfy naturally because of the unnatural circumstances in which they found themselves. Relations with women were supposedly forbidden for the clergy and impossible for other categories of males such as students and soldiers. After they completed their studies and service, they sometimes retained "habits that destroy the sacred fire that enflames each sex for the other."[31] Short of ending sexual segregation in the schools and the army, what other reforms might rescue humans from experience that deformed some of them? The provincial magistrate Bernardi de Valernes suggested:

> Let marriages be facilitated, let the inhabitants of the provinces be prevented from going to bury themselves, along with morals, in huge capitals, let exorbitant wealth not be amassed in the hands of lazy and unmarried men, and one will soon see nature recover its rights.[32]

These lines, including more passive tenses and more wishful thinking, beg several questions: Facilitate marriage by giving young men and women subsidies so they could wed sooner rather than later? Limit immigration and thereby deprive Paris of workers? Compel bachelors to marry? Social causes led one to expect social answers, but the argument that society engendered sodomy did not lead to many if any practical solutions.

Reformers made vague suggestions not only about prevention but also about punishment. Some proposed less severe penalties (legal infamy, galleys, lifelong imprisonment), but more, like the philosophes, endorsed the notion that "crimes against morals should be punished largely if not wholly by public opinion."[33] A lawyer from Rouen, unrepresentative of enlightened opinion, not to mention public opinion, in his own time spelled out how attitudes might shift in the long run. Antoine Nicolas Servin did not dismiss God and nature, but he argued that sodomy did not offend God or nature any more than any other action in which humans used creation, as they did on a daily basis, in ways other than the Creator allegedly intended. Even if it did offend, it was for God and not humans to judge. Humans could condemn and punish only actions detrimental to public welfare in this world. Servin maintained that sodomy, masturbation, bestiality, and other pleasurable but non-procreative practices deprived society of nothing but potential progeny and, if the offenses became public issues, deserved nothing worse than fines. He concluded that the so-called "crime against nature" was "not within the jurisdiction of the judges unless scandal and corruption of the young are involved," in which case it was the scandal or corruption that warranted punishment, not the sexual behavior itself.[34]

That sentence summarizes the outlook of the police, who did not invoke Scripture or nature, not to mention antiquity or procreation, in the 1780s. Through surveillance and imprisonment, they attempted not to purge Paris of sin but to control indecency in public places and to protect minors from seduction and coercion. As the lawyer Peuchet noted, "[i]n the past pederasty was punished by death. Today it is only a matter handled by the police. This vice is regarded as a moral offense rather than an attack on public order."[35] The police did not acknowledge, in principle, that some humans naturally desired members of their own sex or that all humans had the right to seek pleasure as they pleased, as long as they did so discreetly. In practice, however, the police recognized that some men had a taste or inclination that made them different from other men, without feminizing them, a taste that could be easily acquired but not readily corrected, and they rarely tracked such men down behind closed doors.[36] Most philosophes and reformers condemned sodomy *tout court*, but the police made distinctions between sodomites who did and did not deserve punishment for the sake of deterrence. Given the nature and limits of the documents, it is impossible to generalize about popular attitudes, but it is noteworthy that Parisians complained, in a few cases, not about sodomy per se but about men who accosted or molested other males.

In the last analysis, the debates about sodomy in the last decades of the ancien régime were only tenuously connected with the reality of same-sex relations in the 1780s. The Parisian subculture included men from all walks of life, especially from the working classes, not just men culturally segregated from women, formerly or currently, for schooling or by status.

The documents contain more references to predatory teachers who seduced students than to sex among students, as portrayed by Montesquieu and Voltaire. A modest number of pederasts asserted that they had had a taste for men all their lives, but just as many reported that they had acquired the taste through experience. Some, especially older notables, were married. Some, especially younger workingmen, could not afford to marry. And some, more than in the past, were not inclined to marry. Many of them were involved in prostitution, and a few of them were involved in relationships. Philosophes and reformers, without access to the corpus of police reports, discussed fictional sodomites who defied nature and culture, not actual pederasts who enacted liberty without claiming it in so many words by seeking sex in the Tuileries, Palais Royal, and Champs-Elysées. The police knew these men by name, nickname, appearance, and reputation but nevertheless misrepresented them, insofar as they continued to describe same-sex relations in terms of victimization of younger by older males, despite abundant evidence of other patterns in their own records.

Suicide

According to the principles of the ancien régime, suicide, like sodomy, violated divine, natural, and statutory prohibitions. God commanded humans not to kill and provided them with an inherent and tenacious instinct for self-preservation, which supposedly inspired and required them to live as long as He and not they saw fit. Traditionalists regarded self-destruction, which some Greek and Roman philosophers condemned, as a form of cowardice and betrayal of family and society. They recognized that this foolish and selfish crime might tempt humans in distress and understood why it was punished in the most degrading and disgusting manner, for the sake of deterrence. French law deprived those who took their own lives of their good name, property, and burial in consecrated ground. It sentenced their bodies to be dragged through the street on a hurdle, hanged by the feet, and dumped in the refuse. Unless, of course, they were out of their minds, because of disease or despair, when they drowned, hanged, or shot themselves, which, as Jousse noted, "the relatives do not fail to claim in order to save the property of the deceased and the honor of the family."[37] Traditionalists did not berate magistrates for routinely assuming that the dead were non compos mentis when they killed themselves or for abandoning the rituals of exemplary retribution. They did attack the philosophes for leading French men and women astray on the subject of human happiness and liberty.

Despite the attacks, the philosophes did not explain suicide in simple terms or endorse it in general terms. Montesquieu described it as a product of custom, among the virtuous Romans, or illness, among the eccentric English, "who kill themselves without any imaginable reason that leads them to do so."[38] Rousseau had his forlorn Saint-Preux question both divine prohibition and social obligations and conclude that we may "free ourselves from life itself as soon as it is a burden for us, since it is up to us to do so and in doing so we do not offend God or men." Jean-Jacques also had the more temperate milord Edouard refute Saint-Preux's arguments, accuse him of weakness and advise him to make himself useful to his fellow creatures.[39] Even Diderot insisted that "[w]e are not in the world only for ourselves. We are closely connected with other men, our country, our relations, our family. Each requires of us certain duties that we cannot escape by choice."[40] Voltaire admired noble Romans like Cato, who sacrificed themselves for their country, and granted that his own contemporaries acted less nobly: "We others also kill ourselves, but it is when we have lost our money or in a rare fit of foolish passion for something that is not worth it." Humans had plenty of problems, financial, physical, and emotional, but reason should help them remember that problems passed and realize that most of them were not so serious after all:

> Why do we have fewer suicides in the country than in the cities? It is because in the fields it is only the body that suffers. In town, it is the mind. The ploughman does not have time to be melancholy. It is the idle who kill themselves. It is those folks who seem so fortunate to the populace.[41]

According to Voltaire, Parisians took their own lives because they imagined themselves miserable, not because they, unlike peasants, read "philosophical" books.

Most philosophes, in other words, agreed with their ideological adversaries that nature and culture condemned suicide as well as sodomy. They assumed that providence endowed humans with the capacity to recognize right and wrong by consulting conscience or learning through experience and education. Instinct led them to seek pleasure and avoid pain, to be sure, but they could not expect to maximize pleasure and minimize pain as they pleased without regard for their fellow creatures. Overindulgence in pleasure, as many learned the hard way, could be harmful to self, neighbors, and society as a whole. Reason advised restraint, and laws imposed restraint on all humans so they could enjoy pleasure without inflicting pain on others. What about internal suffering caused by illness and passions, as opposed to mistakes in the external calculus of pleasure and pain? If misery stifled the instinct for self-preservation and silenced the faculty of reason, which usually made death look less desirable and necessary than despair suggested, men and women who killed themselves deserved sympathy rather than posthumous punishment. The statutory penalties were useless both because they did not deter individuals who were not in their right minds and unjust because they impoverished the innocent families of those who took desperate measures to escape their problems.

Turning to the materialists, Diderot did not condone suicide, but d'Holbach did. He argued that humans had no unbreakable obligations to nature or society: "A nature that persists in making our existence unhappy orders us to leave it," and "a society that can or will not procure us any good loses all its rights over us." Embodied by nature, neglected by society, unhappy individuals killed themselves for reasons, demonstrable or imaginary, that seemed compelling to them in the circumstances in which they found themselves:

> It is a temperament soured by affliction, it is a bilious and melancholy constitution, it is a defect in the organization, it is a disturbance in the machine, it is necessity, and not reasoned speculations, that give birth in man to the intention of destroying himself.[42]

Diderot suggested that nature itself might incline humans to sodomy, and d'Holbach suggested that nature itself might incline humans to suicide inasmuch as nature constituted and organized human machinery. As for "reasoned speculations," downplayed by d'Holbach, Naigeon did not mention Bentham's subversive essay on pederasty, but he did translate David Hume's scandalous essay on suicide, withdrawn from publication in 1755 and published posthumously in 1783. Hume denied that self-destruction involved transgression of duties to God, society, and self. He famously insisted that "the life of man is of no greater importance to the universe than that of an oyster" and that humans had as much right to end their lives as they did "to build houses, cultivate the ground and sail upon the ocean. In all these actions we employ our powers of mind and body to produce some innovation in the course of nature."[43] For most philosophes, restrictive nature prescribed sociable conduct and provided humans with the instinct and reason they needed to live as long as they could and should. For d'Holbach and Hume, channeled by Naigeon, permissive nature, stripped of its normative powers and functions, made some humans more vulnerable to melancholy than others and gave all humans the liberty to rearrange matter, including their own matter, as they pleased.

Lawyers and judges, like philosophes, expressed a range of views about suicide and agreed only about the abolition of the statutory penalties. Some described it as a crime against religion and society, but others demurred. The lawyer Vasselin declared that

> [t]he man who destroys himself is no longer useful to society, but he does not injure it in any way. He does not disturb public tranquility. He does not offend morality, does not attack the property, security, or honor of his fellow citizens. Perhaps he displeases God, but he does not scandalize religion.[44]

Since self-inflicted deaths did not cause tangible and visible harm to the living, they could not justly be considered criminal misconduct on the part of the deceased. The provincial magistrate Malteste de Villey argued that if it was a crime to kill oneself, it was a less serious one than the idleness of beggars and of people who lived off investments ("a type of suicide, in relation to society") or the departure of emigrants who took valuable skills with them ("another type of suicide with regard to the body politic").[45] Why penalize one type of antisocial conduct so ferociously when humans ignored and renounced their conventional obligations to each other every day in many ways? In the end, according to Servin, only despotic governments, in which "every man is the property of the master," could logically regard self-destruction as a "serious offense" that should be singled out for punishment.[46] Whether they regarded such deaths as the result of weakness, which suggested personal accountability, or madness, which suggested "general impunity" for its victims, most reformers recognized that humans had more liberty in practice than they should have in principle.[47] Some allowed them more latitude to commit suicide than to commit sodomy.

Several lawyers and judges redirected the discussion from personal to collective responsibility more pointedly than the philosophes did and posited, with Brissot, a man of the law turned man of letters, that suicide should be "prevented and never punished."[48] According to the provincial magistrate Bernardi de Valernes, it is "one of those offenses that the legislator should seek to prevent as much as it is possible, by diffusing though every social sector all the happiness it is capable of, but which it is difficult to punish once it is committed." Humans had obligations to each other, to be sure, but society had equally important obligations to its members. Even if it could not ensure health and wealth for all of them, it should do what it could to reduce unhappiness for as many of them as possible. If suicides multiplied, "through unfortunate circumstances,"

> it would be a warning to those who govern that some part of the body politic is out of order, since several of its members scorn the general human attraction to life, to the point of tearing themselves from it through violence. But the legislator's wisdom, even in this case, consists in working back to source of the crime rather than punishing it through penalties.[49]

Doctors could treat the symptoms and causes of illness in the body formed by nature, and rulers should treat the symptoms and causes of illness in the body politic deformed by culture. Given the many possible causes of suicide, of course, it would take some doing to figure out what was wrong in order to figure out how to fix it. Some types of misery lent themselves to social treatment, but others did not. A benevolent legislator might do something about poverty in specific circumstances, but what about inequality more generally, not to mention heartbreak and ennui? Once again, discussion of the social origins of problematic conduct did not yield practical conclusions about social remedies for the problem.

Philosophes and reformers hoped that the innate instinct for self-preservation would prevent most if not all humans in despair from taking their own lives, but Parisians witnessed or at least thought they witnessed an epidemic of self-destruction in the last decades of the ancien régime. Police records document the attempted and completed suicides of hundreds of men and women from all walks of life, especially from the working classes. Only a modest number of them left explanatory notes, which did not, of course, tell the whole truth and nothing but the truth, so we must also rely on testimony from people who knew the departed and the survivors, as well as accounts in memoirs, nouvelles (collections of news and gossip), and journals. Although they no longer needed to do so, to ensure that the bodies were not subjected to posthumous punishment, relatives, neighbors, and friends deposed on the spot inevitably suggested that victims suffered from some type of malady or melancholy and were therefore not in their right minds. But even after witnesses and magistrates turned the non compos mentis exception into a standard assumption in such cases, "the public" continued to discuss moral and social as opposed to legal issues.

Many accounts mentioned mental distress, and a few mentioned the damaging influence of "philosophy," but hardly any invoked personal liberty in so many words. Most involved the mundane causes familiar to preceding and following generations of unhappy Parisians as well as philosophes and reformers: infirmity, poverty, conflict, and grief. Dejection and derangement preceding self-destruction did not preclude assigning other motives to the now deceased or judgment by the living. Contemporaries associated suicide with misery, not ancient heroics or modern idleness, and expressed sympathy for most of its victims except for profligates and criminals. Unlike controversialists, they focused on the personal tragedy rather than the theoretical legitimacy of self-inflicted death. They did not imagine diseased or distraught, destitute or desperate individuals brooding about social duties before reaching for the gun or heading for the Seine. The archival evidence suggests that ordinary men and women did not replay the learned debates about suicide, any more than sodomy, in their own minds and that they knew how to handle both of these marginal practices, when they needed to, in collaboration with the police, by complaining about sexual harassment to protect the young and invoking the insanity defense to protect the dead and their families.

Conclusions

In the course of the disputes about and between church and state that spanned the eighteenth century, the French monarchy and its magistrates effectively renounced responsibility for enforcing ecclesiastical standards of conduct.[50] Sodomy and suicide, whether they actually became more common, seemed more visible and less dangerous after 1750. The police arrested men who sought sex, especially with younger males, in public places and rescued individuals who jumped into the Seine, but the judges had no delusions about suppressing such misconduct through exemplary retribution. They did not enforce the statutes, not because they thought that social causes like sexual segregation and perennial poverty exonerated offenders but because they knew that the likelihood or spectacle of punishment would not prevent others from committing the same offenses and because they feared that publicity surrounding punishment might only persuade unsatisfied and dissatisfied Parisians that they had more options, sexual and terminal, available to them than they had been taught. The authorities could not eradicate the crimes, but they hoped, in vain of course, to obliterate the criminals from public awareness, by interning pederasts and interring suicides. Both set bad examples, with this important difference: suicides shocked, saddened, and mystified others, while pederasts not only offended but also corrupted others.

Some Parisians accosted by pederasts and most Parisians confronted with suicides expressed aversion, but they did not express outrage inspired by traditional Biblical prohibitions. The people and the police did not use religious language to describe and denounce the offenders. Philosophes and reformers ignored Scripture and invoked nature and society in their analyses of the issues. But the secularization of the offenses in the last decades of the ancien régime and the extenuation of the penalties, which antedated 1750, did not amount to wholesale liberalization of attitudes. Most philosophes and reformers considered sodomy unnatural because it diverted the natural instinct for sexual pleasure from its proper object and antisocial because it thwarted procreation. They likewise considered suicide unnatural because it stifled the natural instinct for self-preservation and antisocial because it ruptured the network of bonds that integrated humans into communities. With few exceptions, philosophes declared and reformers agreed that nature did not make men desire men or anyone desire death. They recognized that society deformed some males through separation from females and made life difficult for its less fortunate members, but most agreed that personal trumped collective responsibility for the conduct in question, especially sex between men. They hoped that self-control combined with social control, in the form of public opinion rather than public punishment, would prevent suicide, which inspired dismay, and sodomy, which inspired disgust. That sort of prejudice, along with the noisy attack on prejudice, is part of the lasting legacy of the enlightenment. The test cases of the marginal practices explored in this article suggest that we must look to the materialists, not the mainstream, for a descriptive, inclusive conception of nature that validates human diversity and personal liberty, if we want one, as opposed to a prescriptive, restrictive conception of nature that recycles tradition.

NOTES

1. *Le Pot-Pourri de Loth, orné de figures et de musique* (London, 1781), 3. All of the translations of French texts quoted in this article are my own. This work has been attributed to the notary Pierre Lalleman (Lallemand or Lallemant?), who died in 1811, as well as the playwright Antoine Alexandre Henri Poinsinet, although he died in 1769. The author, whoever he was, set the Lord's words to the old French song "Qu'en voulez-vous dire." The text includes the tunes.

2. At the behest of his father, Frederick the Great (1712–86) married Elisabeth Christine of Brunswick-Wölffenbüttel-Bevern (1715–97) in 1733. After he ascended the throne in 1740, they lived separately.

3. The illustrations were drafted by Antoine Borel (1743–1810) and engraved by François Roland Elluin (1745–1810). The one in question, a rare eighteenth-century French depiction of male same-sex relations, is accessible online.

4. The lines that he quoted come from François Marie Arouet de Voltaire (1694–1778), *Mérope* (1743), 2.7. A recruiting officer who had gambled away the funds entrusted to him for his work attended a performance of this play in Montpellier

in 1778. He took these lines to heart and later shot himself according to *Etrennes de Thalie aux amateurs des spectacles, ou Choix d'anecdotes et de bons mots des théâtres* (Brussels: Lefrancq, 1786), quoted in Louis Sallentin, *L'Improvisateur français*, 21 vols. (Paris: Goujon fils, 1804–6), 17.147. In principle, all property owners who inhabited the city for a year and a day and paid taxes there were entitled to the appellation and privileges of "bourgeois de Paris." In practice, however, this designation was generally applied to non-nobles who lived off their investments. The shoemaker enhanced his status by describing himself in this way.

    5. Louis François Mettra (1738–1805) et al., *Correspondance secrète, politique, et littéraire*, 18 vols. (London: John Adamson, 1787–90), 12: 201–3 (12 December 1781), reprinted in Guillaume Imbert de Boudeaux (1744–1803), *La Chronique scandaleuse, ou Mémoires pour servir à l'histoire des moeurs de la génération présente* (Paris, 1783), 217–9, and recycled in Louis Portelette, dit Louis Ponet, *M. Botte tout seul, ou Le Savetier bel esprit, vaudeville en un acte* (Paris: Fages, 1806). Ponet set the suicide note to the tune of "En quatre mots."

> Nicolas Botte, fifty years of age,
> Makes known the following facts
> To those present in the audience.
> No one should be accused
> Of my death, which I alone have caused.
> I feel so much sorrow that
> Surely no bourgeois de Paris has ever
> Suffered likewise under
> The cruel power of destiny.
> Friends, mourn the sad end
> Of an unhappy human.

    6. Surveys include Robert Aldrich, ed., *Gay Life and Culture: A World History* (London: Thames and Hudson, 2006), and Louis Crompton, *Homosexuality and Civilization* (Cambridge MA: Harvard Univ. Press, 2006); Georges Minois, *Histoire du suicide: Le Monde occidentale face à la mort volontaire* (Paris: Fayard, 1995), translated by Lydia Cochrane as *History of Suicide: Voluntary Death in the Western Culture* (Baltimore: Johns Hopkins Univ. Press, 2001); and Marzio Barbagli, *Congedarsi dal mondo: Il Suicidio in Occidente e Oriente* (Bologna: Il Mulino, 2009), translated by Lucinda Byatt as *Farewell to the World: A History of Suicide* (Cambridge: Polity Press, 2015). The most useful overviews of these subjects in eighteenth-century France are Maurice Lever, *Les Bûchers de Sodome: Histoire des "infâmes"* (Paris: Fayard, 1985), and Dominique Godineau, *S'abréger les jours: Le Suicide en France au XVIIIe siècle* (Paris: Armand Colin, 2012).

    7. Prostitutes frequented the same areas. See Erica Marie Bénabou, *La Prostitution et la police des moeurs au XVIIIe siècle* (Paris: Librairie Académique Perrin, 1987). Women did not seek women in public places, so police records, unfortunately, do not document same-sex relations between women.

    8. On such contests see Jeremy Caradonna, *The Enlightenment in Practice: Academic Prize Contests and Intellectual Culture in France, 1670–1794* (Ithaca: Cornell Univ. Press, 2012).

9. On tensions in and limits of Enlightenment, the works of Lester Crocker remain useful. *Age of Crisis: Man and World in Eighteenth-Century French Thought* (Baltimore: Johns Hopkins Univ. Press, 1959), and *Nature and Culture: Ethical Thought in the French Enlightenment* (Baltimore: Johns Hopkins Univ. Press, 1963).

10. In more than a few texts, "sodomy" includes masturbation, sex between persons of the same sex, and oral and anal sex between men and women. In this article "sodomy" generally means sex between men since most of the texts hardly mention sex between women.

11. I have studied all the extant papers of all the commissaires de police from 1725, 1750, 1770, and 1775 and researched these subjects in other archival sources as well. On sodomy see Jeffrey Merrick, "Sodomitical Inclinations in Early Eighteenth-Century Paris," *Eighteenth-Century Studies* 30 (1997): 289–95; "Commissioner Foucault, Inspector Noël, and the 'Pederasts' of Paris, 1780–3," *Journal of Social History* 32 (1998): 287–307; Sodomitical Scandals and Subcultures in the 1720s," *Men and Masculinities* 1 (1999): 373–92; "'Brutal Passion' and 'Depraved Taste:' The Case of Jacques François Pascal," in eds. Jeffrey Merrick and Michael Sibalis, *Homosexuality in French History and Culture* (New York: Haworth Press, 2001), 85–104; "'Nocturnal Birds' in the Champs-Elysées: Police and Pederasty in Pre-Revolutionary Paris," *GLQ: A Journal of Lesbian and Gay Studies* 8 (2002): 425–32; "Sodomites and Police in Paris, 1715," *Journal of Homosexuality* 42 (2002): 103–28; "Constructions of Sodomy in the Reign of Louis XVI," *Proceedings of the Annual Meeting of the Western Society for French History* 29 (2003): 263–70; "Chaussons in the Streets: Sodomy in Paris, 1666," *Journal of the History of Sexuality* 15 (2006): 167–203; "Patterns and Concepts in the Sodomitical Subculture of Eighteenth-Century Paris," *Journal of Social History* 50 (2016) forthcoming. On suicide, see Jeffrey Merrick, "Patterns and Prosecution of Suicide in Eighteenth-Century Paris," *Historical Reflections/Réflexions historiques* 16 (1989): 153, from which I have borrowed the story of the suicidal shoemaker; Jeffrey Merrick, "Suicide, Society, and History: The Case of Bourdeaux and Humain, 25 December 1773," *Studies on Voltaire and the Eighteenth Century* 8 (2000): 71–115; Jeffrey Merrick, "Le Suicide de Pidansat de Mairobert," *Dix-huitième siècle* 35 (2003): 331–40; Jeffrey Merrick, "Suicide in Paris, 1775," in ed. Jeffrey R. Watt, *From Sin to Insanity: Suicide in Early Modern Europe*, (Ithaca, 2004), 158–74; Jeffrey Merrick, "Suicide and Politics in Pre-Revolutionary France," *Eighteenth-Century Life* 30 (2006): 32–47; Jeffrey Merrick, "Death and Life in the Archives: Patterns of and Attitudes to Suicide in Eighteenth-Century Paris," in eds. David Wright and John Weaver, *Histories of Suicide: International Perspectives on Self-Destruction in the Modern World* (Toronto, 2009), 73–90; Jeffrey Merrick, "'It Is Better to Die': Abbé Rousseau and the Meanings of Suicide." *Historical Reflections/ Réflexions historiques* 42 (2016), forthcoming; "Rescued From the River: Attempted Suicide in Late Eighteenth-Century Paris." *Histoire sociale/Social History* 49 (2016), forthcoming.

12. Daniel Jousse (1704–81), magistrate in the bailliage, siège présidial, et châtelet d'Orléans, "De la sodomie," *Traité de la justice criminelle de France*, 4 vols. (Paris: Debure père, 1771), 4:118. On Jousse see *Daniel Jousse: Un Juriste au temps des Lumières (1704–1781)*, ed. Corinne Leveleux-Teixera (Limoges: Presses Univ. de

Limoges, 2007).

13. Pierre François Muyart de Vouglans (1713–81), lawyer, magistrate in the Conseil supérieur that replaced the Parlement of Paris from 1771 to 1774 and then in the Grand Conseil, "De la sodomie," *Les Lois criminelles de France dans leur ordre naturel, dédiées au roi* (Paris: Mérigot, Crapard, Benoît Morin, 1780), 243. On Muyart de Vouglans see André Langui, "Sentiments et opinions d'un jurisconsulte à la fin du XVIIIe siècle: Pierre François Muyart de Vouglans, 1713–1791," *Travaux judiciaires et économiques de l'Université de Rennes* 35 (1964): 177–274.

14. André Jean Baptiste Boucher d'Argis (1717–94), magistrate in the Châtelet, the royal court with jurisdiction over Paris, "Sodomie ou pédérastie," in *Encyclopédie méthodique: Jurisprudence*, 10 vols. (Paris: Panckoucke, 1782–91), 7: 614.

15. None of the sources noted that the second case, unlike the first and the third, did not involve minors or violence.

16. Nicolas Meusy (1734–72), vicar of the parish of Rupt in Franche Comté, "Des crimes contre nature," *Code de la religion et des moeurs, ou Recueil des principales ordonnances, depuis l'établissement de la monarchie française, concernant la religion et les moeurs*, 2 vols. (Paris: Humblot, 1770), 2: 579.

17. Pierre François Muyart de Vouglans, "De la sodomie," *Institutes au droit criminal, ou Principes généraux sur ces matières, suivant le droit civile, canonique, et la jurisprudence du royaume, avec un traité particulier des crimes* (Paris: Le Breton, 1757), 510.

18. Nicolas Sylvestre Bergier (1715–90), canon of Notre Dame de Paris, "Sodome, Sodomie," in *Encyclopédie méthodique: Théologie*, 3 vols. (Paris: Panckoucke, 1788–90), 3: 518. On Bergier, see Sylvianne Albertan-Coppola, *L'Abbé Nicolas Sylvestre Bergier (1718–90): Des Monts-Jura à Versailles, le parcours d'un apologiste au XVIIIe siècle* (Paris: Honoré Champion, 2010).

19. Fortunato Bartolomeo de Felice (1723–89), publisher, clarified this obscure passage by explaining that sodomy "accustoms males destined to be formed through vigorous and generous exercises to a lax life. As they advance in age, they can no longer make a profit from their bodies and are forced, in order to provide for themselves, to prostitute others and engage in other types of shameful traffic. I do not mention the pride and insolence inspired in young folks by the number of their admirers. Through flattery and shameful complaisance, the latter effeminize the souls along with the bodies of the former so thoroughly that, grown up and abandoned, they continue to cultivate the vices they contracted." "Pédérastie," *Encyclopédie, ou Dictionnaire raisonné universel des connaissances humaines*, 42 vols. (Yverdon, 1770–5), 32: 599.

20. For more on Greeks and Turks, see Jacques Peuchet (1758–1830), lawyer, "Prostitution," *Encyclopédie méthodique: Jurisprudence*, 10 vols. (Paris: Panckoucke, 1782–91), 10: 685–6.

21. Charles de Secondat, baron de Montesquieu (1689–1755), "Du crime contre nature," *De l'esprit des loix*, book 12, chapter 6. In the first edition, 2 vols. (Geneva: Barrillot et fils, 1748), 1:304–6.

22. François Marie Arouet de Voltaire, "Amour socratique," *Dictionnaire philosophique* (1764), *Oeuvres complètes*, ed. Louis Moland, 46 vols. (Paris: Hachette, 1876–90),16: 135.

23. See, for example, Samuel Auguste André David Tissot (1728–97), physician, "Suites de la masturbation chez les femmes," *L'Onanisme: Dissertation sur les maladies produites par la masturbation* (Lausanne: Antoine Chapuis, 1760), 50–3, and Jacques Peuchet, "Amour sapphique," *Encyclopédie méthodique: Jurisprudence*, 10 vols. (Paris: Panckoucke, 1782–91), 9: 320–1. Many sources did not even mention sex between women. Peuchet provides one of the most instructive discussions of "this vice. It is hidden, it is unknown and it is an illness of the imagination, caused by constraint, subjection, effervescence of the senses, rather than an actual disorder. It is common in cloisters and in some societies of women. It is up to religion, good society, natural love to destroy this inclination, much less unnatural than though just as odious as the analogous one among men."

24. For that reason "the interaction of the sexes is necessary to prevent dangerous deviations of instinct during the course of youth." Peuchet, "Prostitution," 686.

25. On this pervasive obsession see Carol Blum, *Strength in Numbers: Population and Power in Eighteenth-Century France* (Baltimore: Johns Hopkins Univ. Press, 2002).

26. The best overview of the diversity and complexity of eighteenth-century attitudes is Bryant T. Ragan, Jr., "The Enlightenment Confronts Homosexuality," in eds. Jeffrey Merrick and Bryant T. Ragan, Jr., *Homosexuality in Modern France* (New York: Oxford Univ. Press, 1996), 8–29.

27. Denis Diderot (1713–84), "Du goût antiphysique des américains," *Fragments échappées de la portefeuille d'un philosophe* (1772), *Oeuvres complètes*, eds. Jules Assézat and Maurice Tourneux, 20 vols. (Paris: Garnier Frères, 1875–7), 6: 452–3. On "antiphysical" and other terms see Claude Courouve, *Vocabulaire de l'homosexualité masculine* (Paris: Payot, 1985) or Jean Luc Hennig, *Espadons, mignons & autres monstres: Vocabulaire de l'homosexualité masculine sous l'ancien régime* (Paris: Cherche midi, 2014).

28. Diderot, *Le Rêve de d'Alembert* (1769), *Oeuvres complètes*, 2: 187.

29. Jacques André Naigeon (1738–1810), man of letters, "Académiciens, Philosophie des," in *Encyclopédie méthodique: Philosophie ancienne et moderne*, 3 vols. (Paris: Panckoucke, 1791–94), 1: 33–9.

30. Louis Crompton, "Jeremy Bentham's Essay on Paederasty," *Journal of Homosexuality* 3.3 (1978): 383–405 and 3.4 (1978): 91–107.

31. *Opuscules d'un free-thinker* (n.p., 1786), 75.

32. Joseph Elzéar Dominique de Bernardi de Valernes (1751–1834), magistrate in the parlement of Aix or Provence, *Les Moyens d'adoucir la rigueur des loix pénales en France, sans nuire à la sûreté publique*, in *Bibliothèque philosophique du législateur, du politique, du jurisconsulte*, ed. Jacques Pierre Brissot de Warville, 10 vols. (Berlin, 1782–5), 8: 110.

33. Jacques Pierre Brissot de Warville (1754–93), lawyer, *Théorie des lois criminelles* (Berlin, 1781), 239.

34. Antoine Nicolas Servin (1746–1811), lawyer, *De la législation criminelle, mémoire fini en 1778, envoyé à la Société Economique de Berne en 1779 et retiré du concours en janvier de l'année présente 1782* (Basel: Jean Schweighauser, 1782), 220.

35. Peuchet, "Prostitution," 687.

36. The evidence of sodomitical effeminacy is concentrated in police reports about assemblies of pederasts in the 1730s and 1740s. See Michel Rey, "Police et sodomie à Paris au XVIIIᵉ siècle: Du péché au désordre," *Revue d'histoire moderne et contemporaine* 29 (1982): 113–24. The multiplication of feminine nicknames by the 1780s suggests some diffusion of habits from these private assemblies throughout the public subculture.

37. Jousse, *Traité*, 3: 134.

38. Montesquieu, *De l'esprit des loix*, book 14, chapter 12. Montesquieu feminized sodomites but not suicides.

39. Jean-Jacques Rousseau (1712–78), *Julie, ou La Nouvelle Héloïse* (1761), book 3, letters 21 and 22. In eds. Bernard Gagnebin and Marcel Raymond, *Oeuvres complètes*, 5 vols. (Paris: Gallimard, 1959–95), vol. 2, 285.

40. Unsigned but usually attributed to Diderot, "Suicide," *Encyclopédie*, 15: 639.

41. Voltaire, "De Caton, du suicide," *Dictionnaire philosophique*, *Oeuvres complètes*, 17: 53, 55.

42. Paul Henri Thiry, baron d'Holbach (1723–89), *Système de la nature, ou Les loix du monde physique et du monde moral*, 2 vols. (London, 1770), 1: 303, 306.

43. Jacques André Naigeon, "Hume, Philosophie de," *Encyclopédie méthodique: Philosophie*, 2.2: 746 and 747, from paragraphs 9 and 18 in the first English edition of Hume's essay.

44. Georges Victor Vasselin (1767–1801), lawyer, *Théorie des peines capitales, ou Abus et dangers de la peine de mort et des tourmens, ouvrage présenté à l'Assemblée Nationale* (Paris: Gueffier, 1790), 56.

45. Jean Louis, marquis de Malteste de Villey (1709–85), magistrate in the parlement of Dijon or Burgundy, *Oeuvres diverses d'un ancien magistrat* (London, 1784), 282. The argument about emigration, developed more fully by Servin, comes from Cesare Beccaria (1738–94), *Dei deletti e delle pene* (1764), chapter 35. None of the reformers cited Beccaria, chapter 36, on sodomy. On his influence see most recently *Cesare Beccaria, la controverse pénale, XVIIIᵉ–XXIᵉ siècle*, ed. Michel Porret et Elisabeth Salvi (Rennes: Presses Univ. de Rennes, 2015).

46. Servin, *De la législation criminelle*, 273.

47. Charles Eléanor Dufriche de Valazé (1751–93), lawyer, *Loix pénales, dédiés à Monsieur, frère du Roi* (Alençon: Malassis le jeune, 1784), 181. When he appeared before the Revolutionary Tribunal along with the other Girondins on 30 October 1793, Dufriche de Valazé committed suicide by stabbing himself.

48. Brissot de Warville, *Théorie*, 323.

49. Bernardi de Valernes, *Moyens*, 109–10.

50. Jeffrey Merrick, *The Desacralization of the French Monarchy in the Eighteenth Century* (Baton Rouge: Louisiana State Univ. Press, 1990).

A *Laissez-Faire* Encyclopedia?
A Comparative View of Diderot
as Editor of the *Encyclopédie*

JEFF LOVELAND

The goal of this article is to evaluate Denis Diderot's work not as the leading contributor to the *Encyclopédie* (1751–72) but as its editor. Such evaluations have been made regularly in studies of Diderot and the *Encyclopédie*, but they are often made in passing and outside of any relevant comparative framework. Here, building on previous research, I will compare Diderot to other seventeenth- and eighteenth-century editors of encyclopedias as well as to later ones. I will begin by reviewing the duties of an encyclopedia's editor in Diderot's time and then examine his work in three different areas: planning; recruiting and managing collaborators; and revising submitted texts to impose homogeneity. In the course of the nineteenth century, these duties were gradually recognized as central responsibilities of an encyclopedia's editorial staff, but in Diderot's time, a more important duty for an encyclopedia's intellectual director was typically to contribute articles. This is the basis on which Diderot's work for the *Encyclopédie* is usually judged. Without disparaging his contribution as a researcher, a thinker, and a writer of articles, I argue here that his work as an editor deserves attention as well. Nor is my attention to his editorship in the sense defined above wholly anachronistic. Diderot mentioned all three of the editorial duties examined in this article as desirable in an editor, and each was performed by at least some editors of contemporary encyclopedias. Although a retrospectively established list of editorial duties carries the

205

risk of anachronism, it helps capture the historical specificity of Diderot and the *Encyclopédie*. In particular, I will show that Diderot's editing of the *Encyclopédie*, while in some ways unremarkable for the editor of an encyclopedia, was in other ways unusual, and that these were connected with the distinctiveness of the *Encyclopédie* relative to other encyclopedias.

The Duties of Encyclopedias' Editors in Diderot's Time

The word "editor" and its equivalents in other languages were not much applied to editors of encyclopedias before 1800. Exceptionally, in records maintained by the *Encyclopédie*'s publishers and in the *Encyclopédie* itself, the co-editors Diderot and Jean Le Rond D'Alembert were frequently referred to as "éditeurs," as was their predecessor in the position, Jean-Paul De Gua de Malves.[1] At times, however, they were referred to in other ways, occasionally with alternative nominal forms such as "chefs de l'*Encyclopédie*",[2] but more often with verbal forms indicating their responsibilities. On the title page, for example, the *Encyclopédie* was said to be "mis en ordre et publié par M. Diderot ... et quant à la partie mathématique, par M. D'Alembert."[3] Meanwhile, the intellectual directors of other encyclopedias were more frequently characterized as authors, revisers, or compilers than as editors, though they were usually also identified with verbs specifying their functions. Taking this logic to an extreme, the title page of the final edition (1727) of Antoine Furetière's *Dictionnaire universel* (1690) announced that the work had been "recueilli et compilé premièrement" by Furetière, "corrigé et augmenté" by Henri Basnage de Beauval, and "revu, corrigé, et considérablement augmenté" by Jean-Baptiste Brutel de La Rivière.[4] As in the case of the *Encyclopédie*, the century's preference for such verbal identifications suggests that the concept of editorship had not yet solidified in the context of encyclopedias.

In any event, the term "editor" had different meanings in the eighteenth century from the ones that it has now. Consider the definition proposed by Diderot in his article "Éditeur" in the *Encyclopédie*: "On donne ce nom à un homme de lettres qui veut bien prendre le soin de publier les ouvrages d'un autre."[5] By this definition, Diderot and D'Alembert were indeed editors, at least early on, entrusted as they were with preparing an enlarged version of Ephraim Chambers' *Cyclopaedia* (1728) for the French public. Still, if they or their publishers had realized from the start how far the *Encyclopédie* would stray from being a mere translation or adaptation of the *Cyclopaedia*, they might have assumed a title other than "éditeur."

In "Éditeur," Diderot distinguished himself from a normal editor in another respect. Specifically, he saw an editor as laboring alone on the works of someone else, whereas the collaborative nature of the *Encyclopédie* limited his ability to take responsibility for it:

> Il y a tel ouvrage dont l'édition suppose plus de connaissances qu'il n'est donné à un seul homme d'en posséder. L'*Encyclopédie* est singulièrement de ce nombre. Il semble qu'il faudrait pour sa perfection, que chacun fût *éditeur* de ses articles; mais ce moyen entraînerait trop de dépenses et de lenteur. Comme les *éditeurs* de l›*Encyclopédie* ne s'arrogent aucune sorte d'autorité sur les productions de leurs collègues, il serait aussi mal de les blâmer de ce qu'on y pourra remarquer de faible, que de les louer de ce qu'on y trouvera d'excellent.[6]

Ironically, the modern notion of editorship is closely linked with collaborative authorship, though an older sense remains of a person responsible for a critical edition.

Bypassing the word "editor," we can learn about editorship through the history of the people responsible for the literary preparation of encyclopedias, regardless of how they were designated by contemporaries. Before the mid-eighteenth century, European encyclopedias tended to be credited to single authors, though they were inevitably collaborative to a degree, whether through the help of "invisible technicians" such as secretaries or assistants or through their borrowing from others' texts.[7] The idea of an encyclopedia produced collaboratively by specialized scholars was set forth as early as the late seventeenth century, but it was slow to be realized.[8] Johann Heinrich Zedler's *Grosses vollständiges Universal-Lexicon aller Wissenschaften und Künste* (1732–50) has been plausibly suggested as the first encyclopedia to have numerous contributors, but we know of only a handful. Zedler himself claimed to have relied on the services of just nine anonymous, specialized "muses."[9]

As a result of the slow transition toward collaborative encyclopedia-writing, the modern concept of editorship did not manifest itself in encyclopedias until the second half of the eighteenth century. Even in the case of the substantially collaborative encyclopedias that began to be published after 1750, the tasks of recruiting collaborators and revising their contributions were seen as secondary among the duties of the work's intellectual leader, a person usually figuring among its main contributors. The publishers who undertook the *Encyclopédie* originally named De Gua editor, for example, but they left him the option of finding collaborators or producing the encyclopedia himself.[10] Diderot and D'Alembert, the subsequent editors, wrote thousands of articles alongside the many more they solicited from others. A few decades later, William Smellie compiled the first edition (1771) of the *Encyclopaedia Britannica* almost single-handedly, but he was nonetheless labeled its "editor" on his tombstone around 1795, perhaps because by that date the *Encyclopaedia Britannica* was being directed by authors who called themselves editors and who saw recruiting specialists as a significant part of their job.[11] Further complicating the situation, eighteenth- and nineteenth-century publishers sometimes took on roles that we now assign to editors. Zedler, for example, apparently picked the contributors to his *Grosses vollständiges Universal-Lexicon*, though he later appointed Carl Günther Ludovici to assume the "directorship" ("Direction") of volumes 19 and up.[12] Similarly, Charles-Joseph Panckoucke, the publisher of the *Encyclopédie méthodique* (1782–1832), became a kind of editor, defining the encyclopedia's organization, writing the preface, and recruiting contributors to handle the volumes on particular subjects.[13]

During the nineteenth century, editors of encyclopedias gradually distanced themselves from the composition of articles and devoted more attention to managing collaborators and their contributions. At the same time, the functions of editing began to be separated and placed in a hierarchy as "general," "managing," and "senior" editors came to direct more specialized ones. Both Zedler and Panckoucke acted as managing editors to a degree, leaving the more textual side of editing to their subordinates. The process was more explicit in the development of the variously titled encyclopedias, or "Konversations-Lexika," published by Brockhaus. After recruiting authors for the second edition (1812–19) himself, the company's founder, Friedrich Arnold Brockhaus, appointed a second editor in 1812 and became the chief editor. Then for the fifth edition (1819–20), he relied on a team of specialized sub-editors as well.[14] Although Brockhaus remained more involved with contributors and their entries than many later senior editors, he prefigured the latter in directing a structured, hierarchical editorial team.[15]

By the end of the twentieth century, the editors responsible for putting out an encyclopedia were myriad. Not atypically, the opening pages of a 1997 edition of *Collier's Encyclopedia* (1949) enumerated thirteen members of the "editorial staff" and divided them up into seven kinds of editors.[16] Here, without engaging in such minute segmentation of the concept of editorship, I will study three aspects of Diderot's work as editor: planning; recruiting and managing contributors; and revising texts to impose homogeneity. In modern terms, these tasks might be assigned to a senior editor, a specialized sub-editor, and a copy editor. To a degree, my attention to these tasks is determined by hindsight: it derives from extrapolation backward, to the eighteenth century, of ideas that took definite form in the early nineteenth century. Yet as we shall see, planning, recruiting, and revising were all seen as essential duties for the editor of an encyclopedia by at least some of Diderot's contemporaries.

Diderot as Editor: Planning the *Encyclopédie*

It is not clear what planning Diderot and D'Alembert did for the *Encyclopédie* once they became co-editors in 1747. The most revealing documents that we have in this regard are Diderot's prospectus, published in 1750 but dated 1751, and D'Alembert's "Discours préliminaire des éditeurs." Both documents were meant as advertisements and thus cannot be taken as simple records of planning, but they do supply information about what the editors had in mind. In particular, Diderot's prospectus indicates that a year before publication started, certain features of the final work were already planned: its emphasis on technology, its visual appeal through numerous illustrations, its inclusion of articles of widely varying lengths, and its dependence on a large team of distinguished specialists, their contributions to be free from meddling by the editors.[17] The prospectus may also have hinted at the work's subversive agenda, namely in announcing that it would destroy errors and prejudice.[18] Perhaps, too, the placement of religion next to divination and black magic in the attached tree of knowledge, the "Système figuré des connaissances humaines," boded an anti-religious outlook, as Robert Darnton has argued.[19] Still, Diderot clearly identified these practices as abuses of religion, and even the work's critics seem to have been little concerned with this detail from the "Système figuré."[20] In short, if the famous radicalism of the *Encyclopédie* was planned from the start, the editors muffled their intentions in both the prospectus and the "Discours préliminaire."

Conversely, Diderot and D'Alembert appear to have planned poorly in other ways. In 1750, above all, Diderot announced a much shorter encyclopedia (specifically, an encyclopedia of ten or eleven volumes) than the one ultimately published.[21] In part, this early under-estimate for the size of the *Encyclopédie* may have been deliberate, an attempt to enroll more subscribers, but it surely also reflected casual planning and a tendency to let the encyclopedia grow by itself.

More seriously, Diderot and D'Alembert's plans for creating systematic order in the alphabetical *Encyclopédie* were unrealistic. In his prospectus, Diderot argued that the "Système figuré" provided a key to the order of the *Encyclopédie* and that this order would be reinforced by cross-references and the organization of articles.[22] D'Alembert went further in the "Discours préliminaire," claiming that systematic coherence was guaranteed by cross-references, the visual overview of the "Système figuré," and parenthetical rubrics in articles ("Géog.," "Hist. nat.," "Marine," and so on) referring to disciplines in the "Système figuré"[23] Alarmingly, D'Alembert admitted that cross-references and rubrics might be missing from some articles, in which case he advised the reader to imagine what they ought to be. In the end, the claim that cross-references and rubrics would create systematic coherence was in conflict with Diderot's policy of declining to tinker with contributors' submissions. As we shall see, the editors' failure to enforce a uniform approach to cross-references or to establish a correspondence between rubrics and the tree of knowledge undermined their goal of making the encyclopedia systematic as well as alphabetical.

In Diderot and D'Alembert's favor, we should remember that they became editors too late to participate in the earliest planning, which fell to the publishers and the first editor, De Gua. In particular, the latter wrote a set of guidelines for potential contributors to the *Encyclopédie* around 1746.[24] Here, among other things, he stressed the importance of imposing homogeneity across different contributors' articles, a policy exactly opposite that of Diderot and D'Alembert. At the same time, he anticipated their plans in insisting on teamwork on the part of specialized contributors and on outdoing the *Cyclopaedia* in coverage of the mechanical arts. Nothing indicates, unfortunately, what Diderot and D'Alembert thought of De Gua's plan or if they were aware of it.[25] In any event, Diderot viewed De Gua's organizational work in a negative light, citing it as an excuse for the imperfection of the *Encyclopédie*: "L'ouvrage auquel nous travaillons, n'est point de notre choix: Nous n'avons point ordonné les premiers matériaux qu'on nous a remis, et on nous les a, pour ainsi dire, jetés dans une confusion bien capable de rebuter quiconque aurait eu ou moins d'honnêteté, ou moins de courage."[26]

In other respects, Diderot's problems with planning were those of the period. When large encyclopedias were issued piecemeal over many years, changes of planning were almost inevitable. As a result, the largest encyclopedias of the period were uneven in content. The *Grosses vollständiges Univeral-Lexicon* changed drastically in volume 19, for example. Henceforth it offered biographies of living persons, divided long articles into sub-sections, and featured submissions from the public at large.[27] Likewise, Johann Georg Krünitz announced his *Oeconomische Encyclopädie* (1773–1858) as an improved translation of a Francophone Swiss version of Noël Chomel's *Dictionnaire oeconomique* (1709), but three volumes in, he abruptly changed course, declaring that the encyclopedia would from then on be original.[28] So too the *Encyclopédie* evolved over time. Early on, like the *Cyclopaedia*, it was supposed to be a dictionary of specialized terms, but it later became a dictionary of ordinary language as well, thereby encroaching on the territory of lexical dictionaries like the *Dictionnaire de l'Académie française* (1694).[29] Early on, it covered plants in accordance with Joseph Pitton de Tournefort's botanical system, but it later interjected significant coverage of Carl Linnaeus's competing system.[30] Similar examples of volume-to-volume evolution are not hard to find.

Even encyclopedias published all at once were not immune to such inconsistencies. The 1708 edition of Furetière's *Dictionnaire* was advertised by the publisher as completely revised, but only the first volume had in fact been revised, whereas the others were reprinted from 1701.[31] Still, as the publisher Friedrich Arnold Brockhaus and his assisting editor Ludwig Hain observed in the early nineteenth century, overall consistency was likely to be better in an encyclopedia that was finished quickly.[32]

Diderot as Editor: Recruiting and Managing Contributors

Diderot was neither the first nor the ablest recruiter for the *Encyclopédie*. De Gua, his predecessor as editor, recruited a few contributors, notably the anatomist Pierre Tarin. He apparently hoped to recruit more, but his eccentricity and tempestuousness probably limited his effectiveness in this regard.[33] By contrast, D'Alembert—a more renowned and more sociable figure in the Académie Royale des Sciences—proved adept at recruiting contributors once he and Diderot took over as editors in 1747. Not only did he win over colleagues from the scientific community, but he also managed to persuade Charles-Louis de Montesquieu and Voltaire to join the project. Diderot, for his part, had been turned down by Voltaire four years before. More generally, with less intellectual and institutional prestige, Diderot had little chance of matching D'Alembert's success in recruiting, but he was nonetheless successful. Among his best-known recruits were his friends Jean-Jacques Rousseau and Frédéric Melchior Grimm. Especially after D'Alembert's resignation and the government's condemnation of the *Encyclopédie* in 1759, Diderot was willing to consider almost anyone with talent or knowledge. For example, he enlisted his landlord—a sometime engineer—and a Polish harpist passing through Paris.[34]

Compared to other editors of collaborative encyclopedias, Diderot recruited collaborators at least as effectively as might be expected. Editors of a few earlier encyclopedias, notably Vincenzo Coronelli's *Biblioteca universale* (1701–06) and the *Grosses völlstandges Universal-Lexicon*, had invited the public at large to submit contributions, at least in the fields of geography and biography. This novel strategy, untried by Diderot, apparently paid off, leading to an increase in contributions and coverage.[35] Preparing the first edition of the *Encyclopaedia Britannica* in Edinburgh in the 1760s, Smellie recruited just a handful of the city's famed intellectuals, perhaps out of diffidence due to his low social standing, perhaps because his publishers had no funds for honoraria.[36] By the late eighteenth century, collaboration had broadened on the *Encyclopaedia Britannica*, though the two or three successive editors of the third edition (1797) together recruited only thirty-five known contributors.[37] In the German states, the first *Deutsche Encyclopädie* (1778–1807) boasted more than sixty contributors, but most of them had a connection with the University of Giessen.[38] Neither Diderot nor D'Alembert had restricted their recruitment to such an extent.

As a manager of contributors, Diderot performed well despite a few flaws. In general, his affability, energy, and seductive intellect won him respect and loyalty from those with whom he worked. He sometimes offered contributors ideas for making articles better, but, in keeping with his policy of editorial non-intervention, he rarely dictated changes.[39] Still, contributors occasionally had grounds for complaint. Rousseau judged him forgetful or negligent regarding compensation. On occasion, moreover, Diderot allowed third parties to alter solicited contributions without securing the approval of their original authors. After convincing the scholar Charles de Brosses to submit a manuscript on the evolution of language, Diderot gave it to others to use in their own articles. De Brosses was annoyed, having assumed that it would appear under his own name and as submitted. Similarly, Diderot let Louis de Jaucourt use an article submitted by the sculptor Étienne-Maurice Falconet, though Falconet blamed Jaucourt rather than Diderot.[40]

In having these authors' work changed, and in considering it communal property, Diderot was violating his policy against editorial meddling, but his actions were unexceptional in the history of encyclopedias. Fortuné-Barthélemy de Félice, the editor of a revised version (1770–80) of the *Encyclopédie* published in the Swiss city of Yverdon, had his contributors sign contracts recognizing his authority to alter submissions. He did not even consult them about changes he made, and he bragged that he revised articles by contributors as prestigious as the astronomer Joseph-Jérôme de Lalande.[41] Likewise, in the early nineteenth century, Brockhaus had editors alter submitted contributions in any way necessary to ensure that the contents of the "Konversations-Lexicon" were uniform and harmonious, but this policy, like Félice's, was a matter of public knowledge, just as it was for the numerous nineteenth-century encyclopedias imitating the "Konversations-

Lexikon." By contrast, Diderot's disrespectful treatment of texts by de Brosses, Falconet, and at least two other contributors ran against his stated policy and took place in secret.[42] It was also hypocritical on the part of an editor who later lamented the printer's censoring of his own articles as "an atrocity unparalleled in the history of the book trade."[43]

Diderot as Editor: Revising Submitted Texts and Imposing Homogeneity

Writing in 1820, Brockhaus and Ludwig Hain attempted to define the division of labor in editing their "Konversations-Lexikon," then in its fifth edition. Whereas Brockhaus's editorial duties were mostly managerial, Hain was responsible for, among other things, revising submitted articles and putting in cross-references to create a kind of harmony within the encyclopedia.[44] From at least this period onward, revising and homogenizing articles were regularly counted among the duties of an encyclopedia's editorial team, though they were eventually assigned to subaltern editors.[45] No doubt many nineteenth-century encyclopedias continued to fall short of Brockhaus's ideal of harmony or homogeneity.[46] Above all, Pierre Larousse's *Grand Dictionnaire universel du XIXe siècle* (1866–76) was famously sprinkled with odd bits of whimsy and subjective playfulness. This work, however, was soon challenged by the more consistently objective *Grande Encyclopédie* (1885–1902) and ultimately all but replaced within the Larousse firm by the homogeneous and serious *Nouveau Larousse illustré* (1897–1904).[47]

Was the duty of imposing homogeneity seen as relevant to editors of encyclopedias in Diderot's time? It is difficult to generalize insofar as the modern encyclopedia was just taking shape, along with its personnel, but some people thought so. In 1686, for example, the scholar Samuel Chappuzeau argued that a single person—in fact, he himself—should write the supplement to Louis Moréri's *Grand Dictionnaire historique* (1674) to maintain "uniformité du style."[48] Similarly, in the preface to his revised editions (1701, 1708) of Furetière's *Dictionnaire*, Basnage apologized for leaving transitional "scars" within certain articles and for not, overall, imposing more homogeneity: "J'aurois bien voulu qu'il y eût plus d'uniformité."[49] Likewise, evidently paying himself a compliment, Chambers wrote that in its second edition (1738) his *Cyclopaedia* had been "rendered more uniform, its parts in many places better disposed, as well as more conformable to each other, and the references reformed throughout."[50]

More telling than such statements of editorial purpose are editorial practices. Let us look at how the *Encyclopédie* was edited relative to other encyclopedias in this respect. Editing, in this sense, was not Diderot's task alone. At the start of project, D'Alembert seems to have helped, as indicated by the references to proofs and errata in one of his letters from 1751: "J'ai pourtant assez d'ouvrage: quatre épreuves à corriger, un avertissement à achever, l'errata du second volume à composer."[51] Already at the time of Diderot's imprisonment in 1749, however, D'Alembert and the publishers evidently saw Diderot as the main editor, the one paid to endure "dix ans à l'ennui de 7 à 8 in-folio," as D'Alembert saw the task.[52] After D'Alembert's resignation as co-editor in 1758, Jaucourt assumed a greater role in the production of the *Encyclopédie*, so much so that some scholars have identified him as a virtual second editor alongside Diderot. Still, little evidence has emerged to support claims for Jaucourt's editorial involvement with anything other than his own seventeen thousand articles.[53] Diderot almost certainly began and ended the project as the person most responsible for coordinating the various articles in the *Encyclopédie*.

To what extent, then, did Diderot coordinate them? As Richard Schwab, Walter Rex, and John Lough have pointed out, the *Encyclopédie* is characterized by considerable formal inconsistency, notably in its manner of indicating articles versus sub-articles, in its application of disciplinary rubrics to articles, and in its means of attributing articles to authors.[54] The fact that disciplinary rubrics varied most at the start of volume 1 is perhaps more a sign of a failure in planning than of failures in editing. Yet even if the *Encyclopédie* became more standardized, articles were apparently never subjected to much editorial revision. As the following paragraphs show, this generalization holds for formal aspects of articles—rubrics, signatures, and cross-references—as well as for their literary and stylistic properties.

Disciplinary rubrics may have become less inconsistent after the opening pages of volume 1, but they remained inconsistent. In theory, by means of such rubrics, each entry was to situate its subject within one or more disciplines in the "Système figuré." True to D'Alembert's warning in the "Discours préliminaire," however, thousands of entries lacked any rubric. More seriously, rubrics were presented in different ways. The first one in the *Encyclopédie*, in the article "A," was extremely explicit, charting an itinerary from the trunk of the tree of knowledge through branches corresponding to the science of man, logic, the art of communication, and, finally, grammar.[55] By contrast, almost all subsequent rubrics were limited to identifying the branch of the tree of knowledge nearest the entry, albeit using different typographical and grammatical conventions, different abbreviations, and different degrees of specificity relative to disciplines in the tree of knowledge. The discipline of history in particular was often presented in rubrics with highly specific modifiers, as in "history of the popes" or "Roman history."[56] The same is true of law, where Luigi Deglia has identified forty different rubrics. Most of them were used just a handful of times.[57] Alternatively, rubrics sometimes varied dramatically within the same field of knowledge. Whereas most entries on plants were tagged as belonging to natural history as well as perhaps botany, for instance, many were tagged as belonging to botany alone, a faraway branch in the tree of knowledge.[58] Finally, a significant number of rubrics did not match any science in the tree of knowledge, including many of the rubrics chosen by Jaucourt.[59] Evidently, Diderot made little if any effort to impose uniformity on rubrics or to supply them when lacking.

Other French dictionaries and encyclopedias used similar rubrics to indicate articles' disciplinary affiliations among other things, but few of them had trees of knowledge to which the rubrics were supposed to correspond.[60] Still, Chambers' *Cyclopaedia*, the other eighteenth-century encyclopedia famous for its division of knowledge, encountered similar problems, albeit on a smaller scale, undoubtedly because Chambers worked mostly alone. Hundreds of keywords in the *Cyclopaedia* were tagged as being terms of "antiquities," for example. Not only, however, was the subject of antiquities not listed in the preface among the forty-seven arts and sciences to be covered, but Chambers asserted there that it was not even a "subordinate art," merely a collection of "numerous remote particulars."[61]

The *Encyclopédie* was the first collaborative encyclopedia to feature indications of authorship within its articles. The front matter of volume 1 included a list of contributors along with the letters by which they were to be identified at the ends of their articles, so that D'Alembert, for example, was to sign with an "O." From the beginning, however, certain contributors signed articles with surnames instead of letters, a discrepancy that persisted in varying proportions throughout the series. Initially, Diderot announced that unsigned articles should be credited to him as an "author," whereas articles beginning with an asterisk should be credited to him as an "editor." In practice, the distinction proved murky. Soon articles by other authors were also appearing without signatures, whether through negligence or a desire to remain anonymous, and Diderot abandoned the asterisk after volume 10.[62] All told, combined with uncertainty about the limits of articles and sub-articles, the *Encyclopédie*'s system of signatures turned out to be less precise than might be expected.

Still, compared with other contemporary encyclopedias, the *Encyclopédie* was a model of precision in its identification of contributors. Zedler, for example, promised that the names of contributors to his *Grosses vollständiges*

Universal-Lexicon would someday be published, but they were not.[63] In Britain, collaborative encyclopedias tended to acknowledge contributors on title pages or in prefaces, but usually without listing their contributions in detail. Likewise, in the early nineteenth century, Brockhaus identified a minority of contributors with symbols at the ends of articles, but valuing the appearance of anonymity as a guarantee of objectivity, the company quit publicizing the key to its signatures and gradually dropped them.[64] Finally, after decades of identifying contributors vaguely in prefaces, the planners of the *Encyclopaedia Britannica* turned to the model of the *Encyclopédie* with the *Supplement to the Fourth, Fifth, and Sixth Editions* (1815–24). So too did many other encyclopedias in the following centuries. The editor of the *Supplement* noted the added editorial labor of providing attributions in an encyclopedia's articles and offered due praise for the editors of the *Encyclopédie*: "The plan of announcing the names of contributors, in connection with their respective articles, was first adopted, and was pretty extensively followed in the French *Encyclopédie*."[65]

Cross-references in the *Encyclopédie* have an exalted reputation, namely for being both systematic and frequently subversive. This reputation derives from programmatic statements by the editors—in the prospectus, the "Discours préliminaire," and especially Diderot's article "Encyclopédie"— as well as the tendency to reduce the *Encyclopédie* to a minimal repertory of appealing extracts centered on the values of enlightenment.[66] This is not the place for a detailed rebuttal of the notion that the *Encyclopédie* is filled with subversive cross-references. Suffice it to note that historians and anthologies continually return to a small number of examples. Ironically, at least one of the most famous examples is misleading. It is true that the article "Anthropophages" refers to "Eucharistie" after evoking pagans' misinterpretation of the Eucharist as cannibalistic. At first glance, the cross-reference might appear to be a subversive critique of Catholicism appended onto an otherwise orthodox article. Unfortunately for the clarity of this interpretation, the article was copied, along with the cross-reference, from Chambers' *Cyclopaedia*.[67] Furthermore, it was signed by the Catholic theologian Edme-François Mallet. As Mallet was still living when the article appeared, he would surely have protested if his signature had been affixed to an article considered injurious to Catholicism.

Nor were the roughly sixty thousand real cross-references in the *Encyclopédie* systematically deployed in the work as a whole. Admittedly, they were sometimes deployed systematically by individual contributors. Not surprisingly, authors tended to refer to their own articles,[68] but some contributors fell into other distinctive patterns. Daubenton, for example, included a cross-reference to "Plante"—an anonymous article when it finally appeared—in nearly all of his articles on plants. Unfortunately, Diderot did not attempt to coordinate different contributors' systems, so that he and Jaucourt almost never referred to "Plante" in their own articles on plants.[69] Furthermore, many of the cross-references in the *Encyclopédie*, like the ones in "Anthropophages," were simply copied from the *Cyclopaedia*.[70] It is likely that Diderot added cross-references to other contributors' articles at least on occasion. Still, he did not edit submitted cross-references to any significant extent.

Besides being unsystematic within the work as a whole, were the cross-references in the *Encyclopédie* also inaccurate? Even Diderot acknowledged that the work's cross-references sometimes took readers on unsatisfying journeys from one cross-reference to another.[71] Worse still, many cross-references went nowhere, pointing as they did to wrongly designated or non-existent articles.[72] In a work as gigantic as the *Encyclopédie*, it is easy to come up with examples of such mistakes, but they need to be contextualized, both against the usual practices of the *Encyclopédie* and against the practices of other encyclopedias. Consider, for instance, the *Encyclopédie*'s last fifty cross-references in the last volume of text. At this point, Diderot could have verified the accuracy of every one of the cross-references since all of the articles referred to had already been printed. Thus, he was no longer at a disadvantage with respect to encyclopedists like Chambers who prepared their whole encyclopedias before publishing any part. In fact, of the last fifty cross-references in the *Encyclopédie*, only two are seriously inaccurate, while five others involve misspellings that the reader could rectify without much effort.[73] Since Jacucourt wrote a large proportion of the articles at the end of the *Encyclopédie*, it might be contended that the general accuracy of the cross-references was due to him and not Diderot. If the sample is extended to include the last fifty articles not signed by Jaucourt, however, only one cross-reference is seriously inaccurate, while five others involve misspellings that the reader could rectify.[74]

It is possible, admittedly, that the cross-references were checked by an unknown assistant or an ambitious corrector employed by the printer, but Diderot himself mentioned checking cross-references as the editor's job in his article "Encyclopédie": "Mais comment un éditeur vérifiera-t-il jamais ces renvois, s'il n'a pas tout son manuscrit sous les yeux?"[75] Likewise, at least a few of Diderot's contemporaries—Alessandro Zorzi, for example, who planned an unpublished *Nuova enciclopedia italiana*, and Felice as editor of the Yverdon *Encyclopédie*—considered handling cross-references a task for an encyclopedia's editor.[76]

Greater accuracy might be expected in the century's smaller encyclopedias, since an editor could more easily verify cross-references in two or three volumes than in seventeen. Indeed, Chambers' *Cyclopaedia* has been praised for the high quality of its editing.[77] By the measure proposed here, however, the editing of the *Cyclopaedia* was not much more accurate than that of the *Encyclopédie*: Of the last fifty cross-references in the *Cyclopaedia*, one is seriously inaccurate, while four others contain misspellings that the reader could easily correct.[78] By contrast, the cross-references in the five-volume second edition (1721) of the *Dictionnaire universel françois et latin* (1704), commonly referred to as the *Dictionnaire de Trévoux*, seem to have been edited with markedly less care than those in the *Cyclopaedia* or the *Encyclopédie*: of the last fifty cross-references, five are seriously inaccurate, and two others have misspellings.[79] It should be remembered that the *Dictionnaire de Trévoux* had begun two decades earlier as a superficially revised, re-Catholicized version of Furetière's Dutch-published *Dictionnaire*.[80] Apparently its editing remained superficial even in the more original second edition. A somewhat better record for cross-referencing can be found in a bigger work from the end of the century, the third edition of the *Encyclopaedia Britannica*: of the last fifty cross-references in this encyclopedia, none are seriously inaccurate, though seven have misspellings.[81]

Surprisingly, Zedler's *Grosses vollständiges Universal-Lexicon*—the eighteenth century's biggest encyclopedia, a work with over six times as many words as the *Encyclopédie*—had no errors at all in its last fifty cross-references.[82] Indeed, its cross-references were safeguarded against errors insofar as they included both the name of the article referred to and its volume and page.[83] Such accuracy may have reflected a German preoccupation with compilation and bibliography, already legendary in the eighteenth century, but it probably also reflected the devotion with which the final editor Ludovici applied himself to editing.[84] In particular, he claimed to have spent a lot of time working on cross-references. More generally, he seems to have dedicated himself wholeheartedly to his duties as editor of the *Grosses vollständiges Universal-Lexicon*, so much so that he stopped publishing anything on his own, despite having laid the foundations for a career in academic philosophy before being appointed editor.[85] Diderot, by contrast, undoubtedly worked hard on the *Encyclopédie*, but he had enough time during his years as editor to publish philosophical essays, plays, and the early *Salons* (1759–81) as well as to write first drafts of *La Religieuse* and *Le Neveu de Rameau*.[86] Furthermore, his attitude toward editing, already casual at the start of the project, may have grown more so with the passage of time. In overseeing the plates from 1759 onward, for example, he was careless about verifying the correspondence between texts and figures.[87] My analysis of cross-references suggests, nonetheless, that he was no more careless in this area than most other contemporary encyclopedists.

Beyond the formal niceties of rubrics, signatures, and cross-references, what did Diderot do or not do to make the *Encyclopédie* homogeneous? As we have seen, he repudiated the very notion of editorial meddling in the article "Éditeur" and elsewhere, stating instead that he would publish articles in whatever form contributors wrote them. This policy may have helped in the recruitment of contributors since the latter could count on being credited for ideas expressed just as they wished. In practice, the editors were not quite so liberal as the policy would have it. As D'Alembert noted in his introduction to volume 3, they reserved the right, in particular, to merge articles on the same subject into a whole, regardless of authorship.[88] Overall, nonetheless, it is striking how much heterogeneity the editors were willing to accept in the *Encyclopédie*. Some articles were written neutrally, while others were filled with overt polemics. Within law, for example, Antoine-Gaspard Boucher d'Argis's articles were of the former variety, while Jaucourt's were of the latter.[89] Similarly, some articles were written in the third person, while others used the first person, whether plural or singular.[90] Lastly, many articles were sober, but some were sarcastic or humorous. Diderot himself composed ironic articles deploring gaps in contemporary knowledge of natural history.[91] Within the parameters of these general variations, certain articles stuck out for their own peculiarities. One notorious example was Joseph-François-Edouard de Desmahis's article "Femme," which shadowed a character named Chloé as part of its effort to support an abundance of generalizations about women. Indeed, Voltaire complained to the editors about their inclusion of the article, insisting that it did not belong in a serious work.[92] More generally, Voltaire felt that the editors should standardize articles in the *Encyclopédie* and offer contributors more guidance.[93]

In the stylistic variety of its articles, the *Encyclopédie* was undoubtedly less homogeneous than many small encyclopedias, including the *Cyclopaedia*. The difference is less striking, though probably still significant, with respect to large and collaborative encyclopedias. Both the *Grosses vollständiges Universal-Lexicon* and the third edition of the *Encyclopaedia Britannica* in particular had quirky articles along with a vast number of conventional ones. In the former work, for example, "Russland" included two contradictory accounts of Empress Elizabeth I's accession to power in 1741, one of them cheerful and analytical, the other one sinister and anecdotal.[94] Likewise, in the third edition of the *Encyclopaedia Britannica*, vivid styles of writing from travelers' accounts found their way into certain geographical articles.[95] It was only in the course of the nineteenth century that the editors of large encyclopedias were able to eliminate such discrepancies of style and approach.

Conclusions

In retrospect, it is hard to criticize Diderot for his work as editor of the *Encyclopédie*: Under his editorship, the work became a best-seller, a model for subsequent encyclopedias in many respects, and a monument to the ideas of contemporary France and the Enlightenment. Diderot was obviously not wholly responsible for the success of the *Encyclopédie*, but his role was decisive.

Regardless, it is worthwhile to evaluate Diderot and compare him with other intellectual directors of encyclopedias in the limited context of editing. The position of editor had not fully emerged for encyclopedias in Diderot's time, but the three principal duties of the modern editorial staff—planning, managing collaborators, and revising submitted texts—were familiar to and variously undertaken by eighteenth-century encyclopedists. Considering Diderot as an editor unfairly distances him from his fame as a thinker and author of articles, but it provides a means of probing similarities and differences between his work and that of other encyclopedias' editors. More generally, it provides a means of better integrating the *Encyclopédie* into the history of encyclopedias.

As an editor, in fact, Diderot shared important characteristics with his contemporaries. Like most editors involved with encyclopedias published over more than a few years, he planned the *Encyclopédie* imperfectly, though he did plan such features as its coverage of technology, its numerous plates, and its reliance on specialists. At the same time, his difficulties with planning were exacerbated by his adherence to two incompatible tenets: an idealistic commitment to systematic unity, and a decision to refrain from revising contributors' articles, even for rubrics and cross-references, where standardization would have helped readers and posed little threat to contributors' autonomy. In the small number of known instances in which he violated his principle by altering texts in a significant way, contributors were justifiably irked. In subsequent centuries, encyclopedias reliant on prestigious, signing contributors often maintained the principle of editorial non-intervention to a degree, but such permissiveness was rarely extended to rubrics, cross-references, or style in general, which were increasingly seen as appropriate for standardization.

In its cross-references, nonetheless, the *Encyclopédie* was apparently no less accurate than other encyclopedias, the *Grosses vollständiges Universal-Lexicon* excepted. Diderot probably deserves some of the credit. Along with D'Alembert, he was also a pioneer in turning the longstanding idea of a broadly collaborative encyclopedia into a reality and in setting up an influential, reasonably accurate method of attributing articles.

Lastly, however inimical to developing strictures about homogeneity in encyclopedias, Diderot's willingness to give free rein to his contributors had positive consequences: it encouraged contributions, especially creative ones, and it made the *Encyclopédie* a lively and diverse repertory of contemporary ideas, notwithstanding its general allegiance to the values of enlightenment.

NOTES

1. See for example Louis-Philippe May, "Documents nouveaux sur l'*Encyclopédie*," *Revue de synthèse* 15 (1938): 18, 21; Jean Le Rond D'Alembert, "Discours préliminaire des éditeurs," in *Encyclopédie, ou dictionnaire raisonné des sciences, des arts et des métiers*, ed. Denis Diderot and D'Alembert, 28 vols. ([Paris]: [Briasson et al.], 1751–72), 1: i; Denis Diderot, "Certitude," in *Encyclopédie*, 2: 846. Spelling and punctuation have been modernized throughout this article except in titles. Translations are my own. I would like to thank Emmanuel Boussuge, Marie Leca-Tsiomis, Irène Passeron, and two anonymous readers for *Studies in Eighteenth-Century Culture* for their help with my research.

2. "... heads of the *Encyclopédie*." See [Louis-Mayeul Chaudon], *La Religion vengée ou réfutation des auteurs impies* 11 (1760): 363.

3. "... put in order and published by Mr. Diderot ... and, as for the mathematical part, by Mr. D'Alembert."

4. "... first collected and compiled ... corrected and enlarged ... revised, corrected, and considerable enlarged ...." See Antoine Furetière, Henri Basnage de Beauval, and Jean-Baptiste Brutel de La Rivière, *Dictionnaire universel contenant généralement tous les mots françois tant vieux que modernes, et les termes des sciences et des arts*, 4 vols. (The Hague: Pierre Husson et al., 1727), 1: title page. For references to editors of encyclopedias as authors, revisers, and compilers, see Dennis de Coetlogon, *An Universal History of Arts and Sciences*, 2 vols. (London: John Hart, 1745),1: iii; Furetière, Basnage, and Brutel, *Dictionnaire universel*, 1: ****1v; *The Present State of the Republick of Letters* 12 (1733): 77.

5. "This name is given to a man of letters who agrees to take charge of publishing the works of someone else." See Denis Diderot, "Éditeur," in *Encyclopédie*, 5: 396.

6. "There are some works whose editing supposes more knowledge that it has been given to a single man to possess. The *Encyclopédie* is emphatically of this number. It seems that it would be necessary, for its perfection, that each person be the *editor* of his or her articles; but this expedient would lead to too much expense and slowness. As the *editors* of the *Encyclopédie* do not appropriate any sort of authority over the productions of their colleagues, it would be just as bad to blame

them for the weak things one will find there as to praise them for the excellent things one will find there." See Diderot, "Éditeur," 5: 396.

7. Jeff Loveland and Joseph Reagle, "Wikipedia and Encyclopedic Production," *New Media and Society* 15 (2013): 1296, 1298–99.

8. Frank A. Kafker and Jeff Loveland, "La Vie agitée de l'abbé De Gua de Malves et sa direction de l'*Encyclopédie*," *Recherches sur Diderot et sur l'Encyclopédie* 47 (2012): 200.

9. Jeff Loveland, "Varieties of Authorship in Eighteenth-Century Encyclopedias," *Das achtzehnte Jahrhundert* 34 (2010): 96–97.

10. May, "Documents nouveaux," 19–20.

11. For references to "editors," see *Encyclopaedia Britannica; or, a Dictionary of Arts, Sciences, and Miscellaneous Literature*, third edition, 18 vols. (Edinburgh: Bell and Macfarquhar, 1797), 1: xii–xiii. Notice in contrast the reference to "compilers" in *Encyclopaedia Britannica; or, a Dictionary of Arts, Sciences, etc.*, second edition, 10 vols. (Edinburgh: J. Balfour et al., 1778–83), 1: vii. On Gleig's attention to recruiting for the third edition, see Kathleen Hardesty Doig et al., "Colin Macfarquhar, George Gleig, and Possibly James Tytler's Edition (1788–97): The Attainment of Recognition and Eminence," in *The Early Britannica: The Growth of an Outstanding Encyclopedia*, ed. Frank A. Kafker and Jeff Loveland (Oxford: Voltaire Foundation, 2009), 162–64.

12. Bernhard Kossmann, "Deutsche Universallexika des 18. Jahrhunderts: Ihr Wesen und ihr Informationswert, dargestellt am Beispiel der Werke von Jablonski und Zedler," *Archiv für Geschichte des Buchwesens* 9 (1969): 1569–70; Johann Heinrich Zedler, "Nötiger Vorbericht," in *Grosses vollständiges Universal-Lexicon aller Wissenschaften und Künste*, 64 vols. (Halle and Leipzig: Zedler, 1732–50), 19:)(1v-)(2r. As Kossmann notes, Jakob August Frankenstein and Paul Daniel Longolius probably acted as editors before Ludovici.

13. Christabel P. Braunrot and Kathleen Hardesty Doig, "The *Encyclopédie méthodique*: An Introduction," *SVEC* 327 (1995): 8–9.

14. Anja zum Hingst, *Die Geschichte des Großen Brockhaus: Vom Conversationslexikon zur Enzyklopädie* (Wiesbaden: Harrassowitz, 1995), 105, 111–12.

15. For Brockhaus's and Ludwig Hain's duties see Hingst, *Geschichte*, 112–13.

16. *Collier's Encyclopedia*, 24 vols. (New York: Collier's, 1997), 1: front matter.

17. [Denis Diderot], prospectus to *Encyclopédie, ou dictionnaire raisonné des sciences, des arts et des métiers* (Paris: Briasson et al., 1751 [1750]), 1–6.

18. [Diderot], prospectus, 4.

19. Robert Darnton, "Philosophers Trim the Tree of Knowledge: The Epistemological Strategy of the *Encyclopedie*," in *The Great Cat Massacre and Other Episodes in French Cultural History* (New York: Basic Books, 1984), 199–200.

20. [Diderot], prospectus, 8, "Système figuré des connaissances humaines." For criticism of the tree of knowledge, see Abraham-Joseph Chaumeix, *Préjugés légitimes contre l'Encyclopédie*, 8 vols. (Brussels: 1758–59), 1: 39–42; Guillaume-François Berthier, review of the prospectus of the *Encyclopédie*, *Mémoires pour servir à l'histoire des sciences et des arts*, January 1751: 302–27.

21. [Diderot], prospectus, [12]; Frank A. Kafker, "*Encyclopédie, ou dictionnaire raisonné des sciences, des arts et des métiers, par une société de gens de lettres*," in *Dictionnaire de Diderot*, ed. Roland Mortier and Raymond Trousson (Paris: Honoré Champion, 1999), 159.

22. [Diderot], prospectus, 11.

23. D'Alembert, "Discours préliminaire," 1: xviii–xix.

24. Christine Théré and Loïc Charles, "Un Nouvel Élément pour l'histoire de l'*Encyclopédie*: Le 'Plan' inédit du premier éditeur Gua de Malves," *Recherches sur Diderot et sur l'Encyclopédie* 39 (2005): 107. See also Robert Favre and Michel Dürr, "Un Texte inédit de l'abbé de Gua de Malves concernant la naissance de l'*Encyclopédie*," *Mémoires de l'Académie des sciences, belles-lettres et arts de Lyon*, third series 55 (2000 [2001]): 51–68.

25. Kafker and Loveland, "Vie," 200–05.

26. "The work we are laboring on is not of our choice: We did not arrange the original materials that were handed over to us, and they were, so to speak, thrown to us in a confusion quite capable of deterring anyone who would have had either less integrity, or less courage." See Diderot, "Encyclopédie," 5: 644*r*.

27. Ulrich Johannes Schneider, *Die Erfindung des allgemeinen Wissens: Enzyklopädisches Schreiben im Zietalter der Aufklärung* (Berlin: Akademie Verlag, 2013), 101, 107–08.

28. Annette Fröhner, *Technologie und Enzyklopädismus im Übergang vom 18. zum 19. Jahrhundert: Johann Georg Krünitz (1728–1796) und seine oeconomisch-technologische Encyklopädie* (Mannheim: Palatium, 1994), 25–28.

29. Marie Leca-Tsiomis, "Langue et grammaire dans l'*Encyclopédie*," in *L'Encyclopédie ou la création des disciplines*, ed. Martine Groult (Paris: CNRS, 2003), 203–14.

30. Jeff Loveland, "Louis-Jean-Marie Daubenton and the *Encyclopédie*," *SVEC* 12 (2003): 188–93.

31. Dorothea Behnke, *Furetière und Trévoux: Eine Untersuchung zum Verhältnis der beiden Wörterbuchserien* (Tübingen: Max Niemeyer, 1996), 150–51.

32. *Allgemeine deutsche Real-Encyclopädie für die gebildeten Stande: Conversations-Lexicon*, fifth edition, 10 vols. (Leipzig: F. A. Brockhaus, 1819–20), 10: VI ("Vorrede").

33. See Kafker and Loveland, "Vie," 192–96, 199–200.

34. Frank A. Kafker, *The Encyclopedists as a Group: A Collective Biography of the Authors of the Encyclopédie* (Oxford: Voltaire Foundation, 1996), 36–41.

35. Loveland and Reagle, "Wikipedia," 1303–04.

36. Frank A. Kafker and Jeff Loveland, "William Smellie's Edition (1768–71): A Modest Start," in *Early Britannica*, 19–20, 67.

37. Doig et al., "Colin Macfarquhar," 169–71.

38. Willi Goetschel, Catriona Macleod, and Emery Snyder, "The *Deutsche Encyclopädie*," in *Notable Encyclopedias of the Late Eighteenth Century: Eleven Successors of the Encyclopédie*, ed. Frank A. Kafker (Oxford: Voltaire Foundation, 1994), 260, 263.

39. See his suggestion to Étienne-Noël Damilaville, only partially accepted, in Denis Diderot, *Correspondance*, ed. Georges Roth and Jean Varloot, 16 vols. (Paris:

Éditions de Minuit, 1955–70), 16: 31 (letter 331*bis*). For an analysis of Damilaville's response, see Emmanuel Boussuge, ed., *Correspondance [de Diderot]*, vol. 29 of *Oeuvres complètes* (Paris: Hermann, 1975–), forthcoming.

40. Kafker, *Encyclopedists as a Group*, 39–40.

41. Alain Cernuschi, "L'ABC de l'*Encyclopédie* d'Yverdon ou la refonte encyclopédique de F.-B. De Felice à la lumière de ses lettres de 1771," *Recherches sur Diderot et sur l'Encyclopédie* 49 (2014): 139–40, 142.

42. Kafker, *Encyclopedists as a Group*, 98–99.

43. Douglas H. Gordon and Norman L. Torrey, *The Censoring of Diderot's Encyclopédie and the Re-Established Text* (New York: Columbia Univ. Press, 1947), 33.

44. *Allgemeine deutsche Real-Encyclopädie*, fifth edition, 10: IX–XI ("Vorrede").

45. See Paul Kruse, "The Story of the *Encyclopaedia Britannica*, 1768–1943," (Ph.D. diss., Univ. of Chicago, 1958), 165; Philippe Castellano, *Enciclopedia Espasa: Historia de una aventura editorial*, trans. Caty Orero Saéz de Tejada (Madrid: Espasa, 2000), 167–69; Heinz Sarkowski, *Das Bibliographische Institut: Verlagsgeschichte und Bibliographie, 1826–1976* (Mannheim: Bibliographisches Institut, 1976), 188. Editors of the *Encyclopaedia Britannica* and other works featuring "treatises" continued to repudiate the uniformity of the German "Konversations-Lexikon" in the length of its articles. See for example James Louis Garvin, ed., *Encyclopaedia Britannica*, fourteenth edition, 24 vols. (London: Encyclopaedia Britannica, 1929), 1: xxi–xxii.

46. See Ulrike Spree, *Das Streben nach Wissen: Eine vergleichende Gattungsgeschichte der populären Enzyklopädie in Deutschland und Großbritannien im 19. Jahrhundert* (Tübingen: Niemeyer, 2000), 284–86.

47. Jean-Yves Mollier and Bruno Dubot, *Histoire de la librairie Larousse (1852–2010)* (Paris: Fayard, 2012), 193–94, 314–15, 319.

48. "… uniformity of style." See J. Caullery, "Notes sur Samuel Chappuzeau," *Bulletin de la société de l'histoire du protestantisme français* 58 (1909): 150–52.

49. "I wish there had been more uniformity." See Antoine Furetière and Henri Basnage de Beauval, *Dictionnaire universel contenant généralement tous les mots françois tant vieux que modernes, et les termes des sciences et des arts*, 3 vols. (The Hague: Arnoud and Reinier Leers, 1701), 1: *2r-v*.

50. Ephraim Chambers, *Cyclopaedia: Or, an Universal Dictionary of Arts and Sciences*, second edition, 2 vols. (London: D. Midwinter et al., 1738), 1: [i] ("Advertisement concerning the Second Edition").

51. "Nevertheless, I have enough work: four proofs to correct, a preface to finish, the errata for the second volume to write." See Jean Le Rond D'Alembert to Renée-Caroline de Froullay Créquÿ, 27 December 1751, vol. 2 of *Correspondance générale*, ed. Irène Passeron (Paris: CNRS Éditions, 2015), 364–65.

52. "… ten years with the boredom of 7 to 8 volumes in folio." See D'Alembert to Jean-Henri-Samuel Formey, 19 September 1749, vol. 2 of *Correspondance générale*, 227; Arthur M. Wilson, *Diderot* (New York: Oxford Univ. Press, 1972), 115.

53. Gilles Barroux and François Pépin, eds., *Le Chevalier de Jaucourt: L'Homme aux dix-sept mille articles* (Paris: Société Diderot, 2015), 7–8.

54. R. N. Schwab, W. E. Rex, and J. Lough, *Inventory of Diderot's Encyclopédie*,

7 vols. (Geneva: Institut et Musée Voltaire, 1971–84), 1: 20, 24–27, 32–53.
    55. *Encyclopédie*, 1: 1. A few dozen other articles can be found with such "super-rubrics," including "Agriculture," "Algèbre," "Analyse," "Anatomie," "Animal," "Appréhension," "Argent," "Arithmétique," "Art," "Bataille," "Botanique," "Catoptrique," "Cosmologie," "Cadran," "Caractère," "Copernic," "Courbe," "Dictionnaire," "Dioptrique," "Dynamique," "Divination," "Étendue," "Fauconnerie," "Fortification," "Géodésie," "Géographie," "Géométrie," "Gnomonique," "Horlogerie," "Hydraulique," "Hydrographie," "Mathématique," "Méchanique," "Musique," "Optique," "Perspective," "Statique," and "Tolérance." See Marie Leca-Tsiomis, "Le Système figuré des connaissances de l'*Encyclopédie*: Théorie et pratique," in *L'Esprit de système au XVIIIe siècle*, ed. Élise Pavy and Sophie Marchand (Paris: Hermann, forthcoming).
    56. Gilles Blanchard and Mark Olsen, "Le Système de renvois dans l'*Encyclopédie*: Une cartographie des structures de connaissances au XVIIIe siècle," *Recherches sur Diderot et sur l'Encyclopédie* 31–32 (2002): 51–52.
    57. Luigi Delia, "Le Droit dans l'*Encyclopédie*, cartographies, enjeux, collaborateurs," *Recherches sur Diderot et sur l'Encyclopédie* 48 (2013): 144–45.
    58. James Llana, "Natural History in the *Encyclopédie*," *Journal of the History of Biology* 33 (2000): 15n; Jacques Roger, "L'Histoire naturelle et les sciences de la vie," in *Essais et notes sur l'Encyclopédie de Diderot et D'Alembert*, ed. Andrea Calzolari and Sylvie Delassus (Milan: Franco Maria Ricci, 1979), 246, 249.
    59. For examples see Blanchard and Olsen, "Système," 51; Marie Leca-Tsiomis, "L'*Encyclopédie* selon Jaucourt," in *Chevalier de Jaucourt*, 79–80; Leca-Tsiomis, "Système figuré," forthcoming.
    60. M. Glatigny, ed., *Les Marques d'usage dans les dictionnaires, XVIIe–XVIIIe siècles* (Lille: Presses Univ. de Lille, 1990).
    61. Jeff Loveland, "Encyclopaedias and Genre, 1670–1750," *Journal for Eighteenth-Century Studies* 36 (2013): 167.
    62. Schwab, Rex, and Lough, *Inventory*, 1: 33, 45.
    63. Schneider, *Erfindung*, 43–95.
    64. *Allgemeine deutsche Real-Encyclopädie*, 10: XII–XVIII ("Vorrede"); Jeff Loveland, "Two French 'Konversationslexika' of the 1830s and 1840s: The *Encyclopédie des gens du monde* and the *Dictionnaire de la conversation et de la lecture*," in *Translation and Transfer of Knowledge in Encyclopedic Compilations, 1680–1830*, ed. Clorinda Donato and Hans-Jürgen Lüsebrink (Toronto: Univ. of Toronto Press, forthcoming); Ines Prodöhl, *Die Politik des Wissens: Allgemeine deutsche Enzyklopädien zwischen 1928 und 1956* (Berlin: Akademie Verlag, 2011), 43–44.
    65. Macvey Napier, ed., *Supplement to the Fourth, Fifth, and Sixth Editions of the Encyclopaedia Britannica*, 6 vols. (Edinburgh: A. Constable, 1815–24), 1: xxxiv.
    66. [Diderot], prospectus, 11; D'Alembert, "Discours préliminaire," 1: xviii–ix; Diderot, "Encyclopédie," 5: 642v–644r.
    67. Marie Leca-Tsiomis, "Le Capuchon des cordeliers," *Recherches sur Diderot et sur l'Encyclopédie* 50 (2015): 350.

68. See Julie Candler Hayes, "Translation (In)Version and the Encyclopedic Network," in *Using the Encyclopédie: Ways of Knowing, Ways of Reading*, ed. Daniel Brewer and Hayes (Oxford: Voltaire Foundation, 2002), 102–04.

69. Loveland, "Louis-Jean-Marie Daubenton," 203–04.

70. Hans-Wolfgang Schneiders, "Le Prétendu Système des renvois dans l'*Encyclopédie*," in *L'Encyclopédie et Diderot*, ed. Peter-Eckhard Knabe and Edgar Mass (Cologne: Verlag Köln, DME, 1985), 259; John Lough, "The *Encyclopédie* and Chambers's *Cyclopaedia*," *SVEC* 185 (1980): 223.

71. Diderot, "Encyclopédie," 5: 644*r*.

72. See the comments in *Nouveaux mémoires de l'Académie royale des sciences et belles-lettres [de Berlin]* 1770 (1772): 53–54.

73. The cross-references can be found in *Encyclopédie*, 17: 721–50. The two serious errors are the references to the non-existent articles "Ornithologie" and "Orbite auditif [*sic*]" in the articles "Zoologie" and "Zygomatique." In the latter case, the anonymous author probably meant to refer to two articles, "Orbites" and "Auditif."

74. The cross-references can be found in *Encyclopédie*, 17: 716–50.

75. "But how will an editor ever verify these cross-references, if he does not have his whole manuscript in front of his eyes?" See Diderot, "Encyclopédie," 5: 643*v*.

76. [Alessandro Zorzi], *Prodromo della nuova enciclopedia italiana* (Siena: Vincenzo Pazzini Carli et al., 1779), XIX; Cernuschi, "ABC de l'*Encyclopédie* d'Yverdon," 138–39.

77. Lael Ely Bradshaw, "Ephraim Chambers' *Cyclopaedia*," in *Notable Encyclopedias of the Seventeenth and Eighteenth Centuries: Nine Predecessors of the Encyclopédie*, ed. Frank A. Kafker (Oxford: Voltaire Foundation: 1981), 125.

78. The cross-references can be found in Ephraim Chambers, *Cyclopaedia: Or, an Universal Dictionary of Arts and Sciences*, first edition, 2 vols. (London: Knapton et al., 1728), 2: 391–92. The one serious error is the reference to the non-existent article "Jugale" in "Zygoma."

79. The cross-references can be found in *Dictionnaire universel, françois et latin*, second edition, 5 vols. (Trévoux: Florentin Delaulne et al., 1721), 5: 687–706. The five serious errors are the references to the non-existent articles "Viète," "Oby," "Chiaurlic," "Sophala," and "Yoiel" in the articles "Zététique," "Ziemnoy poias," "Ziorlo," "Zofala," and "Zuglio" respectively.

80. Marie Leca-Tsiomis, *Ecrire l'Encyclopédie: Diderot: De l'usage des dictionnaires à la grammaire philosophique* (Oxford: Voltaire Foundation, 1999), 91–96; Behnke, *Furetière*, 104–20.

81. The cross-references can be found in *Encyclopaedia Britannica*, third edition, 18: 925–45.

82. Jeff Loveland, "Why Encyclopedias Got Bigger ... and Smaller," *Information & Culture* 47 (2012): 236–37.

83. The cross-references can be found in *Grosses vollständiges Universal-Lexicon*, 64: 1779–92.

84. See for example David A. Kronick, *A History of Scientific and Technical Periodicals: The Origins and Development of the Scientific and Technological Press, 1665–1790* (New York: Scarecrow, 1962), 165–66.

85. Schneider, *Erfindung*, 163–64, 171–72, 177–79.

86. See John Lough, *The Encyclopédie in Eighteenth-Century England and Other Studies* (Newcastle: Oriel, 1970), 229.

87. Madeleine Pinault Sørensen, "Rôle et statut de l'image dans l'*Encyclopédie*," in *Encyclopédie ou la création des disciplines*, 138. More generally, see John Lough, *The Encyclopédie* (London: Longman, 1971), 77–78.

88. Jacques Proust, *Diderot et l'Encyclopédie*, new edition (Paris: Albin Michel, 1995), 136.

89. Delia, "Droit," 166.

90. On the *Encyclopédie*'s use of the first person, see Leca-Tsiomis, *Écrire l'Encyclopédie*, 175–77.

91. Marie Leca-Tsiomis, "De l'abari au baobab, ou Diderot naturaliste ironique," in *Sciences, musiques, lumières: Mélanges offerts à Anne-Marie Chouillet* (Ferney: Centre International d'Étude du XVIIIe Siècle, 2002), 229–38; Llana, "Natural History," 20–21.

92. Frank A. Kafker and Serena L. Kafker, *The Encyclopedists as Individuals: A Biographical Dictionary of the Authors of the Encyclopédie* (Oxford: Voltaire Foundation, 1988), 102.

93. Béatrice Didier, *Alphabet et raison: Le Paradoxe des dictionnaires au XVIIIe siècle* (Paris: Presses Univ. de France, 1996), 96–98.

94. Schneider, *Erfindung*, 123, 140–42.

95. Doig et al., "Colin Macfarquhar," 181.

Drawing the Corporeal: Balance and Mirror Reversal in Jacques-Louis David's *Oath of Horatii*

TAMAR MAYER

In 1784, Jacques-Louis David painted the *Oath of Horatii*, a work that marked him as the leading artist of his generation and became one of his most well-known masterpieces (fig. 1). The painting tells the story of the three Horatii brothers who vow to sacrifice their lives for Rome in a duel with the Curiatii brothers from Alba Longa and end an ongoing war between the two cities. On the left side of the composition, the three sons take an oath, and, on the right side, the women are already mourning the impending death of their loved ones. While several interpretations of this painting have focused on the opposition between these two spheres—the masculine and the feminine— this essay offers ways of reading the composition more continuously by considering the figures' variant modes of stance and stability. By analyzing the many drawings and sketches that David made for this painting, I set to convey new relationships between his preparatory and final work.

Specifically, this essay focuses on several modes of mirror reversal that appear in David's sketchbook, currently held at the Louvre, which contains many preparatory studies for the *Horatii*.[1] The surprisingly rich modes of reversal that appear in this sketchbook, together with drawing practices found in some of David's later books, reveal a deep engagement in David's work with questions of balance and stability. The existence of many drawings of legs and feet in this sketchbook reaffirms that problems of gravity and of

Figure 1. Jacques-Louis David, *The Oath of the Horatii*, ca. 1784. Oil on canvas, 330 x 425 cm. Inv.: 3692. Photo: Gérard Blot/Christian Jean. Louvre, Paris, France. Photo Credit: © RMN-Grand Palais / Art Resource, NY.

establishing figures' relationship to the ground below them were dominant in this process. The focus on the solid stance of the male figures, together with an interest in narrative continuity through gestural movement, helps to generate a new reading of the *Horatii*'s composition. Inspired by Ralph Ubl's groundbreaking work on Delacroix's drawings and by his idea that Delacroix's treatment of the drawn surface helps to reformulate notions of gravity in his pictorial works, this essay seeks to demonstrate similar correlations between drawing and painting in David's work.[2]

It has been claimed that the *Horatii* broke with conventions of pictorial composition by presenting two distinct and unrelated groups, rendering the painting static, rigid, and spatially unharmonious.[3] While this is true, important continuities can be recovered amidst the discord and contrast. Focusing on the father as the key figure that embodies the tension between the two groups, I interpret the *Horatii*'s composition as a chain of decreasing power: from the forceful stability of the sons on the left, through the slight imbalance of their father at center, to the utter collapse of the women on the right. I illustrate this reading by closely comparing David's preparatory compositional drawing and the finished composition. The frieze is the structure within which this compositional dynamics takes place. The dominance of the frieze in the *Horatii* has been established, but it has never been linked with David's preparatory drawings and practices.[4] I argue that acts of 180° reversals in his drawing encapsulate the complex functions of David's frieze-like structure, which, in the *Oath of the Horatii*, is used as a means of achieving two somewhat contradictory ends: both to secure the figure's stable stance and to provide the axis within which the beholder may read the composition as a continuous chain of gestural movements.

By providing a close analysis of David's preparatory procedures for this painting, specifically the drawings of legs and feet that appear in this sketchbooks, I show that issues of stable and solid stance are central to David's *Horatii*. Key to this analysis is the contrast between the standing men and the seated women, and the fact that absolutely all of the drawings in question (twelve altogether) are of the male legs and feet, while drawings of the female feet are absent from this book altogether. For David, composing male figures powerfully standing on the ground required a different approach than the one for presenting seated women. This opposition, the ways it manifests itself in the Horatii sketchbook, and how matters of stance become key for a renewed analysis of the composition, are the subjects of this essay.

These and other newly discovered correlations between drawing and painting in David's work help reintroduce the issue of the artist's operative body into the discussion. Scholarly analyses mostly think of that body as inaccessible in David's work. Thomas Crow, for example, argues that the artist's hand is not visible in David's painting.[5] It is true that the surfaces of many of David's canvases are smooth, the degree of finish immaculate, and the artist's hand appears undetectable. But the artist's operative body does manifest itself, albeit in a different way, through acts of mirror reversal, which are decisive for this painting. Instead of the famous "artist's touch," the operations of drawing reconnect the final composition with the history of its own making. If, as Norman Bryson claims, the *Horatii* is a painting that deals with the contrast between linguistic signs of mortality and the living flesh, it is precisely an interpretation of what that "living flesh" could mean in David's work that this essay provides.[6] Ultimately, the phenomenology of making is closely tied to a phenomenology of viewing. Changes in the viewer's position vis-à-vis David's paintings, which have been extensively discussed in previous research, do reflect changes in the artist's bodily operations while he is drawing.[7] The larger implications of this study do, therefore, help construct new connections between the making and the viewing of David's work.

In recent decades scholars have begun to address the various alterations and transformations that David introduced in the transition from preparatory drawing to painting.[8] For instance, Heidi Kraus demonstrates the types of transformations that took place when David used drawings made in Rome between 1775 and 1780 to paint his *Horatii* and *Sabines*.[9] But the focus here is on a specific type of transformation—mirror reversal—that took place in David's work during the 1780s. An examination of the functions of these mirror reversals helps shed new light on the nature of David's preparatory procedures and their development throughout his career.

Mirror Reversals in the Horatii Sketchbook

Two modes of mirror reversal appear in this sketchbook that David used during his second trip to Rome (October 1784 through August 1785).[10] The book contains figure studies for the *Horatii*, copies of antiques and masterpieces, as well as studies of local landscapes.[11] The majority of the drawings seem more finished and less sketchy than his drawings in later sketchbooks, including carefully studied anatomical details. Unlike some of David's later sketchbooks, this one should be read from left to right, with preference given to drawings on the recto pages (only 33 verso pages are drawn on versus 84 recto pages), in a right-side-up orientation.[12] This way of using the sketchbook is echoed in the sequential and orderly pictorial structure of the *Horatii*, especially the unfolding of its composition from left to right.

The first mode of mirror reversal is straightforward: these are tracings of images on the verso pages of the sketchbook. Out of a total of twenty-two such tracings in all of David's sketchbooks, seven appear in this one. Whether these are tracings of heads for the *Horatii* or architectural details for the *Brutus*, they both relate to the strong frieze-like structure of David's 1780s' compositions (figs. 2–5). Examples from David's later books reveal that many of these later tracings are of standing figures, most of them in poses with a strong lateral orientation (figs. 6, 7).[13] I believe that these partake in a process of evaluating the stability and autonomy of the figure's stance. Delécluze's record of David's own emphasis on the stability of his models' poses and Leonardo da Vinci's theories on the use of mirrors in painting suggest this reading.

Notions of gravity and solidity were crucial for the *Horatii*. The men's feet appear rooted into the hard marble floor (fig. 1). Indeed, these concerns run through David's work and pedagogy. The artist is known to have insisted that models be able to maintain a pose and support their own weight without

Figure 2. Jacques-Louis David, *Head of a bearded old man and a stool.* Horatii sketchbook, R.F. 4506, folio 21r. Photo: Michel Urtado. Musée du Louvre, Paris, France. Photo Credit: © RMN-Grand Palais / Art Resource, NY.

Figure 3. Jacques-Louis David, *Head of a bearded old man and a scene.* Horatii sketchbook, R.F. 4506, folio 21v. Photo: Michel Urtado. Musée du Louvre, Paris, France. Photo Credit: © RMN-Grand Palais / Art Resource, NY.

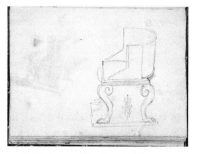

Figure 4. Jacques-Louis David, *Two studies of an antique chair.* Horatii sketchbook, R.F. 4506, folio 55r. Photo: Michel Urtado. Musée du Louvre, Paris, France. Photo Credit: © RMN-Grand Palais / Art Resource, NY.

Figure 5. Jacques-Louis David, *Study of a chair, after the antique.* Horatii sketchbook, R.F. 4506, folio 55v. Photo: Michel Urtado. Musée du Louvre, Paris, France. Photo Credit: © RMN-Grand Palais / Art Resource, NY.

Figure 6. Jacques-Louis David, *Sketch for "Leonidas at the Thermopylae."* Sketchbook dedicated to "Leonidas," R.F. 9136, folio 28r. Photo: Michèle Bellot. Musée du Louvre, Paris, France. Photo Credit: © RMN-Grand Palais / Art Resource, NY.

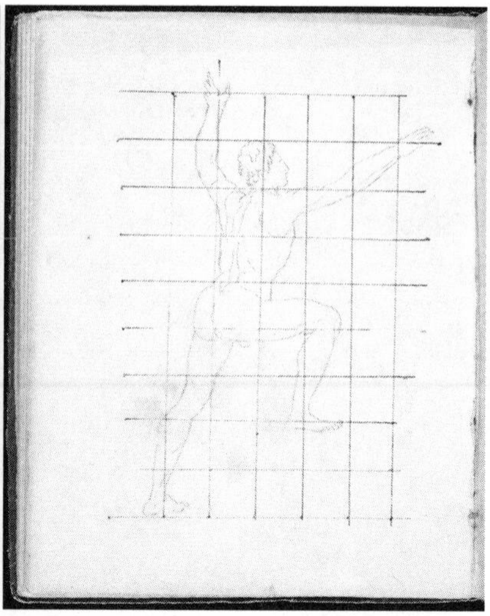

Figure 7. Jacques-Louis David, *Study for "Leonidas at the Thermopylae",* a reprise from the recto. Sketchbook dedicated to "Leonidas," R.F. 9136, folio 28v. Photo: Michel Urtado. Musée du Louvre, Paris, France. Photo Credit: © RMN-Grand Palais / Art Resource, NY.

the assistance of cords or strings so that the pose would seem as natural as possible. This insistence goes against the training of the Académie, of which David disapproved. At the Académie "the professor would give the model an acrobatic pose, which necessitated the use of 'strings' and pulleys so that the model could 'hold the pose.'"[14] In David's view, a figure's stance had to be self-sufficient, autonomous, and stable.[15] Symmetrically reversed tracing could have been a way of examining whether a pose met these criteria convincingly. This practice resonates with Leonardo da Vinci's rationale for examining his own painting with a mirror to detect its faults more easily.

According to Leonardo, "… when you are painting you should take a flat mirror and often look at your work within it, and it will then be seen in reverse, and will appear to be by the hand of some other master, and you will be better able to judge of its faults than in any other way."[16] For Leonardo, the mirror becomes a distancing device: it reveals pictorial errors much more clearly than the human eye because it sets the eye apart from the bodily operations of picture-making. Similarly, when one traces an existing outline, the result is a "surprise," in the sense that it is difficult to anticipate how things will look once reversed.[17] Just as artists often need to step back from their canvas in order to judge the overall effect of what they have created more clearly, so mirror reversals allow artists to clarify that which is (or is not) working well in their paintings.

Dorothy Johnson has explored the extent to which David's use of mirroring was inspired by the new 1796 French edition of Leonardo's *Treatise on Painting*.[18] She claims that David's placement of a large mirror in front of his *Sabine Women* during its exhibition was meant to provide "a tour de force, an aesthetic demonstration of the absolute perfection" of this painting.[19] Johnson notes that "Leonardo's recommendations for using the mirror to assist the artist in perfecting an illusion of nature in painting (…) were already well known in late eighteenth-century France and had been incorporated into the art dictionaries of the period, such as that of Watelet and Levesque.[20] David customarily used mirrors in the processes of painting and exhibiting his works to demonstrate their perfection (e.g., the *Sabines*, the *Coronation*, *Mars and Venus*). David's traced drawings attest to the significance of mirror reversal in his repertoire.

Another source of reversals that inspired David and his fellow artists was engravings. He drew from engravings, but unlike other artists (Fragonard, Watteau), he did not produce etchings or engravings of his own works—they were only copied by others.[21] It may be, therefore, that his familiarity with mirror reversal in his own compositions assumed a key position in David's oeuvre, one that was internal to the preparatory process and preceded the painting rather than followed it. The various detailed leg studies in the Horatii sketchbook form a clear picture of what those practices looked like in the earlier part of David's career.

The association of David's mirror reversals with issues of gravity and stability emerges from the nature of the mirror's interference with corporal structures of picture making. In David's drawings, as in Leonardo's, the mirror breaks the continuum among the viewing eye, the drawing hand, and the drawn figure. The direction and orientation of the drawn figure are not unrelated to the artist's bodily disposition while drawing. Just as the mirror image of a painting estranges the artist's eye from her hand and breaks the continuity of her operative corporeal self, so the reversed tracings undo the spatial coherency within which the orientations of the drawing body and the drawn body are essentially linked. Undoing this spatial link, the directionality of the drawn body becomes independent, and detecting whether it looks unstable becomes easier with mirror reversal. In other words, a convincing rendering of a self-sufficient pose—one where the figure would seem to carry its own weight—will remain convincing in the reversal as well.

The tracings in the Horatii sketchbook include heads and architectural details but no standing figures; nonetheless, they share the most important characteristic of David's later tracings: a dominant lateral orientation. Almost all of David's traced images feature figures, heads, or objects shown either in full profile or in poses that stretch out sideways. It becomes clear that the types of images that David chose to trace are those in which reversal could appear in the most extreme manner, that is, in full 180° degree rotation around the vertical axis of the object. The tracings in the Horatii sketchbook represent very early configurations of a practice that will become decisive to David's creative process. Their laterality implies that they are part of a life-long engagement with problems of stability.

* * *

The second mode of reversal that appears in this book consists in studies of anatomical details drawn in reverse to the way they will appear in the final painting. Interestingly enough, these are all studies of legs and feet, supporting the claim that reversals, in David's preparatory process for the *Horatii*, relate to issues of figures' stance. A strikingly large number of drawings of feet and legs appear in this book (drawn on eleven different folios).[22] Six out of the eight feet of men seen in the painting are drawn here, but only two of them are consistent with the way they appear in the painting itself.[23] The remaining four derive from mirror reversal: left legs in the painting are drawn as right legs in the sketchbook and vice versa.

David's preparatory process for the *Horatii* was largely logical and systematic. The artist first experimented with primary compositional studies that indicate the overall intended structure. He also made comprehensive figure studies (from the model or from antiquity) that allowed for a closer examination of specific figures, and a full ink and wash compositional drawing. Finally, David produced detailed drapery studies of individual figures. This process is both cumulative and rational, with linear structures being set before tonal ones.[24] Given this systematic process, why would David study these anatomical details in an opposite orientation to the one they will have in the final painting?[25] It seems unlikely that he contemplated reversing his composition or changing figures' position considering the many drawings that survived from this preparatory process, none of which includes full figures or groups in reversed orientation to the one they have in the painting.[26] When, in later projects, most prominently in his *Leonidas at Thermopylae* (1814), David mirror-reversed the orientation of certain figures or groups, this process is recorded in multiple full-figure studies of such opposing orientations, as well as group studies and compositional studies. In the process for the *Horatii,* only drawings of body parts, and most significantly of legs and feet, are drawn in reverse—which begs a different explanation.

For example, in the painting, the second son has his left leg stepping forward and his right leg stepping back. In the book, it is exactly the opposite: his front leg is depicted as a right leg (figs. 8–10). All three drawings are from the same ancient sculpture, the Gladiator Borghese, which explains why David could not simply alter the sculpture's pose so that it would fit his pictorial needs.[27] Yet David not only drew the sculpture's leg and later subjected it to mirror-reversal for his painting, he also studied it from an entirely opposite point of view (representing the outer rather than the inner leg). These studies are careful, specific, and exact. Why would he invest so much time if he were not planning to use them, as such, in his painting? At the very least, this practice indicates that the artist found it useful to examine a pose from multiple points of view in order to convey it more convincingly in his painting. To represent a pose in a persuasive manner, David acquired a full understanding of how it affects the entire body, and that knowledge required analyzing the pose from various perspectives. But the care taken with these sketches could have even greater significance.

In all three drawings the leg is presented in profile, fully aligned with the frieze. But two of these drawings (figs. 9, 10) feature the outer rather than the inner leg—a perspective wholly absent from the actual painting. I believe that this feature suggests that David was looking to establish the *outline* of this pose in the *same orientation* as it will appear in the painting (stepping forward, knee bent, pointing to the right side), even if this meant delineating internal anatomical details that would later be excluded from the painting. Despite his great skill in creating mirror-reversed poses, David found value in studying and having a grasp on the correct orientation of the pose as well. He needed to define the *right* orientation of a certain pose in great detail, even if what he was able to take from it, in the end, was only an outline. Together, these three drawings attest to David's resourcefulness in combining an outline that he studied in the same orientation that he would need for his painting with anatomical details that derived from mirror-reversal of another drawing. These drawings imply that mirror reversals were not viewed as having identical value to the original drawing. Tracing may have been a good way of examining whether poses seem convincing once reversed, but in the context of putting together a composition that reads in a particular direction, the orientation of a given figure must have had a surplus value that could not be achieved simply through an act of mirror

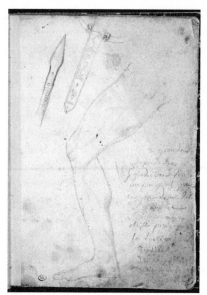

Figure 8. Jacques-Louis David, *Study of weapons, male leg, and autograph annotations (after the "Borghese Gladiator").* Horatii sketchbook, R.F. 4506, folio 2r. Photo: Michel Urtado. Musée du Louvre, Paris, France. Photo Credit: © RMN-Grand Palais / Art Resource, NY.

Figure 9. Jacques-Louis David, *Male leg (after the "Borghese Gladiator").* Horatii sketchbook, R.F. 4506, folio 3r. Photo: Michel Urtado. Musée du Louvre, Paris, France. Photo Credit: © RMN-Grand Palais / Art Resource, NY.

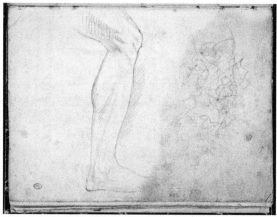

Figure 10. Jacques-Louis David, *Study of a leg and sketches (after the "Borghese Gladiator").* Horatii sketchbook, R.F. 4506, folio 83v. Photo: Michel Urtado. Musée du Louvre, Paris, France. Photo Credit: © RMN-Grand Palais / Art Resource, NY.

reversal. In a composition that dynamically unfolds from left to right, David's grasp of the energetic thrust of a leg pointing in that same direction was valuable (even if it showed the outer rather than inner leg) in ways that are not transferrable through tracing.

The Horatii sketchbook contains similar variations of the front leg of the first son (figs. 11–13). In the painting, this leg is the right leg. In the sketchbook, however, one of the three drawings (fig. 11) presents a right leg in the same orientation as it is in the painting, but a second drawing (folio 25 verso) presents this foot as a left foot, in a mirror reversal of the painted orientation. Rosenberg's and Prat's catalogue does not mention any external source for this drawing, but it does indicate that it is directly related to this figure.[28] This is another example where David chose to draw a foot exactly in reverse to how it will appear in the painting. A final set of studies on folio 83 recto, (fig. 12) shows us the same leg in the same orientation that will appear in the painting, yet it is hard to determine whether it is the outer or the inner leg (the outer leg would be consistent with the painting). I suggest that this ambiguity is emblematic of what we have seen happening in this sketchbook all along: David studied given poses from various points of view and then toyed with them and reversed them according to his needs. Throughout this process, he explored anatomical details and refined the outlines of poses, multiplying and varying both.

Finally, the sketchbook contains two studies (figs. 14, 15) for what seems like the back foot of the second son, once again in a mirror-reversal to the orientation in the painting. In their 2002 catalogue, Rosenberg and Prat do not mention a correlation between these two drawings and the figure of the second son, but we know that they are of the same sculpture of the Borghese Gladiator.[29] On the recto of the same sheet, another drawing of a foot appears in a frontal view (fig. 16). This pose correlates well with that of the back foot of the *third* son, but, in the painting, it is a right foot, while here it is a left one. What becomes apparent is the richness of David's process: a single sculpture with two legs could inspire poses of three different legs in the painting. These drawings exemplify how David studied the sculpture emphasizing the ways the feet meet and connect with the ground—and then played with the orientation in his studies, employing mirror reversal according to his pictorial needs.[30]

David's uses of mirror reversals in the Horatii sketchbook were, therefore, complex. On the one hand they partook in a process of evaluating the stability of forms set along a frieze; on the other hand, they elucidated how, in the context of a pictorial narrative with a particular direction, images of mirror reversal are not simply interchangeable. A close investigation of David's drawings in this sketchbook reveals both the pertinence of 180° reversals for

Figure 11. Jacques-Louis David, *Head of an ancient warrior, and two right legs (Studies for the "Oath of the Horatii")*. Horatii sketchbook, R.F. 4506, folio 12r. Photo: Michel Urtado. Musée du Louvre, Paris, France. Photo Credit: © RMN-Grand Palais / Art Resource, NY.

Figure 12. Jacques-Louis David, *Study of legs and autograph annotations*. Horatii sketchbook, R.F. 4506, folio 83r. Photo: Michel Urtado. Musée du Louvre, Paris, France. Photo Credit: © RMN-Grand Palais / Art Resource, NY.

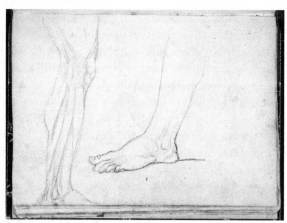

Figure 13. Jacques-Louis David, *Anatomic studies of a leg and a foot*. Horatii sketchbook, R.F. 4506, folio 25v. Photo: Michel Urtado. Musée du Louvre, Paris, France. Photo Credit: © RMN-Grand Palais / Art Resource, NY. Palais / Art Resource, NY.

Figure 14. Jacques-Louis David, *Study of a foot and traces (after the "Borghese Gladiator")*. Horatii sketchbook, R.F. 4506, folio 11v. Photo: Michel Urtado. Musée du Louvre, Paris, France. Photo Credit: © RMN-Grand Palais / Art Resource, NY.

Figure 15. Jacques-Louis David, *A landscape and a foot (after the "Borghese Gladiator")*. Horatii sketchbook, R.F. 4506, folio 76v. Photo: Michel Urtado. Musée du Louvre, Paris, France. Photo Credit: © RMN-Grand Palais / Art Resource, NY.

Figure 16. Jacques-Louis David, *Studies of a left arm, a right hand, and a left foot.* Horatii sketchbook, R.F. 4506, folio 11r. Photo: Michel Urtado. Musée du Louvre, Paris, France. Photo Credit: © RMN-Grand Palais / Art Resource, NY.

establishing a solid frieze-like structure and the importance of directionality for the formation of a unified, continuous composition. I have argued that both the tracings and the reversed leg studies relate to problems of stance and stability, a point I would like to develop with examples from David's later sketchbooks.

In sketchbooks he used while working on his grand Napoleonic commissions, David developed new ways of using the grid as an artistic tool (figs. 17, 18).[31] In the hundreds of squared drawings from those years, the artist always began to draw the grid at the point where the figure's foot meets the ground. This is different from the way he used the grid in his earlier drawings from the 1780s and 1790s.[32] The way David used the grid in the Napoleonic works seems like an attempt to transfer his figures to the canvas as "already standing," as it were, on solid ground, with the lower grid-line referencing that fictive ground. And, if the bottom edge of the foot coincides with the lowest horizontal grid-line, the very top edge of the head coincides with the highest horizontal grid-line. The grid, therefore, is a stabilizing tool, "locking" the figures within its boundaries. Moreover, in these drawings, the very central vertical grid-line marks the figure's imaginary central axis—its balancing point—the one beyond which it would no longer be able to maintain its pose. During the early 1800s, David was, therefore, laboring to regulate his process, responding to the challenge of transferring a vast number of figures, each studied separately, into an already existing composition without producing a "pasted" quality, a lack of gravity, or proportional discrepancies. The grid served to control uniformity of scale, enhance a sense of stability, and render convincingly the figure's ability to support its own weight in a given pose. This latter phenomenon, repeated across hundreds of drawings, helps illuminate how a stable and autonomous stance continued to engage David for decades.[33]

* * *

Back to the *Horatii*: notions of grounding were crucial for the *Horatii* both structurally and metaphorically. They became an important part of the painting's message: an emblem of exemplary ancient dedication to civic ideals.[34] The moment David chose to depict is one that does not appear in the ancient sources.[35] It communicates a message of extreme loyalty to the state, carrying particular resonance in France of the 1780s. On the left side of the canvas, three young men—powerful, noble and determined—represent Roman heroism and patriotism. On the right side, women mourn the future loss of their family. The men are depicted with straight lines and bright

Figure 17. Jacques-Louis David, *A Study for a flag-bearer in the "Distribution of the Eagles"*. Sketchbook dedicated to the "Eagles," 1961.393.1., folio 20r. Helen Regenstein Collection, the Art Institute of Chicago. Photo Credit: © The Art Institute of Chicago.

Figure 18. Jacques-Louis David, *Hortense de Beauharnais, the princess Louis, holding the hand of her son, prince Napoleon-Charles.* Sketchbooks dedicated to the "Coronation," folio 5r. Harvard Art Museums/Fogg Museum, Bequest of Grenville L. Winthrop. 1943.1815.12.5. Photo Credit: Imaging Department © President and Fellows of Harvard College.

colors: they are erect, active, and strong. The women are depicted with curvilinear lines and pastel colors: they are passive, afraid, and do not even dare to look at the scene.[36] These formal contrasts heighten the opposition between the two spheres, conveying the lesson that in the conflict between loyalty to the state and loyalty to one's family, the state must come first. The personal tragedy in this case is even worse due to additional ties between the opponent families: one of the Horatii sisters (Camilla on the extreme right) was engaged to one of the Curiatii brothers, and one of the Curiatii sisters (Sabina, right next to her) was married to one of the Horatii brothers who is killed in battle. The consequence of these marriage relations is, therefore, that the defeat of either side in this battle would be tragic to both.

The tragedy reaches its peak when, after winning the battle, the surviving Horatius returns to Rome to find his sister Camilla mourning the death of her fiancé, and he kills her. This murder earned the last Horatii offspring a sentence of death, which his father then appealed, begging the assembly to spare the life of his only living child. David's earlier compositional sketches for this painting present the victorious Horatius returning to Rome and killing his sister (1781) and the Horatii's father defending his son in front of the people (1782). The difference between these versions and the one David ended up choosing is that the former represent the moment after the battle when the moral conflict has been determined, whereas the final version portrays a dramatically tense moment before the battle, when the future is arguably still open.

The Horatii's choice to sacrifice their lives for a greater purpose had to be made with certainty. These men's forceful determination is made visible in their tight and erect bodies, with feet both strongly rooted in the marble floor and fully aligned with the frieze. Dorothy Johnson has argued that David used feet as corporal signs in the *Horatii*, communicating a message of physical and moral strength.[37] What this essay shows is that notions of grounding and solidity, which were so crucial for the *Horatii*, were closely tied to practices of reversal. I have suggested that the painting's famous frieze-like composition was related to David's habit of mirror-reversing and tracing lateral objects and figures. While the composition itself is far from symmetrical, artistic practices of mirror reversal came to play a decisive role in its development.[38]

Avoiding pure symmetry in the visual arts is associated with the need to maintain a delicate balance between order and movement, between organizational principles and the liveliness of forms. Indeed, the equilibrium between stillness and movement captures something fundamental to David's *Horatii* where the male figures are stable and rooted while the overall composition conveys movement throughout. Having reviewed how drawings derived from mirror reversal relate to the solidity of the male warriors, I now turn to examine how different configurations of stability and gravity inform the entire composition, producing a delicate continuum in movement. What does an understanding of David's operational procedures tell us about his struggle with the formulation of morality in this famous painting? The next section demonstrates how the relationship between the different parts of this composition could be reconfigured once these operations are brought to light.

* * *

The *Horatii*'s Composition, Reread

In 1785, Salon criticisms described the painting as "astonishing, sublime, inspired in its invention; though marred by harsh notes and a declamatory impatience with compositional subtleties, it elevated the mind and moved the emotions away from center stage; the pride and inflexibility of the early Romans, so foreign to modern mores, came alive on canvas."[39] Contemporary critics and recent scholars stress the spatial disharmony and lack of compositional unity in David's paintings. Thomas Puttfarken claims that "David's paintings were generally successful not despite but because of what some critics called their lack of unity."[40] Art historian Thomas Crow notes that

> ... the defiance of convention, the asperities, tenseness, austerity, and awkwardness which [the critics] responded to are there for us to see. The lining-up of the three sons, the gaps which separate the figure groups, the assertively simple and declarative order of the picture as a whole, communicate a willful rejection of compositional complexity and difficulty as values in themselves. Painterly flourishes and obvious demonstrations of virtuosity are absent. There is no seductive variety or texture, either of the objects depicted or of the painted surface itself; the surfaces of things—stone, metal, cloth, flesh—have a brittle, unrelieved hardness.[41]

The composition is considered disjointed because of its opposition of male and female groups. According to Crow, the opposition "... between clenched angularity and supple, curvilinear form, between controlled and uncontrolled emotion, verges on disassociation."[42] Bryson describes it as an opposition between language and silence, or politics and domesticity.[43] This opposition manifests itself in the differences between the figures' feet as well: heroic male dedication is represented in both erect stances and rooted feet, while the seated women's feet are mere extensions of their reclining bodies, softly touching the ground. This difference is also reflected in David's preparatory procedures. Does it not seem odd that a single sketchbook contains twelve different studies of male legs and feet but none of the female? At the very least it shows that David was occupied with male stance and with its impact on the relationship between the figures' feet and the ground, more than he was with the females' feet. As we saw, the prominence of mirror-reversed studies implies that this practice relates to David's attempt to formulate a solid, stable, and autonomous male stance in the *Horatii* painting.

Several triangular structures unify this composition, and the women participate in them: the two female figures on the extreme right lean onto one another to form a triangular shape. Instead of assertively placing their weight onto the ground, which could be seen to represent ancient laws and morals, the women lean on one another. The male and female groups each form a community, but their unification is achieved through different means. The brothers are united through doubling, or their resemblance to one another, to the extent that they seem to stand too close together, rendering the spatial relations between them unreliable. The women, on the other hand, are united through their support of one another's weight, the carrying of each other's grief.[44]

Thomas Crow claims that "the picture refuses to find form for the relationships between men and women which are central to its narrative content."[45] What my argument attempts to do is offer precisely that—a form for this relationship—one that emerges from a continuous reading of the shifting modes of gravity, beginning on the far left and ending on the far right side of the composition. Even as Crow notes that the painting is "dissonant, unnuanced, and disjointed," he observes that its "mathematical rationality, geometrical order, and even surface" unify it.[46] While these unifying principles lean more towards the stylistic, the continuity that interests me emerges from figural dispositions within the pictorial narrative.

Art historian Michel Fried was first to insist on reading the *Horatii* not as a split picture but one that presents unity of effect through absorption. The *Horatii*, according to Fried, is a powerful expression of pictorial drama, an epitome of what anti-theatrical painting looked like in the 1780s. The opposition between men and women in the *Horatii*—the men active and the women passive—is understood as paradigmatic; both are oblivious "to everything but their own thoughts and feelings."[47] Inspired both by Fried's influential theory and by Dorothy Johnson's notable work on corporal communication in David's *Horatii*, this essay analyzes this well-known composition by charting the effects of gestural movement on the viewer's experience.[48] The cumulative effect of the ways figures and masses move against one another as well as against their surroundings creates a fictive sense of continuity across the canvas.

David's decision to paint a moment that took place before the peak of the drama resonates with Lessing's concept of the "pregnant moment."[49] In the *Horatii*, David's introducing something of the poetic (temporal) arts into the plastic (spatial) arts took the form of an unfolding evolution along the frieze. Some of the spatial disharmonies for which the *Horatii* is famous relate to the dominance of the frieze as a construct within which both grounding and movement had to take place.[50] This movement could be considered as a "domino-like" effect of receding strength: the sons are the strongest figures, the father is slightly weaker, and the women are the weakest. This reading situates the father as a key figure—one that marks an indecisive option between the solid determination of the men to the left and the passive collapse of the women to the right. Bryson argues that "the patriarch is now weaker than his sons, his debility stressed by David in the instability of his power: his arms and legs are bent where the legs and arms of the sons are straight, the left foot uncertainly placed, while the feet of the sons are square with the ground."[51] A preparatory drawing of the father's right leg (fig. 11) demonstrates that originally the figure's instability was meant to be even greater.

A comparison between an ink and wash drawing (fig. 19) and the actual painting helps interpret the movement across this canvas. The swords in the father's hand are positioned more on an angle in the painted version and his right knee looks more bent backwards (even if this is an effect of the way David formulated the shading above the knee). Together, these two modifications (from the drawing) create the illusion that, by stretching their arms forward, the sons could have caused their father to shift his weight backwards. The father's retreating pose gives the fictive impression that in their powerful act of oath-taking, the sons gained the ability to initiate movement that could cause their father's slight imbalance.[52]

The sons' ability to "generate" such movement relies on the fact that they are such solid figures. The comparison between the compositional drawing and the painting also reveals David's ways of stabilizing the sons' position on the fictive pictorial ground. In the drawing, the stance of the front son is wider and slightly less balanced; his flowing clothes make it seem as if he is in the midst of taking a step forward, and, accordingly, that his brother must exert greater force when he grips his torso. In the painting, on the other hand, the whole unit of the three sons is more rooted, maybe even more focused on their mission. The fabrics are less flowing, the second son holds onto his brother more subtly than before, and the triangular stance of the front son is more stable.

Dorothy Johnson argues that in this painting, the body itself becomes the primary vehicle of expression, which puts David against an earlier tradition in which pictorial meaning was delivered through the face.[53] In this context, the way that David positioned the feet on the plane of the floor was of utmost importance. The stability of the sons turns them into paradigms of determination and dedication. Against their blinded thrust forward, their father's pose could be conceived as retreat. On the right side of the canvas, the domino effect continues: the movement of the father shifting his weight backwards is dramatized and brought to its full impact in Sabina's collapse

Figure 19. Jacques-Louis David, *Oath of the Horatii*, ca. 1782-4. Pen and brown ink, brown wash, on paper, 22.9 x 33.3 cm. Inv. PL1194. Palais des Beaux-Arts, Lille, France. Photo © PBA, Lille / Dist. RMN-Grand Palais / Art Resource, NY.

into her chair. Once again, compared to the Lille drawing, in the painting we see a shorter distance and more direct alignment (achieved through a strip of shading) between the father's left foot and Sabina's left foot, contributing to this effect. This focus on decreasing modes of autonomy and stability in the *Horatii's* figures allows for a more continuous reading of the whole composition. The father, in his slightly odd pose, serves as an important intermediary figure: he is a recipient of the oath and the one who channels its tragic impact from the left to the right side of the canvas. This tragedy culminates in Sabina's falling back into the chair, losing all uprightness and autonomy of stance.

This fictional movement, however, had to be contained within the painting's boundaries. David could not allow its impact to "spill" outside of the canvas, and the figure of Camilla on the extreme right is positioned to "stop" it, as it were. Curled, leaning against her own sister-in-law, Camilla counterbalances this movement and "closes" the composition. Once again, a comparison between the drawing and the painting helps clarify this point. In the drawing, Camilla's knees are crossed over one another, and her right foot is securely placed on the ground—giving the impression that her lower body is supporting its own weight while her upper body leans against her sister-in-law. In the painting, the crossed knees are gone and both feet are lifted from the ground, making it seem as if Camilla leans her entire body weight onto Sabina. Contributing to this effect are the more pronounced curve in Camilla's back and the way David cropped her figure, not to permit us a view of her body's full contour. Camilla's pose represents complete collapse into agony. She is the closing unit of this composition—a composition that runs from heroic action on the left to human devastation on the right.[54] This movement takes place within the structure of the frieze, illustrated very well by the single line connecting the first son's feet, his father's back foot and Camilla's two feet. Once again, in the painting more so than the drawing, David enhanced this straight line using the architecture of the floor's flagstones.

In conclusion, the operations of tracing and mirror reversal that appear in the Horatii sketchbook engage in the attempt to establish male heroism through a stable and solid stance, and they are reflective of the dominance of the frieze in this composition. The painting's spatial disharmonies become related to the frieze's dual, somewhat conflicting, function: to enhance stability on the one hand yet enable shifts and movements through the pictorial narrative on the other. The painting establishes continuity of gestural movement by situating the father as a key intermediate figure. By stressing the changing relationships between figures and the ground below them, this analysis both generates a more continuous reading of the *Horatii's* composition and exemplifies how, in this painting, gender differences denote dramatically different societal models of community-making.

Coda

Such correlations between the phenomenology of David's creative process and his finished compositions occurred throughout his career. The operative functions of David's drawing procedures are reflected in the orientation of his compositions—the direction from which they could be understood. Later on compositional complexities will become greater—moving from the frieze to structures that include multiple directions and orientations.[55] The ever-growing complexity of David's compositions is closely tied to the development of his reversals. As the modes of reversal that David used in his preparatory processes became more complex and more abstract, his compositions became more multidirectional and round. In order to elucidate what I mean by more abstract modes of reversal, I will introduce a final example from a later sketchbook used in the years 1794–1800 (figs. 20, 21).[56]

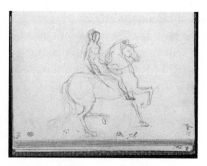

Figure 20. Jacques-Louis David, *Man in armor on a rearing horse, holding a sword, and another horse.* Sketchbook dedicated to the "Sabines," R.F. 9137, folio 31v. Photo: M. Jeanneteau. Musée du Louvre, Paris, France. Photo Credit: © RMN-Grand Palais / Art Resource, NY.

Figure 21. Jacques-Louis David, *Horseman, seen from the right profile.* Sketchbook dedicated to the "Sabines," R.F. 9137, folio 32r. Photo: M. Jeanneteau. Musée du Louvre, Paris, France. Photo Credit: © RMN-Grand Palais / Art Resource, NY.

Figure 22. Same as figure 20 above, rotated 90°

Figure 23. Same as figure 21 above, rotated 90°

The book is dedicated mostly to preparatory drawings for the *Sabine Women* (1799), but the two drawings that interest me are for *Napoleon crossing the Alps* (1801). This painting also concerns issues of stability and balance, as it represents Napoleon, the military genius, staying upright and maintaining control over a wildly rearing horse. It seems like the drawing on the right is a tracing, in mirror reversal, of the image on the left, with a variation in the horse's front legs. But, in fact, these two sheets are adjacent to one another and were drawn separately, with each drawing positioned horizontally, facing outwards (figs. 22, 23). The relationship between them resembles a "virtual trace:" instead of literally tracing an image onto the verso of a sheet, David simply drew a mirror reflection of it onto the adjacent folio. Instead of treating the sheet as a transparent window (used for tracing), the sheet came to function like an opaque mirror, with the neighboring drawing "reflected" on it in reverse.

Whether this configuration was intentional, David could not have drawn the later image without having the former one in sight. Together, these two folios suggest that practices of reversal were so deeply embedded in David's creative process that he could draw free-hand a mirror image of his drawings without the aid of the operational technique of using an external light source to trace his image. This tendency to use reversals in more complex ways continued into David's later career, which was also apparent in the artist's turning the sketchbook upside down and drawing on it from back to front.[57]

These new connections between the phenomenology of David's creative process and his finished compositions could also be extended to the viewing experience of his works. According to Crow, the *Horatii's* pictorial space does not continue the viewer's space—the viewer does not have a path into the painting.[58] Bryson thinks that the painting's space is continuous with the viewer's space but that the viewer is excluded from its drama.[59] Michael Fried places the beholder outside of the painting, stressing the figures' ignorance of any potential viewer who could be watching them.[60] The bodily presence of the *Horatii's* viewer, therefore, remains external to the pictorial structure. This result differs from the type of three-dimensionality reflected in David's later preparatory procedures and compositions, in which the rounded pictorial structure comes to incorporate the viewer in new ways.[61] The phenomenology of making and that of viewing are thus intimately related.

One of the consequences of this focus on modes of mirroring in David's drawing practices is that the artist's entire career can be understood through the schema of an ever-growing compositional complexity of history paintings that are invested in corporeal agency and movement. The final result is that preparatory drawings of David's late career come to influence his painting in new ways. Emphasizing operations of mirroring, this essay has shown how mirror reversal first interfered in the normative dynamics of interchange between the artist's eye, hand, and mind, allowing him to achieve a new, external perspective on his own work. Later, mirror reversal was integrated into the artist's corporeal disposition while drawing and reflected in the compositional evolution of his work. Mirror reversal is a major process that David employed to address the challenges of moving from drawing to painting or from preparatory to final works. It reveals a broader connection between the dynamics of David's graphic and painted works than has hitherto been recognized.

NOTES

I would like to thank my mentors Ralph Ubl and Martha Ward for their guidance, invaluable insights, and ongoing support of this project. I am deeply grateful to Suzanne F. McCullagh and Pierre Rosenberg for generously providing me with essential material to conduct this research. I truly appreciate the support of Robert Pippin and the John U. Nef Committee on Social Thought. I am grateful to Dorothy Johnson and Perrin Stein for reading this work while it was in progress. I thank Daniella Berman, Charles Kang, Ruth Iskin, and Ronit Milano for the opportunity to present earlier versions of this work. And finally, I am thankful to Andrei Pop, Robert Abbott, and *SECC*'s anonymous readers for their useful comments and suggestions.

1. Inv. R.F. 4506, Paris, Musée du Louvre, Département des Arts Graphiques, referred to, hereafter, as the "Horatii sketchbook." This book, purchased by the Louvre in 1918, currently contains 83 folios, sized 18.8cm by 13.5cm.

2. Ralph Ubl points to the stark contrast between the treatment of the pictorial ground in David's work as opposed to Delacroix's; in contrast to the hard marble floor in David's *Horatii*, both figures and ground in Delacroix's *Death of Sardanapalus* are fluid, unstable, and floating. See for example, Ralph Ubl, "Entwurf und Leben: Eugène Delacroix als Zeichner," in ed. Karin Krauthausen and Omar Nasim, *Notizen, Skizzen, Gekritzel. Zeichnen und Schreiben als Entwurfsinstrumente* (Zürich: Diaphanes Verlag, 2010), 189–218.

3. This was claimed by, among others, Thomas Crow. See: "The *Oath of the Horatii* in 1785: Painting and pre-Revolutionary radicalism in France," *Art History* 1, no. 4 (1978): 457.

4. Dorothy Johnson convincingly demonstrates the prominence of the frieze in David's *Horatii*, in her "Corporality and Communication: The Gestural Revolution of Diderot, David, and *The Oath of the Horatii*," *The Art Bulletin* 71, no. 1 (1989): 92–113.

5. David's even and sustained application of paint, Crow argues, "… involves

a suppression of those qualities which make paint a record of the body, of play, of expressive accident, of the sometimes unruly demands of persons and objects perceived individually. The picture, further, works to efface itself as a product of labour, [*sic*] The handling is plain, undemonstrative, neither polished nor broad. Where painting, typically, had flourished the signs of its making, the signs of a particular process of labour, David reduces this to a minimum." Crow, "The *Oath of the Horatii* in 1785," 460.

6. Norman Bryson, "Mortal sight: The Oath of the Horatii," in *Tradition and Desire: From David to Delacroix* (Cambridge: Cambridge Univ. Press, 1984), 63–84.

7. A substantial part of the scholarship on David has focused on the spectatorship of his works. Michael Fried's seminal work interprets David's achievements through the ongoing question of the relationship between his paintings and their potential beholder. Michael Fried, *Absorption and Theatricality: painting and beholder in the age of Diderot* (Chicago: Univ. of Chicago Press, 1988); Michael Fried, "David et l'antithéâtralité," in ed. Régis Michel, *David contre David: actes du colloque organisé au musée du Louvre par service culturel du 6 au 10 décembre 1989* (Paris: Editions de la Documentation Française, Collection des Colloques du Musée du Louvre, 1993), Vol. 1: 199–227; and, most recently, Michael Fried, "David/Manet: the 'Anacreonic' Paintings,'" in *Another Light: Jacques-Louis David to Thomas Demand* (London and New Haven: Yale Univ. Press, 2014), 7–39.

Additionally, Wolfgang Kemp's discussion of *David's Oath of the Tennis Court* stresses the incorporation of a viewer into the painting's circular composition to convey a message of political equality. See his "The Theater of Revolution: A New Interpretation of Jacques-Louis David's *Tennis Court Oath*," in ed. Norman Bryson, Michael Ann Holly, and Keith Moxey, *Visual culture: images and interpretations* (Hanover, NH: Univ. Press of New England [for] Wesleyan Univ. Press, c1994), 202–27.

Ewa Lajer-Burcharth's influential work argues that the placement of a mirror in front of David's *Intervention of the Sabine Women* turned the viewer into a participant in the painting, producing a call for republican patriotism. See her "David's *Sabine Women*: Body, Gender and Republican Culture Under the Directory," *Art History* 14, no. 3 (1991): 397–430 and her *Necklines: The Art of Jacques-Louis David after the Terror* (New Haven: Yale Univ. Press, c1999), chapter 3.

8. Dorothy Johnson's work provides detailed analyses of some of David's drawings and their role in the development of his career. See her *Jacques-Louis David: art in metamorphosis* (Princeton, N.J.: Princeton Univ. Press, c1993) and her "Lines of Thought: David's Aporetic Late Drawings," in ed. Mark Ledbury, *David after David: Essays on the Later Work* (Williamstown, MA: Sterling and Francine Clark Art Institute, 2007; distributed by Yale Univ. Press), 153–69. Another important source on the subject is Pierre Rosenberg, *From drawing to painting: Poussin, Watteau, Fragonard, David, and Ingres* (Princeton, N.J.: Princeton Univ. Press, 2000). Philippe Bordes also elucidates David's preparatory drawings, specifically for his *Tennis Court Oath*. See his *Le Serment du Jeu de Paume de Jacques-Louis David. Le peintre, son milieu et son temps de 1789 à 1792* (Paris, 1983). Perrin Stein focuses on David's drawings for the *Brutus* in her "Crafting the Neoclassical: Two

New Drawings for Jacques-Louis David's *The Lictors Bringing Brutus the Bodies of His Sons*," *Master Drawings* 74, no. 2 (2009): 221–36. Ewa Lajer- Burcharth analyzes David's drawings for the *Intervention of the Sabine Women* in her "The Revolution Glacée," *Necklines*, 1999. Virginia Lee explores David's Versailles sketchbook in her "Jacques-Louis David: The Versailles Sketchbook," *Burlington Magazine* 111 (1969): 197–208, 360–69.

9. Heidi E. Kraus, "David's Roman Vedute," *Studies in Eighteenth-Century Culture* 38 (2009): 173–97.

10. Pierre Rosenberg and Louis-Antoine Prat suggest that this book (R.F. 4506) was given as a gift, which may explain why David removed some numeration from it. Pierre Rosenberg and Louis-Antoine Prat, *Jacques-Louis David, 1748–1825: Catalogue Raisonné des Dessins* (Milano: Leonardo arte, 2002), 891.

11. Unlike his *Roman Albums*, this sketchbook did not serve David merely as a means to assemble a general vocabulary of images but as a way to develop a repertoire for a specific painting. On the structural difference between albums and sketchbooks, and, more broadly, on the specific qualities of artists' sketchbooks, see Miriam Stewart, "Curating Sketchbooks: Interpretation, Preservation, Display," in ed. Angela Bartram, Nader El-Bizri, and Douglas Gittens, *Recto Verso: Redefining the Sketchbook* (Surrey, England and Burlington, VT: Ashgate Publishing Company, 2014), 163–75.

12. All of the recto pages of this book are drawn on in a right-side-up orientation. When David shifted to draw on some recto pages horizontally, it is mostly because the subject of his drawing (a landscape, for instance) called for a wider format. The book's verso pages were drawn on much less, and, despite the fact that some of them were drawn on upside-down as well, these isolated instances do not amount to a continuous shift in the book's orientation. This is very different from what happens in some of David's later sketchbooks, which were treated as truly versatile objects. In these later examples, the recto and verso pages at the beginning of the book mostly share the same (right-side-up) orientation, and those at the end of the book share the same (mostly upside-down) orientation. There is a sequential feeling to each end of the book and a clear transition between these two sequences. The Horatii sketchbook, however, still functions mostly like a standard book—with a prominence to the right-side-up and front-to-back orientations.

13. These two examples are from a sketchbook dedicated mostly to the "Leonidas," inv. R.F. 9136, Paris, Musée du Louvre, Département des Arts Graphiques. It was used in 1808–13 and after, and its folios measure 25.5x20.3 cm.

14. Rosenberg, *From Drawing to Painting*, 83.

15. "[The Model] had to keep the pose without the aid of wedges or cords, so that the movement would seem as natural as possible, even at the cost of his fatigue" (Author's translation). Sidonie Lemeux-Fraitot, "Faire œuvre d'atelier," in Richard Dagorne, *Au-delà du maître: Girodet et l'atelier de David* (Paris: Somogy, 2005), 20. See also: Étienne Jean Delécluze, *Louis David: Son École Et Son Temps: Souvenirs* (Paris, 1855), 47.

16. *The Notebooks of Leonardo da Vinci,* ed. Edward Macurdy (London, 1977), 244.

17. David's mirror reversals in drawing resonate with an entire culture of images from roughly the same period—namely, engravings. In David's lifetime, studies of ancient sources conventionally derived from engravings of ancient masterpieces, which were the most available resource to Parisian artists who did not reside in Italy under the Prix-de-Rome. In these engravings, images always appear in reverse. Artists were, therefore, accustomed to the practice of copying images in reverse to the original, often comparing them with the opposite (correct) orientation once they visited Rome or when they saw drawings of the original works by other artists who had gone to Rome.

18. Dorothy Johnson, "Ideality and the Mirror Image: David's The *Sabine Women* Revisited," in ed. Francis Assaf, *The King's Crown: Essays in French Literature and Art in Honor of Basil Guy* (Leuven: Editions Peeters, 2005), 139–51, and Dorothy Johnson, "Jacques-Louis David, Artist and Teacher: An Introduction," in ed. Dorothy Johnson, *Jacques-Louis David: New Perspectives* (Newark: Univ. of Delaware Press, 2006), 38–39.

19. Johnson, "Ideality and the Mirror Image," 151.

20. Johnson, "Jacques-Louis David, Artist and Teacher," 39.

21. See, for example, the drawing of a sacrificial bull in one of David's Roman Albums, currently at the Fogg Art Museum. In Agnes Mognan, *David to Corot: French Drawings in the Fogg Art Museum* (Harvard Univ. Press, 1996), 41; it is also reproduced in Andrei Pop, *Antiquity, Theatre, and the Painting of Henry Fuseli* (Oxford Univ. Press, 2015), 49. I thank Andrei for bringing this point to my attention.

22. Dorothy Johnson was the first scholar to establish the prominence of feet in David's *Horatii*: "That David sought to make a profound and indelible somatic impression on the spectator explains his attention to the minute details of the extremities. Indeed, he was celebrated in his time as the greatest living painter of the hands and feet, (...). The hands and feet of David's figures, characterized by a notable vitality, are important corporal signs and communicate to the spectator in an even more dramatic and forceful way than facial expression itself. (...) In *The Oath*, David painted the extended foot of Horatius twenty times." Johnson, "Corporality and Communication," 111.

23. Two feet appear twice each, and two appear three times each. The two that are consistent with the way they appear in the painting are the first son's back (left) leg, drawn on folio 2 verso as a left leg, and the father's front (right) leg, drawn on folios 12 recto and 12 verso as a right leg. Interestingly enough, in both of these cases, the foot undergoes some modification: the elevated heel (in the son's case) will be further anchored to the ground, and the elevated toes (in the father's case) will be lowered and become more level with the ground.

24. It makes sense that David's ink and wash compositional drawing precedes his detailed drapery studies; it helps keep individual figures' tonal scales in accordance with one another and maintain the uniformity of lighting effects across the entire composition.

25. The sketchbook was used between October 1784 and August 1785. The definitive compositional drawing, now in Lille (fig. 19), shows the male figures in poses that approximate the ones they have in the painting. The dating of the Lille

drawing is debatable: some scholars date it to 1784, while Antoine Schnapper and Arlette Sérullaz date it to 1782. According to Schnapper and Sérullaz, towards the end of 1782, David already had developed a conception of this composition. See their *Jacques-Louis David, 1748–1825, Catalogue: Musée du Louvre, Département des peintures, Paris [et] Musée national du château, Versailles, 26 octobre 1989–12 février 1990* (Paris: Editions de la Réunion des musées nationaux, 1989), 171 (cat. no. 71).

Following Schnapper and Sérullaz, Rosenberg and Prat also believe that David started to work on this drawing in 1782, took it to Rome, and introduced some changes in 1784. These changes mostly apply to the right-hand-side of the composition; they helped make the figures more identifiable and the opposition between the male and female groups stronger. See Rosenberg and Prat, *Jacques-Louis David, 1748–1825*, 70 (cat. no. 50). Following Rosenberg's and Prat's analysis, the men's poses on the left side of the Lille sheet must be close to what they were in 1782 (or, at least, before going back to work on the drawing in late 1784). Even if David did not reach the most definitive version of his composition before making the individual figure studies contained in the Horatii sketchbooks, it seems safe to assume that he had a clear idea of what the men's poses were going to look like. And still, he invested much time in mirror-reversed studies of their legs and feet. He must have, therefore, found the making of these drawings useful in some way. As late as 1784, David was contemplating changes to his composition, recorded in two drawings now in Paris: one is at the École Nationale Supérieure des Beaux-Arts (inv. 733), and the other is at the Louvre (R.F. 29914); for more, see Rosenberg and Prat, *Jacques-Louis David, 1748–1825*, 86–87. The fact that none of the leg and foot studies in the Horatii sketchbook correlate with poses that appear in these later drawings also helps support the claim that they were, indeed, made in correlation with the poses that David had established in the Lille drawing more than a year earlier.

26. These processes are identified and analyzed in my dissertation chapter on the history of David's *Leonidas*. See Tamar Mayer, *Consequences of Drawing: Self and History in Jacques-Louis David's Preparatory Practices*, Ph.D. Dissertation, University of Chicago (forthcoming).

27. The ability to identify David's drawings as preparatory works for this painting and the sources they rely on is based, by and large, on Rosenberg's and Prat's invaluable catalogue. See Rosenberg and Prat, *Jacques-Louis David, 1748–1825*.

28. Rosenberg and Prat, *Jacques-Louis David, 1748–1825*, 900 (cat. no. 1309).

29. Rosenberg and Prat, *Jacques-Louis David, 1748–1825*, 895 (cat. no. 1295 verso) and 916 (cat. no. 1359 verso).

30. Michael Fried also finds mirror reversal central to David's work but in a very different way. According to Fried, by resisting the convention of reversing the mirror reversal of self-portraits in this period, David's self-portrait from 1794 alludes to an analogy between the artists' own portrayal and his portrayal of his friend and political martyr Marat from a few years earlier. See Michael Fried, "David/Marat: The *Self-Portrait* of 1794," in ed. Ledbury, *David after David: Essays on the Later Work*, 191–203.

31. The first example (fig.17) is from a sketchbook dedicated to the "Distribution of Eagles," used c. 1810, currently at the Art Institute of Chicago. Its folios measure 24.3x19.2 cm. The second example (fig. 18) is from a sketchbook dedicated to the "Coronation" used in 1805–1807, currently at the Fogg. Its folios measure 23.7x17.9 cm.

32. I refer mostly to the detailed drapery studies that David produced in preparation for the *Horatii, Socrates, Brutus,* and the *Sabines.* The grid is used much like it was in many Renaissance drawings—to cover an entire surface rather than establish conformity in proportion across hundreds of individual drawings.

33. I develop these ideas in a dissertation chapter dedicated to David's preparatory processes for the *Coronation* (1808) and the *Eagles* (1810). David's use of the grid features in an analysis with a detailed account of his shifting configurations of Napoleon's figure in the *Coronation.* These changes, recorded across more than a dozen drawings (eight of which are from a single sketchbook), illustrate David's negotiations of stability and movement in this central figure as well. See Mayer, *Consequences of Drawing,* forthcoming.

34. The emphases on the figure's ability to appear grounded and to carry its own weight convincingly are not unrelated to enlightenment ideals of the same period. The eighteenth century saw the rise in popularizations of Newtonian theories of gravity and renewed interest in ancient principles of solid human rationality. David's tracings and mirror-reversed drawings were, therefore, part of a process of realizing these ideals visually, in the genre of history painting.

35. See Edgar Wind, "The Sources of David's Horaces," *Journal of the Warburg and Courtauld Institutes*, Vol. 4, No. 3/4 (Apr., 1941–Jul., 1942): 124–38, and F. Hamilton Hazlehurst, "The Artistic Evolution of David's *Oath*," *The Art Bulletin*, Vol. 42, No. 1 (Mar., 1960): 59–63.

36. Dorothy Johnson mentions the "… bicameral opposition of gender groups, the angular, masculine vigor of Horatius and his sons contrasted with the passive submission of the curvilinear forms of the women and children" in "Corporality and Communication," 107.

37. Dorothy Johnson, "Corporality and Communication," argues that "David had used every aspect of corporality—the foot and the hand as well as the face —to produce anatomies that could counter this threat [of physical as well as moral degeneracy]. The figures in The Oath communicate to the spectator on a physical and, one might even say, a visceral level. The response to the pantomime of the figures is an instinctive, somatic one: the corporal signs are immediately absorbed and understood without recourse to verbal explanation" (110).

38. These developments should be put in the context of the re-emergence of symmetry in late eighteenth-century and early nineteenth-century art and architecture as a reaction against rococo traditions of disorderly excess. Neoclassical art reintroduced classical principles of order, perfection, harmony, and logic. Contemporaries believed that symmetry was aesthetically most effective when it included a few asymmetrical elements; pure symmetry was considered static because it led to the danger of "deadening" the pictorial structure. See Robert Rosenblum, *Transformations in Late Eighteenth Century Art* (Princeton: Princeton Univ. Press,

1967), 157; Alexander Voloshinov, "Symmetry as a Superprinciple of Science and Art," *Leonardo* 29, no. 2 (1996): 110.

39. Thomas Crow, *Emulation: David, Drouais, and Girodet in the art of revolutionary France* (New Haven: Yale Univ. Press; Los Angeles: in association with The Getty Institute, 2006), 43.

40. Thomas Puttfarken, "David's *Brutus* and Theories of Pictorial Unity in France," *Art History* 4, 1981, 293.

41. Thomas Crow, "*The Oath of the Horatii* in 1785," 457.

42. Thomas Crow, "*The Oath of the Horatii* in 1785," 464.

43. The *Horatii*, according to Bryson, is "an image of visuality for the subject living under patriarchy." Females are denied political authority: they are "consigned to silence, to the interior, to reproduction," while the men are in the realm of language and power. Norman Bryson, *Tradition and Desire*, 70.

44. Gender differences are prominent in David's work particularly his history paintings. Several of the most intriguing studies of the past two decades offer gendered readings of David's work. See Burcharth, "David's *Sabine Women*," 1991, and her *Necklines*, 1999; Erica Rand, "Boucher, David, and the French Revolution: Politics and Gender in Eighteenth-century French History Painting" (PhD Diss., University of Chicago, 1989); Alex Potts, *Flesh and the ideal: Winckelmann and the origins of art history* (New Haven: Yale Univ. Press, 1994); and, Satish Padiyar, *Chains: David, Canova, and the fall of the public hero in postrevolutionary France* (University Park: Penn State Univ. Press, 2007). Finally, David's studio as an all-male environment is one of the main foci of Thomas Crow's seminal work, *Emulation* (2006).

45. Thomas Crow, "*The Oath of the Horatii* in 1785," 457.

46. "First of all, there is the picture's visibly mathematical rationality, the rigorous geometrical structure which underlines the composition: the spacing of the figure groups, the perspective construction, the heights of the columns, even the angles of limbs, swords, and spear are interrelated in a precisely adhered-to geometry based on the golden section (this has been described and charted by Hautecœur)." There is also the evenness of paint, clarity of description, sharp delineation, and, as Rosenblum notes, "intellectual control." Thomas Crow, "*The Oath of the Horatii* in 1785," 459–60.

47. Michael Fried, *Another Light*, 12.

48. Dorothy Johnson, "Corporality and Communication," 92–113.

49. See Lessing, *Laocoon* (Mineola, NY: Dover Publications, 2005). This choice is characteristic of David's paintings of the 1780s: David's *Socrates* also depicts a moment before the peak of drama, when the ancient philosopher reaches out for the cup of hemlock. David's *Brutus*, on the other hand, describes a moment of contemplation that comes after the execution is over. As aforementioned, in the case of the *Horatii*, the current composition came after David examined a couple of other, more dramatic, options for this scene.

50. On the frieze in the *Horatii*, Bryson writes: "the plane of the frieze cuts across the Roman interior like a blade. Like a sword; it comes almost from another spatial universe." According to Bryson, the structure of the frieze competes with that of the

veduta, and the combination of the two creates an anamorphosis, where the point of view from which one could see the image properly is the vanishing point inside the painting itself, a point the beholder cannot occupy (Norman Bryson, *Tradition and Desire*, 80). Within Bryson's semiotic reading, the inability to see is at the core of the *Horatii's* meaning: for the men, visuality is blinded by signs—outwardly they project the signs of strength and inwardly their vision is paranoid—representing a crisis in subjectivity. The women, for their part, are blinded—they are seen but do not see (Norman Bryson, *Tradition and Desire*, 74).

51. Norman Bryson, *Tradition and Desire,* 70–71.

52. Crow also puts emphasis on the relationship between the father and the sons, but he interprets it quite differently: "(…) the outstretched hands of the sons *just* fail to meet the hands of their father—a whole drama of anticipation and release in this small incident, one which, however small, creates a sensible rift down the center of the tableau. Even the bond between the father and sons is interrupted." Crow, *"The Oath of the Horatii* in 1785," 459.

53. Dorothy Johnson, "Corporality and Communication."

54. A hint about continuity in the *Horatii*, one that places the women at the very end of its inner-movement, is found in Bryson's discussion of the painting as a chain of substitutions/dislocations. Bryson regards the women as victims; they do not "participate in this system of metonymies." They are the "marginalized object of power and vision, yet featuring in the system and in this particular narrative as the final, the ultimate image, at the end of the chain" (Norman Bryson, *Tradition and Desire*, 73). Bryson's analysis is, at its core, psychoanalytical and semiotic; my version of continuity, however, derives from a methodology that considers the relationship between a phenomenology of drawing and shifting modes of corporeal agency in David's painting.

55. Ewa Lajer-Burcharth interprets the *Sabines'* composition as one in which female bodies are "gathered into a circular nugget around the central figure of the striding Hersilia," disrupting the painting's frieze-like structure (Necklines, 150–153).

56. These two examples are from a sketchbook dedicated mostly to the *Sabines*, R.F. 9137, Paris, Musée du Louvre, Département des Arts Graphiques. Its folio measure 17.7 x 13.4 cm.

57. I have developed these and related points in a dissertation chapter on David's preparatory process for his last grand history painting, *Leonidas at Thermopylae* (1814). The many transformations that this painting underwent disclose David's attempt both to stabilize and dramatize his composition: he turned the entire scenic point of view ninety degrees, he subjected many of the figures to mirror reversal, and he moved them from one side of the composition to the other. The painting's rounded composition reflects this mode of reversal in which the three- dimensional book was flipped and turned in the artist's hand. See Mayer, *Consequences of Drawing*, forthcoming.

58. "In this heightened, overall equivalency of vision, the picture stands for an impassive and impervious "otherness" of things. The space of the picture is not an imaginary continuation of the viewer's own; it is another space, and a somehow

daunting one." Crow, "The Oath of the *Horatii* in 1785," 461.

59. According to Bryson, the conflict between the frieze and the veduta places the viewer in an impossible place. Bryson, *Tradition and Desire*, 76.

60. Michael Fried, *Absorption and Theatricality* (1988), and *Another Light* (2014), 7–16.

61. In another dissertation chapter, I analyze the composition of David's *Leonidas* to show how the viewer is implied in regard to it. Godehard Janzing also believes that the viewer of *Leonidas* becomes the protagonist's counterpart, albeit his compositional analysis is different than my own. Godehard Janzing, "Leonidas at the Crossroads: The Crux of the Composition," in ed. Ledbury, *David after David: Essays on the Later Work,* 83. See Mayer, *Consequences of Drawing*, forthcoming.

Contributors to Volume 46

R. S. Agin is Associate Professor of French and Italian at Duquesne University. His research focuses on the aesthetic and scientific cultures of enlightenment Europe. He is the editor of *Sex Education in Eighteenth-Century France* (2011) and, more recently, the translator, with Maria Elena Versari, of Umberto Boccioni's *Futurist Painting Sculpture (Plastic Dynamism)* (2016).

Amelia Dale is a Lecturer in the English Department at the University of Sydney. Recent publications include "'*Acting it As She Reads*': Affective Impressions in *Polly Honeycombe*" in *Passions, Sympathy and Print Culture* (2015) and "Dolly's Inch of Red Seal Wax: Impressing the Reader in *Tristram Shandy*" in *Sterne, Tristram, Yorick* (2016). She is an associate investigator with the Australian Research Council Centre of Excellence in the history of emotion. She is currently working on a monograph on impressions and reproduction in eighteenth-century British quixotic narratives.

Elena Deanda-Camacho is Associate Professor at Washington College, and she specializes in eighteenth-century pornographic literature in Spanish and Spanish American literature. She has published in academic journals in Mexico, United States, and Canada. In 2014, she edited the Vanderbilt e-Journal of Luso-Hispanic Studies, "Silence Revisited: Regulation, Censorship, and Freedom of Speech" (v.10). The essay for SECC derives from her NEMLA-sponsored research at the Vatican Library and France's Bastille Archives in 2014.

Julia Doe is Assistant Professor of Music at Columbia University. She is a specialist in the music, literature, and politics of the French Enlightenment, with a particular focus on lyric theater and the history of theatrical institutions. Her current book project examines the influence of Bourbon patronage on the development of opéra-comique in the final decades of the ancien régime. Excerpts from this work have appeared in *The Journal of the American Musicological Society* and *The Opera Journal*.

Richard Frohock is an English Professor and Department Chair at Oklahoma State University. He is the author of *Heroes of Empire (2004)* and *Buccaneers of America (2012)*, as well as various articles on the literary history of the early Americas, particularly the West Indies. He currently is at work on a book on English piracy narratives of the early eighteenth century.

Michael B. Guenther is an Assistant Professor of History at Grinnell College, where he teaches courses in environmental history, science and technology studies, and the broader Atlantic World. He is currently finishing a book project entitled *Science and the Civic Awakening: The Politics of Knowledge in the Age of Improvement* that examines the ways that the expanding culture of science transformed the social, environmental, and political landscape of Anglo-American society in the eighteenth century.

Aaron R. Hanlon is Assistant Professor of English at Colby College. His book project *The Politics of Quixotism* is a study of Don Quixote's contributions to political theory, particularly to British and American exceptionalisms in the long eighteenth century. In addition to published work in *The Eighteenth Century: Theory and Interpretation, Studies in the Novel,* and elsewhere, he has forthcoming articles in *New Literary History* and *Modern Philology.*

Catherine Jaffe is Professor of Spanish at Texas State University. Her research focuses on women writers, quixotism, gender, translation, and reading in the eighteenth and nineteenth centuries. She is the co-editor, with Elizabeth Franklin Lewis, of *Eve's Enlightenment: Women's Experience in Spain and Spanish America, 1726–1839* (2009). She is preparing an edition and biography of María Lorenza de los Ríos, Marquesa de Fuerte-Híjar (1761–1821), for which she received an ASECS Women's Caucus Editing and Translation Fellowship.

Rita Krueger is Associate Professor of History at Temple University. She is the author of *Czech, German, and Noble: Status and National Identity in Habsburg Bohemia* (2009), and she co-edited, with Ivo Cerman and Susan Reynolds, *The Enlightenment in Bohemia: Religion, Morality, and Multiculturalism* (2011). Her current project is a biography of Empress Maria Theresa. She will be a Faculty Fellow at the Center for the Humanities at Temple University during 2016–2017.

Elizabeth Franklin Lewis is Professor of Spanish at the University of Mary Washington in Fredericksburg, VA. She is the author of, *Women Writers in the Spanish Enlightenment: The Pursuit of Happiness* (Ashgate, 2004) and the co-editor with Catherine Jaffe of *Eve's Enlightenment: Women's Experience in Spain and Spanish America 1726–1839* (Louisiana State Univ. Press, 2009).

Jeff Loveland is Professor of Romance Languages and Literatures at the University of Cincinnati. He is the author of two books: *Rhetoric and Natural History: Buffon in Polemical and Literary Context* (2001) and *An Alternative Encyclopedia? Dennis de Coetlogon's Universal History of Arts and Sciences* (2010). He is currently doing research on European encyclopedias from the mid-seventeenth century to the present.

Tamar Mayer is a Ph.D. candidate in Art History and Social Thought at the University of Chicago and the recipient of a Chester-Dale Fellowship in the Department of Drawings and Prints at the Metropolitan Museum of Art. Her research focuses on drawing practices in French art c. 1800. This article is derived from the first chapter of her forthcoming dissertation, entitled "Consequences of Drawing: Self and History in Jacques-Louis David's *Preparatory Practices.*"

Jeffrey Merrick is Professor of History Emeritus, University of Wisconsin-Milwaukee, researches political culture, marital separations, sodomy, and suicide in eighteenth-century France.

Rebecca Messbarger is Professor of Italian, Art History, History, and Women's Studies at Washington University, specializing in the Italian enlightenment. She is author of T*he Lady Anatomist: The Life and Work of Anna Morandi Manzolini* (2010), a finalist for the College Art Association Charles Rufus Morey Award. She co-edited with Christopher Johns and Philip Gavitt *Benedict XIV and the Enlightenment: Art, Science and Spirituality* (2016) and with Paula Findlen *The Contest for Knowledge* (2005). Her essays include "The Re-Birth of Venus," *Journal of the History of Collections* (May 2012), winner of the James L. Clifford Prize and the Percy Adams Prize.

Heather Morrison is Associate Professor of history at State University of New York at New Paltz. She writes about the enlightenment in Vienna: a 2013 article in *Central European Studies* explores changes to authorship during censor reforms of the 1780s, and a 2012 *Journal of Social History* article analyzes freemasonic drinking songs published by an enlightenment lodge. "Dressing Angelo Soliman" appeared in *Eighteenth-Century Studies* in 2011 and focuses on self-fashioning and the fashioning of others through clothing by examining the exceptional case of an African who lived and died in Vienna. She is working on a book about a plant-collecting voyage that left Vienna to circumnavigate the globe in the 1780s. The Botstiber Institute for Austrian-American Studies supported the research for this project. She has also benefited from the continuing scholarly support of the Richard Plaschka Fellowship, run by the Austrian Exchange Service.

Adam Potkay is Professor of English and William R. Kenan, Jr. Professor of Humanities at the College of William & Mary in Virginia. His books include *The Fate of Eloquence in the Age of Hume* (1994); *Black Atlantic Writers of the Eighteenth Century* (1995), co-edited with Sandra Burr; T*he Passion for Happiness: Samuel Johnson and David Hume* (2000); *The Story of Joy from the Bible to Late Romanticism* (2007), winner of the Harry Levin Prize of the American Comparative Literature Association, and translated into Portuguese, Romanian and Polish, and *Wordsworth's Ethics* (2012). He is currently working on a study of ethics in literature.

ASECS Executive Board 2016–2017

President: **Dena Goodman**, Professor of History and Women's Studies, University of Michigan
First-Vice President: **Susan Lanser**, Professor of Comparative Literature, English, and Women's Studies, Brandeis University
Second-Vice President: **Melissa Hyde**, Professor of Art History, University of Florida
Treasurer: **William F. Edmiston**, Professor of French, University of South Carolina
Executive Director: **Byron R. Wells**, Professor of Romance Languages, Wake Forest University

Members-at-Large

Misty Anderson, Professor of English, University of Tennessee, Knoxville,
Laura Auricchio, Professor of Art History, The New School
Julia Douthwaite, Professor of French, University of Notre Dame
Lisa Freeman, Professor of English, Univeristy of Illinois at Chicago
Julia Simon, Professor of French and Italian, University of California, Davis
Mary Terrall, Professor of History, University of California, Los Angeles

Administrative Office
Office Manager: **Vickie Cutting**, Wake Forest University

For information about the
American Society for Eighteenth-Century Studies, please contact:
ASECS
P.O. Box 7867
Wake Forest University
Winston-Salem, NC 27109-7867
Telephone: (336) 727-4694
Fax: (336) 727-4697
E-mail: asecs@wfu.edu
Web Site: http://asecs.press.jhu.edu

American Society for Eighteenth-Century Studies

Patron Members 2016–2017

Hans Adler
Richard Shane Agin
Stephen Ahern
Stanford Anderson
Mark S. Auburn
Paula Backscheider
Eve T. Bannet
Joseph F. Bartolomeo
James G. Basker
Denise Baxter
Barbara Benedict
Oliver Berghof
Kevin Binfield
Martha F. Bowden
Theodore E.D. Braun
Fritz Breithaupt
Peter M. Briggs
Jane K. Brown
Marshall Brown
Michael Burden
Joseph A. Byrnes
Ann Campbell
Susan Carlile
Vincent Carretta
Jeng-Guo Chen
Julie Choi
Brian A. Connery
E. Heckendorn Cook
Kevin L. Cope
Brian Cowan
Margaret Mary Daley
Marlies K. Danziger
Jenny Davidson
Joan DeJean
Robert DeMaria, Jr.
Julia Douthwaite
William F. Edmiston
Roger J. Fechner
Frances Ferguson
Riikka Forsstrom

Bernadette Fort
Patsy Fowler
Christopher Fox
Jennifer E. Frangos
Gorden Fulton
Robert Glen
Charles E. Gobin
Scott Gordon
Sayre Greenfield
Monika Greenleaf
Loyd Grossman
Anita Guerrini
Phyllis Guskin
Susan Gustafson
Basil Guy
Knud Haakonssen
Wolfgang Haase
Martha Hamilton-Phillips
Corrine Harol
Phillip Harth
Donald M. Hassler
Julie C. Hayes
Charles Hinnant
Robert D. Hume
Lynn A. Hunt
J. Paul Hunter
Sheila M. Hwang
Catherine Ingrassia
Malcolm Jack
Margaret C. Jacob
Regina Mary Janes
Alessa Johns
Sandro Jung
George Justice
Sarah Kareem
Gary Kates
Michael Keevak
Shirley Strum Kenny
Thomas Keymer
Heather King

Charles A. Knight
Jocelyne Kolb
Scott Krawczyk
Thomas W. Krise
Susan Lanser
Meredith Lee
Elizabeth Liebman
Devoney K. Looser
Aino Makikalli
Elizabeth Mansfield
Robert Markley
Jean I. Marsden
Marie E. McAllister
Christie McDonald
Paula McDowell
Dennis McEnnerney
George C. McElroy
Alan T. McKenzie
James C. McKusick
Heather McPherson
Donald C. Mell Jr.
Eun Kyung Min
Dennis Moore
Anja Mueller-Muth
Yvonne Noble
Felicity Nussbaum
Mary Ann O'Donnell
Frank Palmeri
Virginia J. Peacock
Ruth Perry
Jane Perry-Camp
Stuart Peterfreund
R.G. Peterson
George W. Poe
John Valdimir Price
Ruben D. Quintero
John Radner
Bryant T. Ragan
Tilottama Rajan
Paul Rich

Patron Members 2015–2016 (Con't)

Joseph Roach
James Rosenheim
Laura Rosenthal
Roseann Runte
Elizabeth Samet
Carole Fungaroli Sargent
Steven D. Scherwatzky
Harold Schiffman
Volker Schroder
Norbert Schurer
Richard Sher
Eleanor F. Shevlin
John C. Shields
Craig A. Simmons
Robert Louis Smith

G.A. Starr
Susan Staves
Kristina Straub
Masashi Suzuki
Mika Suzuki
Ruud N.W.M. Teeuwen
Linda V. Troost
Randolph Trumbach
Bertil Van Boer
David F. Venturo
Joachim Von der Thusen
Cynthia S. Wall
Howard D. Weinbrot
Byron R. Wells
Betty E. White

J. Edmund White
Lance Wilcox
Annie Williams
Karin E. Wolfe
Larry Wolff
Servanne Woodward
James Woolley
Karin Wurst
Myron D. Yeager
Janet E. Aikins Yount
William J. Zachs
Lisa M. Zeitz

Sponsoring Members 2016–2017

Paul Alkon
Misty G. Anderson
Robert Bernasconi
Thomas F. Bonnell
Leo Braudy
Daniel Brewer
Charles Burroughs
Samara Cahill
Michael J. Conlon
Brian Corman
Joyce East
Clarissa C. Erwin
Daniel Timothy Erwin
David Fairer
Jan Fergus
Lisa Freeman

Jack Fruchtman
Michael Genovese
George Haggerty
Daniel Heartz
Deborah Kennedy
Issac Kramnick
Joan Landes
R.W. McHenry
Maureen E. Mulvihill
Melvyn New
David Oakleaf
John C. O'Neal
Douglas Lane Patey
Adam Potkay
Suzanne R. Pucci
Larry L. Reynolds

John Richetti
Albert J. Rivero
Wendy W. Roworth
Treadwell Ruml II
Peter Sabor
Laura Schattschneider
Barbara B. Schnorrenberg
William C. Schrader
Julia Simon
John Sitter
Jeffrey Smitten
Ann T. Straulman
Astrida Tantillo
Dennis Todd
Raymond D. Tumbleson
Ann Van Allen-Russell
Kenneth Winkler

Institutional Members 2016-17

American Antiquarian Society
Colonial Williamsburg Foundation, *John D. Rockefeller, Jr. Library*
Folger Institute
Fordham University
Newberry Library
Ohio State University Libraries, *Thompson Library*
Omohundro Institute for Early American History, *Kellock Library*
Princeton University
Smithsonian Institute, *AAPG Library*
Stanford University, *Green Library*
UCLA, *William Andrews Clark Memorial Library*
University of California, Santa Barbara*, Division of Humanities and Fine Arts*
University of Kentucky, *Young Library*
University of North Carolina, *Davis Library*
University of Pennsylvania Library
University of Rochester Library
University of Victoria, *McPherson Library*
Yale University Library

Index

Every effort has been made to include references to all identifiable persons living before or during the long eighteenth century, as well as to often cited contemporary critics and commentators, and to provide a selective listing of relevant concepts and keywords. Readers may also wish to consult the endnotes of each essay for more comprehensive information.